The Economy
of Desire

THE CHURCH
AND POSTMODERN
CULTURE

James K. A. Smith, series editor
www.churchandpomo.org

The Church and Postmodern
Culture series features high-profile
theorists in continental philosophy
and contemporary theology
writing for a broad, nonspecialist
audience interested in the impact of
postmodern theory on the faith and
practice of the church.

Also available in the series

Merold Westphal, *Whose Community? Which Interpretation?
Philosphical Hermeneutics for the Church*

James K. A. Smith, *Who's Afraid of Postmodernism? Taking
Derrida, Lyotard, and Foucault to Church*

John D. Caputo, *What Would Jesus Deconstruct? The Good
News of Postmodernism for the Church*

Carl Raschke, *GloboChrist: The Great Commission Takes
a Postmodern Turn*

Graham Ward, *The Politics of Discipleship: Becoming Post-
material Citizens*

The Economy of Desire

*Christianity and Capitalism
in a Postmodern World*

Daniel M. Bell Jr.

Baker Academic
a division of Baker Publishing Group
Grand Rapids, Michigan

Published by Baker Academic
a division of Baker Publishing Group
P.O. Box 6287, Grand Rapids, MI 49516-6287
www.bakeracademic.com

Printed in the United States of America

Library of Congress Cataloging-in-Publication Data
Bell, Daniel M., 1966–
    The economy of desire : Christianity and captialism in a postmodern world / Daniel M. Bell, Jr.
        p.   cm. — (The church and postmodern culture)
    Includes bibliographical references and index.
    ISBN 978-0-8010-3573-9 (pbk.)
        1. Economics—Religious aspects—Christianity. 2. Capitalism—Religious aspects—Christianity. 3. Consumption (Economics)—Religious aspects—Christianity. 4. Desire—Religious aspects—Christianity. 5. Postmodernism—Religious aspects—Christianity. I. Title.
    BR115.E3B377 2012
    261.8′5—dc23   2012022143

12   13   14   15   16   17   18   7   6   5   4   3   2   1

In keeping with biblical principles of creation stewardship, Baker Publishing Group advocates the responsible use of our natural resources. As a member of the Green Press Initiative, our company uses recycled paper when possible. The text paper of this book is composed in part of post-consumer waste.

Contents

Series Preface

Current discussions in the church—from emergent "postmodern" congregations to mainline "missional" congregations—are increasingly grappling with philosophical and theoretical questions related to postmodernity. In fact, it could be argued that developments in postmodern theory (especially questions of "post-foundationalist" epistemologies) have contributed to the breakdown of former barriers between evangelical, mainline, and Catholic faith communities. Postliberalism—a related "effect" of postmodernism—has engendered a new, confessional ecumenism wherein we find nondenominational evangelical congregations, mainline Protestant churches, and Catholic parishes all wrestling with the challenges of postmodernism and drawing on the culture of postmodernity as an opportunity for rethinking the shape of our churches.

This context presents an exciting opportunity for contemporary philosophy and critical theory to "hit the ground," so to speak, by allowing high-level work in postmodern theory to serve the church's practice—including all the kinds of congregations and communions noted above. The goal of this series is to bring together high-profile theorists in continental philosophy and contemporary theology to write for a broad, nonspecialist audience interested in the impact of postmodern theory on the faith and practice of the church. Each book in the series will, from different angles and with different questions, undertake to answer questions such as What does postmodern theory have to say about the shape of the church? How should concrete, in-the-pew and on-the-ground religious practices be impacted by postmodernism? What should the church look like in postmodernity? What has Paris to do with Jerusalem?

The series is ecumenical not only with respect to its ecclesial destinations but also with respect to the facets of continental philosophy and theory that are represented. A wide variety of theoretical commitments will be included, ranging from deconstruction to Radical Orthodoxy, including voices from Badiou to Žižek and the usual suspects in between (Nietzsche, Heidegger, Levinas, Derrida, Foucault, Irigaray, Rorty, and others). Insofar as postmodernism occasions a retrieval of ancient sources, these contemporary sources will be brought into dialogue with Augustine, Irenaeus, Aquinas, and other resources. Drawing on the wisdom of established scholars in the field, the series will provide accessible introductions to postmodern thought with the specific aim of exploring its impact on ecclesial practice. The books are offered, one might say, as French lessons for the church.

Series Editor's Foreword

James K. A. Smith

One of the reasons "postmodernism" is misused and misunderstood is that the term is often associated with what we might call a "disruption thesis": the notion that "postmodernism" names something entirely new and radically different—that postmodernism names a "now" that is somehow discontinuous with all that has gone before. When people hear "postmodernism" bandied about in this way, they look around, see an awful lot that is all too familiar, and dismiss such claims as overwrought, the sorts of things you can convince yourself of if you've spent a little too long in Left Bank cafés (or graduate school).

But the best thinking that employs the heuristic term "postmodernism" doesn't subscribe to such notions of discontinuity. To the contrary: the subtitle of Fredric Jameson's classic work, *Postmodernism*, describes it as "The Cultural Logic of Late Capitalism." On this account, postmodernism is not *less* modern but *more* modern—a kind of *hyper*-modernism, the intensification of forces unleashed by a variety of "revolutions": Copernican, Industrial; French, American; Digital, Sexual.

This is especially true in fiction: those sometimes described as "postmodern" novelists—Thomas Pynchon, David Foster Wallace, Don DeLillo—paint pictures of worlds dominated by consumption

9

and the unique malaise that characterizes "late capitalism." Indeed, in Wallace's *Infinite Jest*, time itself is organized by corporate sponsors. The calendar no longer belongs to the gods and emperors (Janus, Mars, Julius, Augustus) but rather is owned by corporations—the new divine powers. (Most of the action in *Infinite Jest* takes place in the "Year of the Depend Adult Undergarment.") This world is "postmodern" not because it signals some romantic escape from the modern or some jarring break with modernity but because it is one completely saturated and dominated by the forces of modernity. Postmodernity isn't a world where modernity has failed; it is the world where modernity is all in all. Or as Daniel Bell puts it below, it's the world where "we're all capitalists now."

Most Christian thinking about discipleship and spiritual formation has failed to appreciate this reality. Indeed, much of contemporary North American Christianity not only blithely rolls along with these realities; in many ways, it also encourages and contributes to it with a vast cottage industry of Christianized consumption. By locating the challenges for Christian discipleship in arcane cults or sexual temptation or the "secularizing" forces of the Supreme Court, evangelicalism tends to miss the fact that the great tempter of our age is Walmart. The tempter does not roam about as a horrifying monster, but as an angel of light who spends most of his time at the mall.

These are lessons I first learned, in a significant way, from Dan Bell's first book, *Liberation Theology after the End of History*. You might not guess a book of that title would strike such a "practical" nerve, but at the core of Bell's analysis and argument is a concept that should revolutionize how you think about discipleship and spiritual formation: *desire*. And it is that core intuition that he translates and extends here in this new book, utilizing the theoretical resources in thinkers such as Gilles Deleuze and Michel Foucault that enable us to see anew just what's at stake—and what's going on—in the banality of consumption that surrounds us. Bell helps us to appreciate that there is an *economics* of desire—that our desire is primed and pointed by "technologies" that habituate us toward certain ends. The question isn't *whether* we'll be subject to an "economy," but *which*.

Many Christians have failed to see what's at stake in contemporary "postmodern" life—dominated as it is by a globalized market and the rhythms of consumption—because we still tend to think that Christian faith is an "intellectual" matter: a matter of what propositions we believe, what doctrines we subscribe to, what Book we adhere to. And conversely, we tend to think of economics as a "neutral" matter of distribution and exchange. Because of these biases, we can too easily miss the fact that Christian faith is at root a matter of what we *love*—what (and Whom) we *desire*. If we forget that, or overlook that, we'll also overlook all the ways that the rituals of "late capitalism" shape and form and aim our desire to worship rival gods. Hence Bell's argument is not just critical; it is also constructive. He invites us to see the practices of Christian discipleship and the rituals of Christian worship as the lineaments of an alternative economy—a "kingdom come" economics that orders the world otherwise, bearing witness to the strange, upside-down economy of a crucified-now-risen King.

This book excites me not just because it will impact on-the-ground approaches to Christian discipleship but also because it should encourage a paradigm shift in how we stage conversations between Christian faith and economics. As Christian liberal arts education continues to grow and mature, we are seeing more and more mature Christian reflection across the disciplines, including economics. A burgeoning conversation at the intersection of Christian faith and economics—fostered by the Association of Christian Economists—would profit from critical engagement with Bell's thesis and analysis, even though his model and approach will also challenge some of the working assumptions of the "faith and economics" paradigm. Bell has immersed himself in economic theory and made himself accountable to research beyond his discipline, so he can't be dismissed as a mere amateur preaching from his theological soapbox. As he emphasizes below, he is not advocating some romantic, simplistic "withdrawal" from the market; nor is he suggesting that we somehow just "replace" economics with theology. Christian economists who want to disagree with Bell will need to work *through* his argument and analysis, and their foundational reflection on economics from a Christian perspective will be better for it.

I have long considered Dan Bell one of my teachers. My own thinking has been deeply marked by the impact of his work. And so it is a joy and a pleasure to now have his wise voice as part of the choir that is the Church and Postmodern Culture series. He invites us to nothing less than a *holy* economy.

Preface

> The composition of this book has been for the author a long struggle of escape, and so must reading of it be for most readers if the author's assault upon them is to be successful,—a struggle of escape from habitual modes of thought and expression. The ideas which are here expressed so laboriously are extremely simple and should be obvious. The difficulty lies, not in the new ideas, but in escaping from the old ones, which ramify, for those brought up as most of us have been, into every corner of our minds.[1]

Thus the noted economist John Maynard Keynes begins his most famous work. In many ways it expresses my sentiments regarding this project. This was a difficult book to write, not because what it says is hard to grasp, but because the "old ideas" it challenges are so deeply ingrained in my life, character, and desire.

I take heart, however, from the words of the Brazilian theologian Jung Mo Sung, who observes that it is not the theologian who creates practices of solidarity and liberation, but the Spirit.

1. John Maynard Keynes, *The General Theory of Employment, Interest and Money* (1936; repr., Amherst, NY: Prometheus Books, 1997), xii.

To the theologian, he says, falls the work of critiquing that which obscures our perception of the Spirit's blowing and of sowing new categories that help better understand the Spirit's activity in our midst.[2] I should be delighted if this modest work contributes to the church's vision in that way.

To the extent that it does, it is due to the wisdom and examples of others who both think about and live this life far better than I. Included here is the work of Hugo Assmann, Franz Hinkelammert, Julio de Santa Ana, and Jung Mo Sung. I have learned much as well from conversations with Joel Shuman, D. Stephen Long, Kelly Johnson, Chris Franks, and Brent Laytham. I am also grateful to Chris Keller and the good folks at *The Other Journal* who invited me many years ago to wrestle with the kernel of ideas brought to fruition here.

Some of the ideas and material developed here first appeared in Daniel M. Bell Jr., *Liberation Theology after the End of History: The Refusal to Cease Suffering* (New York: Routledge, 2001), and "What Is Wrong with Capitalism? The Problem with the Problem with Capitalism," *The Other Journal* 5 (May 2005): 1–7. They are used by permission of the publishers.

Jamie Smith, the series editor, and Bob Hosack, at Baker, deserve more than a word of thanks for their long-suffering patience. The book is dedicated to Phil Baker, whose spirit exemplifies the generosity of God's economy.

2. Jung Mo Sung, *Economía, Tema Ausente en la Teología de la Liberación* (San José: DEI, 1994), 209.

Introduction

What Has Paris to Do with Jerusalem?

Welcome to Postmodernity

Where am I? I thought as I wandered lost through the spacious glass hallways, utterly confused and feeling more than a little like a rat in a beautiful maze constructed by some mad scientist for her amusement. The building was a fine example of postmodern architectural style—intentionally disorienting and illogically laid out, confusing the inside and the outside, space and order, and even time—as the carefully induced vertigo dissolved my meticulous calculations to arrive early at a meeting.

Other incidents struck me with increasing frequency: On the first day of class I walk into a room only to stop short, wondering what *year* it is because the folks gathered before me are attired in an eclectic array of clothing and hairstyles that span at least the 1950s through the 1990s. An email informs me a friend is involved in prosecuting a case of slavery in the very shadow of one of the most technologically advanced industrial areas in the country. A local school garners national headlines as professors argue over what constitutes great literature and whether and how many of Shakespeare's works should be required reading. As I walk through a town in Honduras, just minutes from a village where I saw gut-wrenching poverty, I pass by laptop computers alongside Mayan handcrafts on the sidewalk.

I sit down to relax, and the music on the radio sounds like a conglomeration of steel drums, a synthesizer, and whales. A student
meets with me to complain that I do not appreciate that his style
of thinking and writing is "nonlinear." At the gym, contemplating
my own petty troubles, I bump into a person whose job of several
decades has just been sent overseas. At a political march, the group
next to me is pretty clearly *against everything*, as they wander off
down various random side streets singing and carrying on, oblivious
to the direction and purpose of the march. I turn on the television
and surf through one hundred–plus channels in search of news, and
when I stop I cannot tell if I have inadvertently landed in the middle
of a music video or my television has merely gone on the fritz as the
screen jumps from the scene of horrible devastation wrought by a
hurricane in a foreign country, to a sports car adorned with a model,
to Christmas preparations at the Mall of America, to Hungarian folk
music, to the sex life of penguins all in the space of a few minutes
(because the talking head with the frozen expression remains the
same during all these sound bites, I conclude it is the news and turn
up the volume). A newsletter informs me my denomination is fighting over whether there are moral absolutes, and my local church is
locked in a bitter debate over the appropriateness of contemporary
music, casual attire, and a flexible structure to worship that deletes
creeds and adds coffee and bagels.

There is a carnivalesque feel to postmodernity, a kind of anarchic
exuberance, where all that was solid seems to melt into air, where
the old order is submerged in disorder, where the traditions and
foundations of the past seem to crumble into so many fragments
that do not disappear so much as float on the chaotic surface of
the tides and currents of a hyper-individualistic, hyper-libertine,
hyper-suspicious age. And, the futurists tell us, the current volatility,
uncertainty, and ambiguity are going to only intensify.[3]

What Should We Fear?

For several hundred years, much of Christianity has been heavily
invested in the project that was modernity. Desperate to find shelter

3. See Bob Johansen, *Leaders Make the Future* (San Francisco: Berrett-Koehler,
2009), xiv.

from the remnants of a fading medieval order, Christianity embraced modernity's patterns of thought, its political arrangements, its economic organization. Furthermore, the church perceived itself to be one of the necessary pillars of the modern world, a crucial contributor to the success and flourishing of modern society. Whether it was a matter of contributing energy and ideas to solving the social problems of the day, Christianizing the social order, or serving as a custodian of spiritual values and safeguarding the soul of the nation by keeping prayer in schools, values in the family, God in the Constitution, Christ in Christmas, and the national borders well-armed against the bearers of atheistic and idolatrous ideologies, Christianity was deeply inscribed in the patterns and processes of the modern Western world.

Against the pagan philosophies of his day, the early Christian theologian Tertullian once famously exclaimed, "What indeed has Athens to do with Jerusalem?"[4] In the face of postmodernity, we may be tempted to repeat his rejection. Having identified so closely with modern forms, and having sanctified this relationship by bestowing on it *divine* sanction, the overturning of modern structures can hardly seem anything other than a frontal assault on the rock of faith by the shifting sands of chaos and anarchic relativism. Like Pilgrim in Bunyan's classic, we are tempted to merely pass through this (post)modern-day Vanity Fair, keeping our distance with a stridently defensive posture of steadfast endurance.

But is this fear and suspicion, this defensive posture, justified? After all, on the one hand, there is evidence to suggest that modernity was *not* as hospitable to a robust orthodox faith as was often presumed. We are beginning to see more clearly now that even as the church tried to "be relevant" and fit into the niche allotted it by modernity, even as the church sought to embrace the cultural, political, and economic forms and institutions of modernity, a high price was exacted for such accommodation. Certainly the end of modernity is *not* noteworthy for the triumph of Christianity; today it seems that the good news has been trivialized and marginalized to the point that the astounding truth of God with us cannot hold the attention of the typical young adult or teenager.[5]

---

4. Tertullian, *De praescriptione haereticorum* 7, in *The Ante-Nicene Fathers*, ed. Alexander Roberts and James Donaldson (Peabody, MA: Hendrickson, 1994), 3:246.

5. See the results of the National Survey of Youth and Religion as reported by Christian Smith and Kenda Creasy Dean. Christian Smith with Melinda Lundquist Denton, *Soul Searching: The Religious and Spiritual Lives of American Teenagers* (New York:

On the other hand, postmodernity has declared itself much more open to religion. Whereas modernity accommodated religion so long as religion could show itself reasonable, not mysterious, or so long as it could deliver the votes, postmodernity places no such strictures on Christianity. In the carnival that is postmodernity, the sublime, the sacred, the charismatic, and the ecstatic may all join the ball.

Already we see the fruits of this postmodern congeniality to the theological in emergent church forms and practices. Worship, church architecture, and, increasingly, Christian political and economic positions are being permeated by postmodern currents and trends, from eclectic music styles, the recovery of premodern spiritual disciplines in contemporary forms, and flexible worship spaces that blur the inside and outside architecturally and electronically (via the Web, Twitter, etc.) to the embrace of pop culture and new political alliances and economic configurations that defy modernity's denominational, ideological, and national boundaries.

The suspicion of postmodernism, however, is not baseless. To the extent that the *post*modern is actually *hyper*modern, it is in many ways an intensification of modern themes. Thus the carnival that is postmodernity remains a parody of Christianity that *uses* rather than *embraces* religion. It may be but a kind of postmodern Trojan horse, a postmodern form of co-optation and conquest of religion.[6] Moreover, while its openness to the theological differs from modernity's atheism, it remains problematic to the extent that it more closely resembles a renewed polytheism or perhaps even Nietzschean super-humanism than true openness to the supernatural.

The Church and Postmodernity

What then are we to make of postmodernism? Should Christians embrace it or resist it? The Church and Postmodern Culture series

Oxford University Press, 2005); Christian Smith with Patricia Snell, *Souls in Transition: The Religious and Spiritual Lives of Emerging Adults* (New York: Oxford University Press, 2009); Kenda Creasy Dean, *Almost Christian: What the Faith of Our Teenagers Is Telling the American Church* (New York: Oxford University Press, 2010).

6. The noted postmodern philosopher Savoj Žižek, who has been at the forefront of engaging Christianity, is bluntly honest in this regard, asserting that the only way to fight the "obscurantism" that is the Christian religion is to embrace it, thereby taking it away from "the fundamentalist freaks"—by which he means anyone who actually believes it. See *The Fragile Absolute* (New York: Verso, 2000), 1–2.

is clearly premised on the notion that postmodernity has something to teach the church. As Jamie Smith says, referring to the nationality of the philosophers engaged by the series, it is offered as a kind of "French lessons for the church."[7] This, however, could be misunderstood. For taking postmodern philosophers to church is not a matter simply of uncritically embracing them. Rather, it is about fostering a more discerning view of postmodernity. In place of a simple rejection of an unmitigated threat, this series presents postmodernity as an opportunity for the church to enhance its ministry and mission in, to, and for the world. Another way of putting this is to say, as Smith does, that we seek to avoid simple dichotomies that either demonize or baptize postmodernism.[8]

This is an especially important point to be clear about at the outset of this particular book because it engages the thought of two of the leading Marxist thinkers and vehement atheists of the late twentieth century. While it uses their work, it is far from simply embracing them. Instead, it attempts, in the words of St. Augustine, to "plunder the Egyptians" as the Israelites did on their way to the Promised Land. Christians have always drawn on and learned from the work of pagan philosophers, frequently putting their insights to uses and ends that they would not or could not have imagined.

In this case, I engage the thought of Foucault and Deleuze on human desire and the postmodern, capitalist economy as a contribution to rethinking and renewing Christianity's relation to political economy. More specifically, I engage Foucault and Deleuze on desire and economy for the sake of recalling the ways the church's life is part of a divine economy of desire—one that redeems desire from the postmodern capitalist economy that would distort desire in ways that hinder humanity's communion with God, one another, and the rest of creation.[9]

Capitalism and Christianity

Put simply, this work is a contribution to the conversation about the relationship of Christianity to capitalism with a postmodern

7. James K. A. Smith, *Who's Afraid of Postmodernism?* (Grand Rapids: Baker Academic, 2006), 10.
8. Ibid., 15.
9. Space limitations preclude directly addressing communion with the rest of creation. Nevertheless, this is an important dimension of the divine economy.

twist. Frequently, this conversation has unfolded in terms of the relative merits and demerits of capitalism and socialism and which economic order best corresponds to Christian beliefs and convictions. At one level, this book continues this conversation, although it changes the focus from capitalism versus socialism to capitalism versus the divine economy made present by Christ and witnessed to by the church.

While comparing ideas and beliefs is important, however, it is insufficient. This is where the postmodern twist to the conversation comes in, and where Deleuze and Foucault prove particularly helpful. For a long time, the conversation about the relation between capitalism and Christianity has presumed that getting our economic lives in order was primarily a matter of comparing and contrasting ideas and beliefs in order to decide which beliefs and ideas were best, and then simply willing ourselves to act on such beliefs and convictions. There are several problems with this approach.

First, capitalism is quite adept at absorbing critique, even packaging and marketing it as one more opportunity for acquiring profit. Thus, even where conflicting convictions and beliefs may be articulated, they do not necessarily generate change or resistance. Think of the way various "independent" musicians, who have prided themselves on their oppositional stance to the current social and/or economic order, have been thoroughly incorporated into the capitalist market as just another consumer good. Perhaps the most striking recent example of this ability to incorporate and then profit from critique was the marketing a few years ago of Ernesto "Che" Guevara—an icon of the modern Marxist and anticapitalist left—now reduced to a capitalist brand and promotional gimmick.[10]

Second, the moral life in any age, let alone a capitalist one, is plagued by the disconnect between belief and practice. This is to say, holding right beliefs or ideas is no guarantee of right actions. Thus Scripture speaks of practical atheists who profess God with their lips and yet deny God with their actions (Titus 1:16), and Paul famously recounts the conflict whereby one does what one does not want to do (Rom. 7:14–25). In addition to the problem of hypocrisy, there is also the reality that conflicting beliefs and

10. Naomi Klein gives example after example of this co-optation of opposition in her *No Logo* (New York: Picador, 2002).

practices can coexist in a life in a kind of unexamined juxtaposition, which some label a characteristic of "folk religion."[11] This is to say, one can sincerely assent to various beliefs and convictions without ever reflecting upon how those convictions may be at odds with various practices and lived realities that characterize one's life. Thus, for example, I could profess that Jesus is Lord or Christ is King without it ever crossing my mind, much less affecting my behavior, that such a profession might preclude my pledging allegiance to other lords or kings.

A third form of disconnection between belief and practice could be called the problem of the consumption of religion.[12] As Vincent Miller points out, the habits we learn as consumers in the market economy tend to carry over to other dimensions of life. Thus we are conditioned to approach religion as a commodity, as just another consumer good alongside toothpaste and vacation homes. Think, for instance, of the commonplace practice of "church shopping." This is to say, capitalism encourages a shallow, decontextualized engagement with religious beliefs. Like the vast array of exotic cultural products from around the world that appear side by side on the shelves of the import franchise at the mall, in a consumer culture, beliefs tend to become free-floating cultural objects.[13] These objects do not require anything of me; they entail no particular commitment or engagement. They do not bind me to any particular people or community. Rather, they function only to serve the end(s) or purpose(s) I choose, which, in the case of religious choices, might include shoring up my self-image as "spiritual," or providing meaning amid the stresses of my middle-class life or the right values for my children, and so on. (Consider the popular standard for evaluating worship: "Does it meet my needs?") Reduced to a religious commodity, Christian beliefs can be held in the midst of a political economy that runs counter to those beliefs without any tension at all.

11. Roger E. Olson, *The Mosaic of Christian Belief* (Downers Grove, IL: IVP Academic, 2002), 18.

12. This section owes much to Vincent J. Miller, *Consuming Religion* (New York: Continuum, 2004), 84–94.

13. Ibid., 84. This may go some way toward accounting for the eclectic character of much contemporary Christianity. See the discussion of the deregulation school of religion in ibid., 92. See also Roger Fink and Rodney Stark, *The Churching of America 1776–1990* (New Brunswick, NJ: Rutgers University Press, 1992).

It is at this point that the postmodern twist to the standard argument and benefit of engaging Deleuze and Foucault come to the fore. Although this book considers beliefs and ideas in order to counter in part the unexamined profession of beliefs that characterizes "folk religion" and in part the arguments of some Christian thinkers whose defense of capitalism depends on problematic theological claims, it moves beyond contested convictions and beliefs. Learning a lesson from Deleuze and Foucault, it moves beyond beliefs to consider the fundamental human power that is desire and how that desire is shaped not only by beliefs and convictions but also by practices and institutions. Indeed, in those places where I treat beliefs and convictions, the point is not simply to make sure we get our beliefs right. Rather, the point is to encourage examining the practices, habits, and institutions that constitute our economic lives and shape our desire.

Which Capitalism?

At the outset it is worthwhile to say a word regarding what I mean by capitalism. Capitalism often goes by the name "free-market economy," which is helpful insofar as it highlights the centrality of the market. Although markets of various shapes and sizes have existed for ages, with the advent of capitalism, the market becomes central to the life of the household and society.[14] Whereas markets existed as long ago as the Stone Age, they were by and large incidental to economic life—trading primarily in luxury items and various extravagances.[15] This pattern continued in the West until the later Middle Ages, when a money/profit/market economy emerged and slowly assumed a more important role in everyday life, bringing us to the cusp of capitalism announced by the likes of James Steuart and Adam Smith in the eighteenth century. As James Fulcher observes, "Markets, like merchants, are nothing new, but they are central to a capitalist society in a quite new and more abstract way. . . . Instead of being a place where you can buy some extra item that

14. See Karl Polanyi, *The Great Transformation* (Boston: Beacon, 1944), from which this paragraph is drawn. See also C. B. MacPherson, *The Rise and Fall of Economic Justice and Other Essays* (New York: Oxford University Press, 1987), 1–20.
15. See Lester K. Little, *Religious Poverty and the Profit Economy in Medieval Europe* (Ithaca, NY: Cornell University Press, 1978).

you do not produce yourself, markets become the only means by which you can obtain anything."[16] Not only is the market central, but it is (or aspires to be) "free" as well, that is, free from external constraints and obstacles to its full and uninhibited functioning. Thus capitalism marks the advent of a world where, as Deleuze will argue, not only is the market central to everything, but everything is also subject to the rule of the market.

Identifying capitalism with the dominion of the market is an important but insufficient step in defining capitalism. After all, capitalism is not a monolithic entity, both in the sense that it has not remained unchanged since it first appeared (the dating of which is itself a matter of much debate) and in the sense that there are competing theories of what capitalism is and how it functions. Economists and others are fond of devising schemata for describing the various kinds and stages of capitalism. One can find capitalism linked to a nearly endless array of adjectives: primitive, advanced, late, anarchic, managed, remarketized, organized, disorganized, savage, casino, global, Fordist, post-Fordist, Keynesian, and neoliberal, just to name a few.

Given the diversity of interpretations of capitalism, it is perhaps unavoidable that some will suggest that I have set up a straw figure, that my interpretation is dated and simplistic. However, notwithstanding the array of interpretations and existence of alternative schools of economics,[17] it is possible to identify a significant consensus on the foundational assumptions of contemporary capitalist or free-market economics. These are apparent in introductory economics textbooks as well as in the economists and theologians on which I draw. Moreover, notwithstanding the diverse schools of economic thought, there is widespread—indeed I am tempted to say "universal"—recognition that what goes by the name of neoliberalism is and has been the dominant theoretical and practical (as in policy-setting) vision since at least the late 1970s. As one economist puts

16. James Fulcher, *Capitalism: A Very Short Introduction* (New York: Oxford University Press, 2004), 16.

17. See, e.g., David L. Prychitko, ed., *Why Economists Disagree: An Introduction to the Alternative Schools of Thought* (Albany, NY: SUNY Press, 1998), or Robert H. Nelson, *Economics as Religion: From Samuelson to Chicago and Beyond* (University Park, PA: Penn State University Press, 2001). See also Steve Keen, *Debunking Economics* (New York: Zed Books, 2001), 300–311. The extent to which alternative schools are indeed alternatives, and not merely variations on the dominant vision, is debated.

it, "The mainstream . . . is so dominant that the other streams have become mere trickles."[18] As much as proponents of other streams may object, and whatever their future impact may be, the neoliberal vision continues to be the dominant paradigm of capitalism today.

Although the term "neoliberalism" first attained wide circulation as critics of capitalism in the global South used it pejoratively to refer to the "Washington Consensus"—that ensemble of policies and institutions supported by the United States for the sake of advancing the spread of capitalism around the globe—it has since become a common way of referring to the neoclassical vision of capitalism associated with the University of Chicago and especially Friedrich von Hayek and Milton Friedman.[19] Politically, it is associated with the economic agendas of Ronald Reagan and Margaret Thatcher, as well as Bill Clinton and Tony Blair.

At its most general level, neoliberal capitalism is about the complete marketization of life. In particular, it is about overcoming the obstacles to and inefficiencies introduced into the market by the Keynesian or welfare-state economics of the previous generation and increasing the integration of the entire globe into the capitalist market. Although it is frequently cast as "antigovernment" by both its advocates and proponents, it is in fact fond of a lean, strong state that is "small" with regard to its interference in market processes while nevertheless retaining and even enhancing its strength for the sake of security, particularly in the face of threats to the market.

Neither Escape nor Nostalgia

Having introduced what is meant by capitalism, it is only fitting to say a word about Christianity and how it is set against capitalism. Given that we are all capitalists now, as the theologian Michael Novak has observed,[20] and so certain habits of mind understandably

18. Stephen A. Marglin, *The Dismal Science: How Thinking Like an Economist Undermines Community* (Cambridge, MA: Harvard University Press, 2008), 6.

19. See Enrique Dussel, *Ética de la liberación en la edad de la globalización y de la exclusión* (Madrid: Editorial Trotta, 1998), 574. For an introduction to neoliberalism, see Manfred B. Steger and Ravi K. Roy, *Neoliberalism: A Very Short Introduction* (New York: Oxford University Press, 2010).

20. Michael Novak, *The Catholic Ethic and the Spirit of Capitalism* (New York: Free Press, 1993), 101.

incline one to think that the way things are is the way things must basically be, especially when the marketization of society is so deep and its bounty so integral to our lives, positing any kind of substantial conflict between capitalism and Christianity cannot help but appear to many as (irresponsible, unrealistic) escapism. Certainly it is the case that the Christian tradition contains within its folds voices and movements that thought that to withdraw or escape was indeed the prudent and necessary path in order to defeat avarice and associated economic vices. It is not my intent that my voice should be added to their number, not least because such withdraw, I believe, would be unfaithful to the church's mission in and for the world.

In a related vein, even as the critique of capitalism developed here draws on the precapitalist tradition, this is not symptomatic of a wistful nostalgia for a pristine past.[21] In this fallen world there is no pristine past; certainly the church has struggled with matters economic from the get-go, as the story of Ananias and Sapphira reminds us (Acts 5). Moreover, humanity has been given many goods—even if they have yet to be shared with all of humanity—in the age of capitalism, goods we would be foolish to refuse in any kind of effort to go backward.

Instead, I appeal to the past because in the church the past is never merely the past but always contributes to the present and the future. In other words, the tradition—be it the Bible, Augustine and Aquinas, the medieval monastics, or the mendicants—contributes to our present understanding and enhances the possibilities for acting and living differently in the world *today*. The tradition, if you will, is a kind of antidote to the overwhelming inertia of the status quo—the way it is is *not* the way it always has to be because it is not the way it has always been.

Appealing to a precapitalist tradition for the sake of opposing capitalism, however, is not just a matter of motivating us to do economic things differently. There are crucial theological claims being made about God and what God has and is making possible here and now.

Besides fleeing to the desert and going backward in time, there is another, subtle form of escapism that is properly resisted. As

21. For a critique of such romantic anticapitalism, see Julio de Santa Ana, *La práctica económica como religión* (San José: DEI, 1991), 15–16, and Jung Mo Sung, *Economía, Tema Ausente en la Teología de la Liberación* (San José: DEI, 1994), 99–100.

suggested above, capitalism is totalizing. The free market is a total market, a market that is at the center of life and society. By setting Christianity against this I am suggesting that the market should be neither total nor free. That is, it should not be the central institution in life and society, nor should its capitalist logic go unchecked. More specifically, I am suggesting that the market, and indeed the discipline of economics, should be subordinate to theological concerns.

Such a claim could be another form of escapism were it an attempt to construct an economy entirely from the confessions and traditions of the faith, bypassing altogether the discipline of economics and the wisdom of economists, not to mention that of laborers, managers, and owners who do not have the benefit of formal theological training.

This is not an effort to replace economics with theology or the market with the church. If in challenging the "total market" I might be said to be resisting "economics alone," even as I turn to the tradition, I reject any kind of fideism that suggests economics can be a matter of "faith alone." Rather, Christianity has always (if not universally and consistently) acknowledged the value of the gift of reason and so of the disciplines besides theology. Economics is one such discipline, and it has much to offer any effort to develop a theological vision and practice of economy. To take just one example, theologians and professional religious types are not infrequently accused of ignoring the general equilibrium results of the various and sundry proposals they espouse regarding social justice in economics. So in the name of charity or justice, they advocate rent controls so that poor persons may secure affordable housing, all the while oblivious to the possibilities that as a result, landlords will cut corners on maintenance or perhaps make fewer rental units available.[22] Put differently, deprived of hard-nosed economic analysis, too often religious efforts proceed under the illusion that solutions to various economic problems can proceed easily or painlessly.

Thus, even as I set capitalism and Christianity in opposition, I am not setting Christianity against economics in its entirety. Rather, I am suggesting that economics and economy are properly subordinated to theology in three possible senses, corresponding to three different

22. D. Stephen Long and Nancy Ruth Fox, *Calculated Futures* (Waco, TX: Baylor University Press, 2007), 32.

understandings of economics and economy. First, although the number is shrinking, many economists still insist that economics—like the free market itself—is a neutral, value-free enterprise that is amenable to most any ends.[23] The efficiency calculus at the heart of market economics does not care what you are producing, it is claimed; it simply provides a value-free assessment of whether you are producing it efficiently. To these folks I am suggesting that the ends of economy are not properly wide open, but given in the Christian confessions. Second, there are some who suggest that economics and economy are not in fact value free and morally neutral but rather depend on values supplied from the extraeconomic realms of culture and religion. To these I am suggesting that economics is subordinate to theology in the sense that theological concerns set the moral parameters for the functioning of the market (which would no longer be "free" in the classical sense). Third, some admit that economics is value laden and then argue that what is needed is a religion—Christianity, a church—shaped to serve those economic values. This is to say, theology should be subordinate to economy. I am suggesting just the opposite: the market economy should be subordinate to and so reinforce the virtuous life. For Christians the normative vision of economics should comport with Christian confessions and virtues.

Yet another form of escapism involves attributing too much significance to capitalism and its dissolution. Economists occasionally sound as if the market economy can solve all our problems. Critics of capitalism, likewise, can give the impression that all that stands between us and an era of prosperity and justice where the impoverished would be raised up and greed and envy would be no more is the abolition of capitalism. This work rests on no such illusion. Even as it is critical of capitalism, it does not begin from the premise that capitalism is the source of all evil. It is not the source of all poverty or economic injustice in the world. As the Christian tradition suggests—not to mention the tapestry of history—the peril of wealth, of the disordered desire that is avarice, precedes and will no doubt outlive capitalism. However, that capitalism is not the root of all economic evil does not mean that it gets a pass, any more than the suggestion that the poor will always be with us means we can safely ignore them.

23. See Marglin, *Dismal Science*, 173–75.

Diaspora Economics

One might assume that opposing capitalism and escapism requires setting forth a blueprint for an alternative global economic order. While there is much in these pages that suggests the nature, dispositions, and practices that mark a faithful alternative to capitalism, the purpose and point is not to present a blueprint. Indeed, I suspect that there is not one single order but many forms of economic life that can aid desire in attaining its true end and rest.

Thus, rather than articulating a single alternative, the purpose is to provoke further reflection on the difference Christ makes to the economic life of those called as disciples of Christ. Said a little differently, it is not a blueprint for the world but a call for Christians to consider our economic lives in light of the faith we pray and practice. It is about the ordering of our desires so that we desire the good that is God and the role that economies play in that ordering.

In this regard, recall the Scripture where the prophet announces the expectation that even the household pots and pans shall be holy (Zech. 14:20). Such is the expectation not because God is a fastidious nag but because the material arrangements of our households—and incidentally, the original meaning of the word "economy" is the law or order of the household—matter. The material ordering of even the mundane tasks of our daily lives both reflects and shapes the desires of our hearts.

This, however, is only part of the story. If economy matters with regard to our loving God, then economy matters because if we love God, we will love our neighbors (1 John 4:20–21). For this reason, I suggested earlier that to withdraw would be unfaithful to our mission. Just as the Jews and early Christians were scattered (the Diaspora) for the sake of the spread of the good news of God's favor toward all, so the church today does not seek to withdraw from the global economy to some desert but is intentionally in this capitalist world as a matter of witness or evangelism. Paul says we are the ones on whom the ends of the ages have come (1 Cor. 10:11). Discipleship is about the Christian community living now in accord with God's economy in the midst of the worldly economies. This is to say, we labor and produce, acquire and distribute, buy and sell, trade and invest, lend and borrow, but we do so in a manner that is different from others insofar as we do so in a manner informed by a desire schooled in virtues such as charity, justice, and generosity. This means that in many cases, our laboring and producing and acquiring and exchanging and investing and lending will look very different from that of disciples of the free market.

In this way, as we journey through this world and its economies, we hope others will see how we order our pots and pans, how we deal with material goods, and so turn and join us on our way in giving thanks to God in heaven, who is the giver of every good gift.

Outline

This inquiry into the economic form of faithful discipleship in the midst of a postmodern capitalist economy begins with a plunge into Deleuze and Foucault in the first two chapters. Wading through their accounts of capitalism, the state-form, technologies of the self, desire, and so forth can feel like slogging through a foreign language and a strange land. But as John Maynard Keynes pointed out in the epigram that opened this book, the difficulty has as much to do with the depth and tenacity of the hold that the old ideas, the ways we are used to thinking about economy, have on us. The difficulty of thought in Deleuze and Foucault is part of the struggle of breaking free of old habits of mind, spirit, and body. They push us to bring desire and its formation to the forefront of our thinking about discipleship and economics in a postmodern world.

This leads to chapters 3–4, where capitalism is subjected to a moral evaluation. This evaluation, however, does not proceed in the usual way, asking *if* it works. Rather, it builds on the insights of Deleuze and Foucault and asks, What work does it do? How does capitalism shape human desire and so human relations with others, including God? The conclusion is that even if capitalism works and produces a superabundance of material goods, it is still wrong for the ways it deforms human desire and so warps relations with oneself, others, and God.

Chapters 5–7 appropriate the lessons of Deleuze and Foucault for the sake of envisioning the church as an alternative economy where desire is being healed by participation in the divine economy of God's eternal generosity. Chapters 5–6 introduce Christianity as an economy of desire, and chapter 7 reflects on how Christian confessions and practices anticipate this renewed desire.

Chapter 8 introduces the practice of the works of mercy as the diaspora or pilgrim form that the divine economy takes in the midst of the world's economies.

1

The Multitude

The Micropolitics of Desire

The Battle in Seattle[1]

It is dark, except for the dim orange glow of the sodium-vapor street lamps reflected off pavement damp from the ubiquitous drizzle; the sun has not yet begun its climb over the horizon. The stillness of the early morning is broken by a solitary shape moving along the sidewalk. A few minutes later another shape appears, then another, and another. A few more minutes pass and a small cluster of nondescript shapes emerges from an alley and moves along the same sidewalk. They converge at the intersection. The same thing happens at another intersection and then another, all across the area. As the sun rises in sync with increasing din of the hustle and bustle of a

1. The portrait that follows is drawn primarily from *30 Frames a Second: The WTO in Seattle*, directed by Rustin Thompson (2000); *Breaking the Spell: Anarchists, Eugene, and the WTO*, directed by Tim Lewis, Tim Ream, and Sir Chuck A. Rock (1999); *This Is What Democracy Looks Like*, directed by Jill Friedberg and Rick Rowley (2000); Seth Ackerman, "Prattle in Seattle," *FAIR EXTRA* (January/February 2000); Jeffrey St. Clair, "Seattle Diary: It's a Gas, Gas, Gas," *New Left Review* 1/238 (November–December 1999): 81–96; Naomi Klein, "Seattle: The Coming-Out Party of a Movement," in *Fences and Windows: Dispatches from the Front Lines of the Globalization Debate*, ed. Debra Ann Levy (New York: Picador, 2002), 3–6.

busy modern metropolis, flows of people join these clusters, now no longer concealed by the darkness but still nondescript, anonymous, dressed in black, wearing goggles, scarves, and masks, some with their arms joined together by concrete and plastic tubing to form giant human chains. A swarm of young people join from the north, while from the south comes a multitude of people from third-world countries. They are joined by the young and old, rich and poor, by different nationalities and ethnicities. There are stages, speakers, singers. There are parades of steelworkers, environmentalists, anarchists, laborers, students, veterans, academics, carpenters, feminists, Native Americans, machinists, farmers, Protestants, Catholics, Muslims, and Jews. Among them are police, journalists, private security agents, television crews, politicians, diplomats, vigilantes, soldiers, bystanders and onlookers, imaginary ninjas armed with Molotov cocktails. Mingling too in this human potpourri are permanent residents of such urban environs—the homeless, panhandlers, local youths looking for a thrill, street venders hawking souvenirs of this event-in-the-making. The sound of drums rises above the dull roar of city life; then horns, trumpets, bullhorns, whistles, horses, rattles, diesel engines, guitars, shattered glass, cow bells, copper kettles, a band, a mobile rapper, and at least one conch shell add to the mix, as do the songs ("The Star-Spangled Banner," "Jingle Bells," "We Shall Overcome"), the chants and shouts ("What do we want? Less war," "Don't consume their TV," "Go home," "Die, die, die," "This is a peaceful protest—do not retaliate," "Disperse!" "Shame! Shame!" "Tonight we're gonna f—k s—t up!" "No violence!" "Power to the people," "This is what democracy looks like"), and the noise that accompanies tens of thousands jumbled together in the narrow valleys between glass skyscrapers that amplify the cacophony. Banners and signs and placards of all shapes and sizes and colors are unfurled and uncovered and hoisted in the air. They are festooned with vampires sinking their teeth into the globe, ghostlike men in suits, fish skeletons, butterflies, boot prints, flowers, doves, fists and chains. They proclaim "Sea Turtles and Teamsters: United at Last," "Insurrection," "Awaken," "Don't Trade on Me," "¡Basta Ya!" "Trade with Cuba," "Vegan Resistance," "No Sweatshops," "Free Tibet," "Make Globalization Work for Working Families," "Yeshua," "Revolution," "Drop the Debt," "Chiapas," "No Pollution," "God Is Angry," "Free Leonard Peltier," "Dykes Revolt," "Jesus Died for Your Sins," "Raging Grannies," "Support Hemp," "No WTO."

Complementing them are the posters with similar slogans papering the walls and light posts along with colorful tags and graffiti declaring "no sweatshops," or "WTO" with a line through it on windows, cars, and buildings. There are earth flags, flags with the anarchists' symbol, upside down American flags, American flags with the stars replaced by corporate logos, rainbow flags, Canadian flags, plain black flags. In the midst of these, floating on the surface of this sea of humanity, are balloons, a giant earth beach ball, a banana, half a dozen coffins with "sovereignty" or "clean air" or "biodiversity" painted on their sides, enormous yellow or orange butterflies, at least one giant green condom that reads "WTO: Practice Safe Trade." In the crowds are people with painted faces, devil masks, purple hair, clerical collars, Dr. Seuss hats, stilts and sheets, Groucho Marx glasses, or little at all, as topless women transform their torsos into poster boards for freedom or against bovine growth hormone or Nike. People are costumed as giant corn cobs, long-horned beetles, sea turtles, Santa Claus, wolves in business suits, small children dressed as yellow and red butterflies with enormous paper wings. A group of giant gagged heads floats by as does an enormous Grim Reaper. A masked and shirtless man runs while twirling a hula hoop around his waist. A hand puppet mimics the riot-gear-clad police. The trees lining the streets glimmer and sparkle festively with the colored lights of the Christmas season. People are dancing, arguing, fighting. A burlesque dancer gyrates in front of a line of the riot-gear-clad police. Someone else attempts to hand them flowers. A sea turtle with a bullhorn is locked in an intense conversation with a police officer also using a bullhorn standing a foot away.

Newspaper vending boxes are overturned; dumpsters are rolled into the streets. The concussion of rubber bullets, stun grenades, pepper spray, and tear gas canisters joins this city symphony. Batons swing through the air. Windows are broken, shops looted. A fire starts. Someone yells, "You are not burning anything recyclable are you?" A young father stands atop an overturned dumpster with his infant child strapped to his back as tear gas and smoke mingle around him. A young man on a skateboard wearing a gasmask scoots by, grinding on a curb. In the middle of the street, amid the clouds of pepper spray and tear gas, a woman kneels in prayer. And everything goes on as before: the drums and horns and bells and dancing and singing do not miss a beat. The banners, balloons, puppets, beach ball, and hula hoops continue with barely a pause.

What's Going On?

Such was the scene for nearly a week in late November and early
December of 1999 in the area around the Washington State Con-
vention and Trade Center in Seattle, site of the third World Trade
Organization ministerial conference. What was going on? Was it
a riot? A rally? A carnival? A protest? A parade? Was this just the
reactionary and rather pointless acting out of immature and self-
centered malcontents? The mindless mischief and vandalism of
loopy, doped-up, and unwashed new-agers? One more opportunity
for all-purpose agitators, whom Thomas Friedman of the *New York
Times* memorably called a "Noah's ark of flat-earth advocates," to
push into the limelight for a few minutes of fame?

An onlooker in downtown Seattle observed that there were just
too many opinions expressed on the streets during those days for
there to be one clear message.[2] A Seattle headline declared simply
that chaos had enveloped the downtown area.[3] Yet participants
regularly suggested that whatever it was, it was the beginning of
something new. The beginning of a new order, an upsurge of a dynamic power constituted by a network of alliances and affiliations
that would lead to the formation of a more open and participatory
world order, a democratic order where people (re)gained control
of their own lives. The anarchists whose tactics included breaking
the windows of select businesses couched it in terms of "breaking
the spell" of corporate domination. Describing the freedom they
sought, one says: "There is nothing in the world like running with
a group of two hundred people, all wearing black, and realizing
each of you is anonymous, each of you can liberate your desires,
each of you can make a difference."[4]

The sights and sounds on the streets of Seattle did not fit neatly in
any ordinary social or political vocabulary. Indeed, it seemed to most
closely resemble all of the things mentioned above, but not blended
together into something that if spread across a canvas would display
a consistent hue and texture. Rather, it was all these different things
at the same time: a riot, rally, carnival, protest, and parade, as if each
were a transparency laid atop the others, like one of those human

2. *30 Frames a Second.*
3. Ibid.
4. Ibid.

body transparency books that so fascinate children. But when the pages of this transparency are stacked together they do not resemble anything, at least anything in the social-political lexicon of modernity.

The Multitude

"Multitude" is the name that the postmodern political theorists Michael Hardt and Antonio Negri give to the novel reality on display in Seattle.[5] By this they mean a newly emerging social subject composed of irreducibly different singularities that, notwithstanding their differences and without losing those differences in a kind of melting pot, come together in a common project. There is no unified vision or all-encompassing purpose that would make these singularities "one." They retain their differences, a fact on display in many colors and words—some of them heated, as when, for example, some of the protestors attempted to prevent the destruction of property. Likewise, the common is not so much a shared goal or purpose as it is the process of all these expressive singularities collaborating, communicating, and creating relations. As the bystander cited above noted, there were too many opinions expressed to be reducible to a single shared axiom. Nevertheless, those diverse persons with an array of visions and voices were able to collaborate in drawing the attention of the WTO and the world. And Hardt and Negri agree with those who were chanting, "This is what democracy looks like." Which is to say, the communicative, collaborative interaction of the diverse desires on display in Seattle is what they call "democracy."

I begin this first chapter with the events in Seattle and the interpretation of those events offered by Hardt and Negri because they so adeptly mark the parameters of the first two chapters: economy, desire, and resistance. Moreover, they bring to the fore economy, desire, and resistance in a distinctly postmodern manner, highlighting how the Multitude defies the political forms of modernity, which were clearly definable by party, class, nationality, and ideology (like capitalism or socialism), as well as the moral forms of modernity, captured as they are in transcendent, unifying ideals and

5. Michael Hardt and Antonio Negri, *Multitude: War and Democracy in the Age of Empire* (New York: Penguin, 2004). See 285–88 for the most sustained treatment of Seattle. See also 86, 191, 215, 217, 266–68, and 315.

values, like "justice" and "rights."[6] Indeed, it is not insignificant that "mindless chaos" is such a tempting label for that event, precisely because the expressiveness, the desire, on display there in manifold ways refused to be neatly contained in the grand ideals of modern political morality. "People power" is both real and difficult to get a handle on, much like the unfolding events in Seattle, as the police and politicians belatedly discovered. For different reasons and to different ends, the people who converged on Seattle, and not only on Seattle but at various similar meetings around the globe in the years that followed, discovered a common project of resisting the current form of the global economic order, and they did it not simply in the name of justice or for the sake of ending poverty but also for the sake of "liberating desire," as the young anarchist put it, freeing desire by means of an in-the-process-of-being-discovered form of open and participatory politics.

Beginning with the events of Seattle viewed through the lens of Hardt and Negri is salutary as well, simply for the fact that Seattle puts faces, flesh, color, and sound to the political economy of desire articulated in very abstract language by Deleuze and Foucault. It is to their account of the postmodern political economy of desire that we now turn, beginning in this chapter with desire.

Who Are Deleuze and Foucault?

Before Michel Foucault died in 1984 and Gilles Deleuze in 1995, they were leading French philosophers who between them published hundreds of books and articles. More than this, they were *political* philosophers. This is to say they consciously did philosophy as part and parcel of a political struggle. At first glance, this may strike us as odd, insofar as what we know of the discipline of philosophy, with its focus on abstract questions like the nature of being and what is real and problems of logic, suggests it is the most *a*political, if not downright irrelevant of disciplines. Yet at the very core of Deleuze's philosophy is the claim that "politics precedes being,"[7]

6. This is not to suggest that values like justice and rights did not drive some of the participants. Rather, it is to suggest that such values and ideals did not provide the transcendent unity that they are supposed to in modern thought and politics.

7. Gilles Deleuze and Claire Parnet, *Dialogues*, trans. Hugh Tomlinson and Barbara Habberjam (New York: Columbia University Press, 1987), 17; Gilles Deleuze and Félix

which means that philosophy is always already political, from the very start of its deliberations. This is the case because every social or political order is built upon (perhaps unconscious or implicit) philosophical convictions, presuppositions about the nature of reality, about what is real, about what people are and how they relate to one another. And different philosophical visions result in the construction of different social, political, and economic orders. For instance, if one believes that matter is an illusion or a corruption of spirit, the body and the material world will be valued and treated differently than a social order erected on the presumption that this material realm is all there is and that matter has its own immanent power or force. Likewise, the philosophical presupposition that being is fundamentally peaceful will result in very different social and political orders than a philosophy that begins with the presupposition that being is fundamentally violent and conflictual. The importance of the recognition of philosophy as intrinsically political will become clearer as we proceed.

Not only were Deleuze and Foucault self-consciously political philosophers, but they were Marxists as well. Since it is commonplace in the West to think that with the pulling down of the Berlin Wall and the collapse of the Soviet Union Marxism has been unequivocally judged as utterly devoid of insight or usefulness, it is worth spending a moment to consider their relation to Marxism. To begin with, Marxism is not one unchanging thing. Rather, it is a tradition, and like any tradition, it contains within it different schools and strands of belief and practice. In this regard, it is not unlike Christianity. Christianity is a tradition that contains within its boundaries Catholics, Baptists, Methodists, and so forth. The same holds for Marxism. Moreover, again like Christianity, there are debates and disagreements within Marxism over just about everything.

Therefore, although many of us may indeed be convinced on both historical and theological grounds that Marxism is not a vision that holds out much promise for the future, that does not mean that all Marxists were (or are) without any insights that may be of use to Christians. Indeed, even as Marxism was dealt a harsh blow in the last decades of the last century, there were Marxists who foresaw that crisis and argued for changes within the Marxist tradition in

---

Guattari, *A Thousand Plateaus: Capitalism and Schizophrenia*, trans. Brian Massumi (Minneapolis: University of Minnesota Press, 1987), 203.

the hope that it would make the most of the social, political, and economic transformations they saw occurring around the world. Deleuze and Foucault were two such Marxists. In the 1960s and 1970s, when the world economy was undergoing transformation into the globalized order that it is today, both Deleuze and Foucault challenged Marxists to rethink how the economic order both advances and how it might be overcome. Perceiving the bankruptcy of both social democracy and Soviet state socialism as forms of resistance to and liberation from the advancing global capitalist order, they began an effort to "think otherwise," to explore new ways of conceiving human relations and revolutionary practice.[8] Central to this rethinking was Deleuze's treatment of desire and capitalism and Foucault's treatment of power, technologies of the self, and governmentality.

Together, their work sheds light on the postmodern economy of desire. Specifically, their work suggests that the contemporary global economic order is not merely economic. The global capitalist order is not only a matter of straightforwardly economic things like modes of production, the efficient manipulation of labor, and the creation of wealth—but rather is also ontological, which is to say that capitalism has to do with the very order of being, the arrangement of the basic stuff and power of reality. Capitalism's global extension hinges on its successful capture and discipline of the constitutive human power that is desire. In other words, capitalism is not merely an economic order but also a discipline of desire.

The questions immediately before us are, what do Deleuze and Foucault mean by desire, and how does capitalism capture and shape it? We begin with Deleuze.

Beyond Statecraft: Micropolitics

The philosophical point of departure for Deleuze's work is the claim that "politics precedes being." This enigmatic statement was partially explained above by suggesting that philosophical reflection is always already endowed with political significance. Beyond

8. In the course of this study I will refer to several works in which Deleuze collaborated with another author, the most notable example being his work with Félix Guattari. I do not attempt the futile task of sorting out the voices; instead, I will simply refer to the texts as being Deleuze's. For Deleuze's remarks on his collaborative efforts, see Deleuze and Parnet, *Dialogues*, 16–19, and Deleuze and Guattari, *A Thousand Plateaus*, 3.

recognizing that there is no such thing as political neutrality, even in a discipline as seemingly abstract and immaterial as philosophy can be, for Deleuze this statement functions as the foundation of his critique of the would-be revolutionaries of his day. It was tantamount to saying to them that if they wanted to resist capitalism, they would have to dig deeper into thought than they were accustomed to doing. Specifically, he was challenging them to move beyond the standard way of thinking about social and political change that was simply taken for granted. For those whom Deleuze was challenging, the standard way of thinking about revolution and social change involved what is called "statecraft" or "politics as statecraft."

The modern vision of "politics as statecraft" was given its classic articulation by the famous late-nineteenth- and early-twentieth-century sociologist Max Weber, when he defined politics as "the leadership, or the influencing of the leadership, of a *political* association, hence today, of a *state*."[9] "Politics as statecraft" is the conception of politics that emerged with the Enlightenment and the birth of the modern world that holds that the realm where persons come together in a polity, in a politics, is rightly overseen by and finds its highest expression in the state; it is the investiture of the state with sovereign authority over society and, consequently, privileging the state as the fulcrum of social and political change.

Think about it this way. When you ponder the "big problems" that confront humanity and society, like poverty or disease or environmental degradation or even the economic crisis, inevitably where does your thinking turn? To the state and the proper policies it should enact. You do not think first and foremost, "What should the church do?" or "What should General Motors do?" Instead, you think about governmental policies and action. It is a habit of mind that is deeply ingrained. We are used to thinking of the state as the chief social actor. Even those who espouse the currently popular view that the state should have a smaller economic footprint do not really relinquish politics as statecraft insofar as they do not really want the state to surrender its supervisory control of society; rather, they want it to enforce policies that protect and preserve the market. That "small state" advocates remain proponents of politics

9. Max Weber, "Politics as a Vocation," in *From Max Weber: Essays in Sociology*, ed. and trans. H. H. Gerth and C. Wright Mills (New York: Oxford University Press, 1946), 77. Italics in original.

as statecraft is perhaps seen nowhere more clearly than in the way advocates of a smaller, less obtrusive state rarely if ever have in mind reducing the military and penal capacity of the state. What is desired is a state that is oriented fundamentally toward enabling and preserving the market. Hence what is desired is not so much a reduction of state power and influence as a reconfiguration of that power and redirection of that influence in accord with different policies and toward different ends. Thus whether we espouse "big government" or "small government" is irrelevant; we continue to think of social change first and foremost (even if not exclusively) in terms of the state and its policies.

Modern revolutionaries, including the folks with whom Deleuze was engaged, are no different in this regard. They thought of revolution in terms of statecraft. They thought that the way to overcome capitalism was primarily a matter of gaining access to the levers of power nested in the nation-state and then using state power to ensure that the right policies, laws, and so forth were enacted and enforced.

Deleuze's assertion that "politics precedes being" challenges this state-centered vision of social, political, and economic change by proposing instead what he calls a "micropolitics of desire."[10] The term "micropolitics" implies a politics of a smaller scale than that of large entities like nation-states. Certainly it is the case that micropolitics involves local and what are called grassroots politics, and even things like nongovernmental organizations. But micropolitics is not first and foremost about scale or size; it is not really about a politics that is *smaller* than nation-states. Rather, it is about a *style* of organization. Micropolitics are politics that are not state-centered in the sense that they are decentered, diverse, disorganized, democratic. Seattle is a good example. What confronted the city and the WTO was not another single, unified, hierarchical organization, but a diverse multitude of forces and voices that had no central core exercising a unified and unifying control. Characteristic of micropolitics is the extension of relations and connections, collaborations. If one were to draw a picture of it, it would look more like a web or a network than the solid blocks that might represent modernity's politics of nation, party, class, and ideology.

Moreover, as Seattle suggests, micropolitics is *not* necessarily smaller or weaker than statecraft and in fact it may be larger, as the

---

10. Deleuze and Parnet, *Dialogues*, 17; Deleuze and Guattari, *A Thousand Plateaus*, 203.

network or web of micropolitical forces can be global, exceeding national, party, and ideological boundaries as well as encompassing vast numbers of people, perspectives, and resources.

Deleuze's point in advocating a micropolitics is precisely (if not *only*) that political struggle and the effort at social change are not exhausted by the struggle to command the power of the state, that conceiving of politics as statecraft in essence leaves resources on the table, untouched and overlooked, through which the effort to effect change can be advanced. He was in effect telling the revolutionaries of his day that their vision of revolution was too small, too narrow, that it needed to be expanded beyond the goal of influencing the direction of state. It needed to be expanded to encompass a revolution at the level of the very motive power that moves human beings: desire. Thus Deleuze advocates a micropolitics of desire.[11]

The Politics of Desire: The Joyous Sociality of Love

Beyond the claim that philosophy is always already implicated in politics, "politics precedes being" says something fundamental about reality, about the basic stuff of reality that is called "being." If we think of "politics" in its most straightforward sense, that is, not in its debased form as the machinations of contemporary politicians and parties but as having to do with the ordering of life in community (a *polity*), we can begin to grasp the deeper meaning of Deleuze's statement. He is in effect saying that being or reality *does not* come with a polity or organization "built in" to it from the start but rather that being must always be organized into a politics. Said a little differently, there is not one political order that is natural or just "given" as the way things ought to be. Instead, because there is no political order intrinsic to being, being must always be politically organized, and such organization can take diverse forms. Hence the revolutionary force of the claim that "politics precedes being." Because there is no one single political form that is "built in" to being, no natural political order, any political order or arrangement is subject to challenge and change.

---

11. This micropolitics does not rule out macropolitical struggle against the capitalist order, since "every politics is simultaneously a *macropolitics* and a *micropolitics*," but, as we shall see, it does dramatically change how one goes about such struggle (Deleuze and Guattari, *A Thousand Plateaus*, 213).

More specifically, and to the point of his argument with the would-be revolutionaries, politics as statecraft is not the only kind of politics. The organization of social space with the state at its summit is not the natural, given order of things. Quite to the contrary, this particular conception of politics and concomitant arrangement of social space is a contingent development, one that did not have to be and that can be otherwise. That we cannot imagine this, that we cannot imagine a world without nation-states that is *better* than the current order of things, suggests just how deeply all of us—even those of us who are "small state" advocates—have been captured by a statist habit of mind. Yet, Deleuze insists, breaking this habit of mind is important if we are to begin to imagine a different way of living, a different politics, than the politics of capitalism.

In addition to challenging the givenness of politics as statecraft in favor of a diverse, decentered micropolitics, Deleuze's claim that "politics precedes being" suggests that the fundamental character of reality be rethought. It is commonplace in the modern West to think about reality and existence in terms of "being." Thus when Shakespeare's Hamlet waxes philosophical, he declares, "To be, or not to be, that is the question,"[12] and one of great theologians of modernity describes God as the "ground of being" and human life as a matter of "the courage to be."[13] When Deleuze declares that politics precedes being, he is suggesting that reality is better conceived in terms of a dynamic power, movement, or energy that he calls desire. Everything is desire, flows of desire, desire organized or assembled into the manifold forms, shapes, and things that are. Reality is not a matter of being, which tends to give the way things are a kind of static weight that resists change and flux. Rather, reality is constituted by desire, by dynamic flows of desire in an infinite multiplicity of becomings. Hence Deleuze calls his politics a "micropolitics of desire."

Thinking about reality in terms of desire instead of being is counterintuitive in the modern West and may be suspect in the eyes of some Christians. As will be discussed later, however, there is a long and fruitful tradition in the church of thinking about life and reality in terms of desire. In fact, what is striking about Deleuze's philosophy of desire is that he draws inspiration for it from, among others, the great medieval Christian theologian Duns Scotus. In

12. Shakespeare, *Hamlet* 3.1.
13. Paul Tillich, *The Courage to Be* (New Haven: Yale University Press, 1952).

particular, Scotus provides Deleuze with a way of thinking about the basic substance and structure of reality that celebrates difference, multiplicity, becoming, and flux. It may be a surprise to some to learn that this atheistic Marxist, postmodern philosopher's vision of a fluid, flexible, decentralized micropolitics of desire that resembles ever-expanding and changing networks and webs of collaboration over against the oppressive, rigid forms of modernity, has roots in the work of the Christian theologian Scotus.

At the time that Scotus worked, there was an argument going on among philosophers and theologians regarding the nature of being. Specifically, there was a question about the relation of the being of humans to the being of God. Was it the same being or were God and humans made up of different kinds of being? Scotus argued that being was "univocal."[14] What Scotus meant was that there is only one kind of being, and all things—human, animal, angelic, divine—share the same being.[15]

At first glance, Deleuze's embracing Scotus on the sameness of being seems to be a very odd move. Embracing the *sameness* of being is a rather strange way to begin a politics that celebrates multiplicity and *difference*. It would seem to make a great deal more sense to begin with an account of being that said being was equivocal, that is, fundamentally different.

Moreover, once Deleuze accepts the univocity, or sameness, of being, the problem arises of how he accounts for difference. If being is univocal, then what could the difference between beings be? Deleuze takes his answer from Scotus and argues that difference is a matter of degrees of power, or, rather, degrees of desire.[16] What distinguishes desire, what establishes difference, is a matter of degree. Univocal being, desire, is differentiated by degrees of intensity. Thus Deleuze writes, "Between a table, a little boy, a little girl, a locomotive, a cow, a god, the difference is solely one of degree of power in the realization of one and the same being."[17] The difference

14. Gilles Deleuze, "Seminar Session on Scholasticism and Spinoza," trans. Timothy S. Murphy, last accessed March 8, 2012, http://www.webdeleuze.com/php/texte.php?cle=176&groupe=Anti Oedipe et Mille Plateaux&langue=2.

15. For Deleuze's treatment of Scotus and the emergence of the univocity of being along the trajectory of Scotus, Spinoza, and Nietzsche, see Gilles Deleuze, *Difference and Repetition*, trans. Paul Patton (New York: Columbia University Press, 1994), 35–42.

16. Deleuze, "Seminar Session on Scholasticism and Spinoza," 4.

17. Ibid.

between things is not qualitative—different kinds of being—but quantitative—a matter of degrees.

Thinking about being not in terms of inert "stuff" but rather in terms of degrees of power or intensities puts us in a position to better understand Deleuze's claim that desire is productive. Being is not inert, motionless material that is waiting to be moved by some outside force. Rather, being as desire, as an intensity of power, is in motion, active, creative, productive. Deleuze calls production the immanent principle of desire. By this he means that desire is fundamentally a creative power. As such it is not, as we are likely to think of it, desire for something unattained. Not so for Deleuze. The motive power of reality is not a lack, an absence, a deficiency, or a desire born of a longing for that which it does not have.[18] Desire, accordingly, is not about possession or the drive to possess. Nor is it a matter of meeting needs or seeking pleasure; both of those remain matters of lack and acquisition. Rather, desire produces; it gives. It works. It creates.[19] Desire is a positive force, an aleatory movement that neither destroys nor consumes but endlessly creates new connections with others, embraces difference, and fosters a proliferation of relations between fluxes of desire. As such desire is the power of collaboration and sociality, and to such power Deleuze gives the name "love" and "joy," while the sociality he equates with playing and dancing.[20] And we are reminded of the festivity, the songs, and the dancing in the streets of Seattle.

18. Deleuze and Parnet, *Dialogues*, 91; see also Deleuze and Guattari, *A Thousand Plateaus*, 154.

19. By positing the ontological primacy of productive desire, Deleuze runs the risk of sounding like a vulgar Marxist who reduces everything to the economic forces of production and their shadows. However, Deleuze's account of productive desire does not equate, in any uncomplicated way, productive desire with the modes of production. Drawing the facile equation "productive desire equals modes of production" overlooks the way in which Deleuze's ontology of desire collapses any distinction between a productive base and a nonproductive superstructure. Everything is desire, hence everything is productive: productions of productions, productions of consumptions. The economy produces, but so too does culture, and religion, and the family, and so forth. See Gilles Deleuze and Félix Guattari, *Anti-Oedipus: Capitalism and Schizophrenia*, trans. Robert Hurley, Mark Seem, and Helen R. Lane (Minneapolis: University of Minnesota Press, 1983), 4.

20. *Anti-Oedipus*, 347; Gilles Deleuze, *Nietzsche and Philosophy*, trans. Hugh Tomlinson (New York: Columbia University Press, 1983), 194; Gilles Deleuze, *Expressionism in Philosophy: Spinoza*, trans. Martin Joughin (New York: Zone Books, 1992), 246; Gilles Deleuze, *Spinoza: Practical Philosophy*, trans. Robert Hurley (San Francisco: City Light Books, 1988), 126.

The world, then, is constituted by flows of intensities of desire.
The movement of desire, however, is not anarchic. While desire as
construed by Deleuze is inherently anarchic, it is nevertheless always
already organized or assembled in particular ways. This is yet another sense in which "politics precedes being." There is no "pure
desire" that is not subject to being organized or assembled such
that it flows in some ways and does not flow in others. For instance,
any and every society is an assemblage of desire.[21] Societies are an
ordering and harnessing of the productive power that is desire into
the various social, political, economic, and cultural forms that constitute that society. Laws are a good example of this. Every society
has laws or rules that shape how the productive power of desire is
spent and not spent. Deleuze goes further to emphasize that even the
human person is an assemblage of desire. No less than society, human
subjectivity is the product of desire under determinate conditions.
Thus, for example, whether I think of myself as first and foremost
an autonomous, self-made individual, as a North American, as one
part of a corporate self called the body of Christ, or as a worthless
and wicked person deserving of the blows I receive at the hands of
an abuser, is the effect of the ways the desire that constitutes my
being has been shaped and formed (assembled, to use Deleuze's
mechanical language) by various forces around me. Admittedly this
remains a bit vague right now; when we turn to Foucault shortly, we
will consider this formation of desire in more detail and concretion.
    That desire is always already assembled, however, does not mean
that it is necessarily assembled in one particular way (one privileged
form of society, one privileged human subjectivity). This returns us
to where we began, with the statement "politics precedes being."
That politics precedes being means that any and every assembly or
organization of desire is inherently unstable. Desire is a dynamic
power that resists any and every "capture" in a determinate social,
political, economic, or cultural form. Therefore, resistance and
revolution are always possible.
    This is the case because in Deleuze's philosophy of being, desire
is definalized; it is shorn of any teleology. This is to say that desire
has no pregiven end or purpose beyond its own experimental expressiveness. As previously suggested, desire resists any and every
end, any and every assembly and organization. Simply by virtue

21. Deleuze and Guattari, *Anti-Oedipus*, 29.

of its being the intrinsically productive, creative, anarchic force that it is, desire is antagonistic to every attempt to tie it down to a specific form or purpose. As a consequence, at any moment in any organization or social order, desire may find a line of flight, a crack in that order, and explode that order. As a consequence, every organization, every social formation, every subjectivity is a contingent, unstable assemblage of desire, whose duration is always uncertain, lasting a day, a season, a year, a life, and order is nothing but a temporary check on disorder.[22]

"Behead the King"

Deleuze developed a political philosophy around the notion of desire for the sake of rethinking revolutionary resistance to the advancing global economic order. Foucault used different language and concepts for the same end. In particular, his vision revolved around not desire but power, and he argued that would-be revolutionaries needed to "behead the King."[23] With this reference to regicide he meant to point out that in the 1970s resistance to an oppressive order was hindered by an obsession with the state and a vision of power to effect social change that was concentrated in the state, in its laws and prohibitions. This is to say, with this royal reference Foucault was chastising those who hoped to bring about social change primarily by means of the power of sovereign states to enact laws and enforce various prohibitions. This is a vision of society and of social change where all power originates at the top of a pyramid, if you will, in the state and flows downward to society. Furthermore, power is understood primarily as negative, coercive, restrictive, and repressive, as a limit embodied in the heavy hand of the law. The state wields its power in the form of law, and it does so to prohibit or stop you from doing something.

To those whose imaginations were captured by this royal vision of power, Foucault urged, "Behead the King." By this he decidedly

22. Brian Massumi, *A User's Guide to Capitalism and Schizophrenia* (Cambridge, MA: MIT Press, 1992), 58–59.

23. Michel Foucault, *Power/Knowledge: Selected Interviews and Other Writings 1972–1977*, ed. Colin Gordon (New York: Pantheon, 1980), 121; Michel Foucault, *The History of Sexuality*, vol. 1, *An Introduction*, trans. Robert Hurley (New York: Vintage, 1990), 88–89.

did not mean that the old king should be replaced with a new king. Rather, he meant that the entire model of power as residing in and originating from the summit of the state should be replaced by a completely different vision of social relations and social change.

This royal model of power should be done away with because it conceals many ways in which power is present and actually exercised. By focusing so narrowly on the state as the fulcrum of social change, Foucault suggests that revolutionaries risk "overlooking all the mechanisms and effects of power which don't pass directly via the State apparatus, yet often sustain the State more effectively than its own institutions, enlarging and maximizing its effectiveness."[24]

For this reason, Foucault argues that those who would resist an oppressive order need to move beyond the state. He explains,

> I don't want to say that the State isn't important; what I want to say is that relations of power, and hence the analysis that must be made of them, necessarily extend beyond the limits of the State. In two senses: first of all because the State, for all the omnipotence of its apparatuses, is far from being able to occupy the whole field of actual power relations, and further because the State can only operate on the basis of other, already existing power relations. The State is superstructural in relation to a whole series of power networks that invest the body, sexuality, the family, kinship, knowledge, technology and so forth. True, these networks stand in a conditioning-conditioned relationship to a kind of "meta-power" which is structured essentially round a certain number of great prohibition functions; but this meta-power with its prohibitions can only take hold and secure its footing where it is rooted in a whole series of multiple and indefinite power relations that supply the necessary basis for the great negative forms of power.[25]

What Foucault is arguing is that the state is not the source and center of power. While it is an important and powerful social agent or actor and so should not be ignored, the state does not generate and dispense all power. Rather, the state exists on a field that is crossed by power, by relations of power, that are already present and active in society in relations like the family and technology and the production and dispersion of knowledge and so forth. (More will be said about this shortly.)

24. Foucault, *Power/Knowledge*, 73.
25. Ibid., 122.

The Ubiquity of Power

According to Foucault, power is better understood as omnipresent, as always already everywhere, with no single point of origin or source. As such, power is not something that could be possessed and hence contained in an entity like the state. Rather, power is a network of relations sprawling across society. Power is dispersed, coextensive with the social body, ubiquitous—everywhere.

Power is omnipresent, however, not because it has captured and subjected everything to itself, like we might imagine a dictatorship or concentration camp. Rather power is omnipresent because it is produced from one moment to the next, at every point, in every relation.[26] Power is everywhere because it comes from everywhere. It has no single point of origin, no unique source of sovereignty from which secondary and descendent forms emanate.[27] For this reason Foucault writes that in thinking of power, "I am thinking rather of its capillary form of existence, the point where power reaches into the very grain of individuals, touches their bodies and inserts itself in their actions and attitudes, their discourses, learning processes and everyday lives . . . a synaptic regime of power, a regime of its exercise *within* the social body, rather than *from above* it."[28]

Insofar as the state exercises power, therefore, it does so only to the extent that when it arrives on the social field, it manages successfully to harness or capture some of those already existing forces. The state, in other words, does not possess any power in its own right. It is not the fount of all power. Even when power does take a hierarchal or pyramidal form in institutions like the army, factory, or state, the summit is not the source of a power that trickles down to subordinate levels. The summit and subordinate positions in the hierarchy stand in a relation of mutual support and conditioning. Thus the state is not a unified pillar of sovereign power. Instead, like every institution, it is an ensemble of power relations.[29] Attacking the mythical sovereign power of the state, Foucault says:

> But the state, no more probably today than at any other time in its history, does not have this unity, this individuality, this rigorous

26. Foucault, *History of Sexuality*, 1:93.
27. Ibid.
28. Foucault, *Power/Knowledge*, 39.
29. Ibid., 159.

functionality, nor, to speak frankly, this importance; maybe, after all, the state is no more than a composite reality and a mythicized abstraction, whose importance is a lot more limited than many of us think. Maybe what is really important for our modernity—that is, for our present—is not so much the *éstatisation* of society, as the "governmentalization" of the state.[30]

What Foucault means by "governmentalization" will be a significant part of the focus of the next chapter. For the time being, what we should take from this is that the state does not embody the sovereign center of social power.

Foucault's emphasis on the ubiquity of power has prompted serious objections. In particular, it is thought that by making power omnipresent, by insisting that power is not the possession of a sovereign state but always already spread across society, he has undermined the prospects for social change. After all, when power was identified with the state, it might have been possible to avoid that power and to find or create spaces where that power was either absent or weak. But the ubiquity of power would appear to foreclose any space or possibility of resistance to or escape from the negative, coercive power of the state. How does Foucault's vision of power nurture instead of crush resistance and social change?

To begin with, the claim that Foucault's account of power is an inadvertent apology for a totalitarian state fails to grasp that the state is *not* the source of power and that all power is not finally controlled by the state. The state has and exercises power, but state-funded power is not the only power that exists. As Foucault said, power is *produced* in every moment from every point; it has no single source such as the state. Power is multiple.

Hence, to claim that power is always already everywhere is decidedly *not* to say that the negative, coercive power of the state is always already everywhere and cannot be escaped. To the contrary, the ubiquity of power means that at any time and place, resistance is always possible.[31] "Where there is power," writes Foucault, "there is resistance."[32] When confronted with the coercive arm of the state

---

30. Michel Foucault, "Governmentality," in *The Foucault Effect: Studies in Governmentality*, ed. Graham Burchell, Colin Gordon, and Peter Miller, trans. Rosi Braidotti (Chicago: University of Chicago Press, 1991), 103.
   31. Foucault, *History of Sexuality*, 1:95–96.
   32. Ibid., 1:96.

and its law, no matter how comprehensive that power feels, resistance is always possible. The multiplicity of power—its multiple forms and origins or sources—means that the negative power of the state is never as comprehensive or total as the state would wish one to believe.

Moreover, the multiplicity of power means as well that power relations are not always negative and coercive. Notwithstanding the negative connotations that frequently cling to notions of "power," and notwithstanding the way the juridical power of the state is largely a matter of a negative power of prohibition, according to Foucault power itself is not negative. Coercion or domination is only one form that power can take; it is not the essence of power. As Foucault writes, criticizing those who imagine a utopian world without relations of power:

> This is precisely a failure to see that power relations are not something that is bad in itself that we have to break free of. I do not think that any society can exist without power relations, if by that one means strategies by which individuals try to direct and control the conduct of others. The problem, then, is not to try to dissolve them in the utopia of completely transparent communication, but to acquire the rules of law, the management techniques, and also the morality, the *ethos*, the practice of the self, that will allow us to play these games of power with as little domination as possible.[33]

Foucault's vision is of a world populated by individuals who are always already immersed in power relations, who are unavoidably enmeshed in webs of influence that they simultaneously exert and respond to, and his hope is for a world where those power relations do not take form as domination, whereby the expressiveness and freedom of some individuals are subjected to the control of others.

Conclusion

The similarities between Deleuze and Foucault are readily apparent.[34] They hold in common a vision of reality inhabited by individuals,

33. Michel Foucault, *Foucault Live*, ed. Sylvère Lotringer (New York: Semiotext(e), 1996), 446.
34. An astute reader will note that I have conflated Foucault's work on technologies and power with Deleuze's ontology of desire to arrive at "technologies of desire." It

individuals who are constituted by a positive, expressive power or desire. They also share a judgment, to this point admittedly more implicit than explicit, that the political-economic forms of the modern world oppress and distort this most basic expressive power or desire by subjecting it to the ends of the capitalist order. Based on this judgment and the analysis of how this oppression occurs, they proffer similar criticisms of those who would topple the current order. Specifically, they share a criticism of revolution, of social change, that presumes statecraft, that presumes power resides in and flows from control of the helm of state. Instead, they argue that desire is eternally restless and not so easily captured or contained in a sovereign state, that power is multiple and omnipresent so that social change can be effected anywhere at any time and does not hinge on seizing the negative power of the state.

Granted, their work is quite abstract and difficult to comprehend. That is why the chapter began with the "Battle in Seattle." Deleuze and Foucault offer a philosophical lens through which to make sense of the kind of postmodern event that took place on the streets of Seattle in late 1999. But more important, the Multitude concretizes the heady abstraction of Deleuze's and Foucault's thought by offering a real-life display of the kind of postmodern politics they envision.[35] On the streets of Seattle, a multitude of expressive singularities, anarchic and discordant flows of desire, spontaneously came together in a common effort to effect social change, not by seizing the state but simply by temporarily occupying a half dozen

---

should be noted that although Deleuze and Foucault were close friends, at least until the final years of Foucault's life, and deeply admired each other's work, there were differences between them. For the purposes of my project, however, the substance of these differences and the ways in which Foucault might object to his being assimilated into Deleuze's ontology of desire are not important. For a concise account of their relationship and the compatibility of their work, see Philip Goodchild, *Deleuze and Guattari: An Introduction to the Politics of Desire* (Thousand Oaks, CA: Sage Publications, 1996), 131–35, as well as the conversation between Deleuze and Foucault, published as "Intellectuals and Power" in *Language, Counter-Memory, Practice*, ed. Donald Bouchard (Ithaca, NY: Cornell University Press, 1977), 205–17. For an example of how Deleuze used Foucault, see his work, *Foucault*, trans. Seán Hand (Minneapolis: University of Minnesota Press, 1988). See also the essay by Deleuze, "Desire and Pleasure" in *Foucault and His Interlocutors*, ed. Arnold I. Davidson (Chicago: University of Chicago Press, 1997), 183–92.

35. The affinity between the micropolitics of Deleuze and Foucault and that of Hardt and Negri is stated most explicitly in Hardt and Nengri's earlier collaboration, *Empire* (Cambridge, MA: Harvard University Press, 2000).

streets and intersections, to the dismay and befuddlement of the state-force marshaled against them.

What are we to make of all of this? How does this illuminate the form of faithful discipleship in a postmodern economy? The chapter clearly raises more questions than it answers. Introducing Deleuze and Foucault, it has studiously set aside any kind of theological or moral evaluation. Furthermore, it has simply taken for granted their objection to capitalism. Both of these issues will be addressed as we proceed.

All this chapter has really done is introduce the basic philosophical landscape of their work. Nevertheless, it does provide some grist for the Christian theological mill, prompting us to contemplate our investment in politics as statecraft as well as the relationship between economy and desire.

Having introduced Foucault and Deleuze on the micropolitics of desire, we now turn to their account of how desire is organized or disciplined. In particular, we consider how capitalism is a discipline of desire.

2

Capital Desire

Capitalism as an Economy of Desire

Desire Gone Wild

One is hard-pressed to tell that it is night from the middle of this street, teeming as it is with a mass of humanity that undulates like a great tide forced by the buildings that line it like uncertain levees into a narrow channel. The surface of this sea glows yellow, red, green, and white, bathed in hues cast off by street lamps, neon signs, and strings of flashing lights that adorn everything as if it were Christmas. It seems to lap up the sides of the levees, leaving eddies of humanity dripping off the lacy-wrought and cast-iron balconies adorned with medieval armor, bromeliads and begonias, artwork, and posters declaring "Girls Gone Wild," all of which advertise a bar, a band, cold beer. The air is filled with the rhythms of jazz, blues, zydeco, rock 'n' roll, and chants of "show us your tits" followed by an exuberant cheer, whistles, and exclamations. Floats cut through this sea, with krewes decked out in festive masquerade costumes of all kinds and colors, casting bead necklaces, doubloons, and toys into the boisterous sea of humanity, setting off a frenzied scramble to collect the throws among the masses, many of whom are also costumed in all manner of colors and themes, with tangles of beads around their necks so thick they look like they're wearing oxen's yokes. In a doorway someone vomits; on a street corner someone else performs a sex act on a stranger while others cheer and cameras flash.

This chapter is about how, according to Deleuze and Foucault, desire is organized or disciplined by capitalism. Like the previous chapter, it begins with a snapshot, a concrete display meant to illuminate some of the basic themes and points of the chapter. In this case, that display is provided by Mardi Gras, the New Orleans carnival synonymous with floats, masks, beads, and sexual exhibitionism.

This, however, raises a problem. For while the chapter purports to be about capitalist disciplining of desire, in the cultural lexicon Mardi Gras is associated not with capitalism and most certainly not with discipline but its opposite: escapism, liberation, freedom, and transgression. Indeed, the folks who engage in such sexual exhibitionism often use the language of liberation and freedom from all restraint and discipline to describe their actions. One such person says of her behavior: "The city that I live in, it's very Christian! But my friends and I have agreed not to tell anyone what we've done in New Orleans. . . . It's all about losing your inhibitions. . . . It's liberating."[1] This is echoed by another who explains engaging in a public sex act thus: "I am a very strong Christian, like totally believe in morals and all that. Strong morals. So for me to do that, totally New Orleans!"[2] Another reports that outside of Mardi Gras, "I'm just normal. I'm law-abiding. I go to church. I follow the rules. I have a 9–5 routine. . . . I love this. I love coming out here and just being free. It's a feeling of freeing yourself and just letting yourself go."[3]

Hence Mardi Gras would appear to exemplify not capitalist discipline but hedonism, plain and simple. As such, the "playful deviance"[4] on display there hardly promises to bolster the argument of this chapter. For this reason, we need to step back from what happens on the streets of New Orleans during a few weeks every spring and take a longer view.

1. David Redmon, "The Liberation Thesis: Secret Deviance, Disciplinary Power, and Escapism," Carnivalesque Films, 16, accessed October 5, 2009, http://www.carnival esquefilms.com/.
2. David Redmon, "Playful Deviance as an Urban Leisure Activity: Secret Selves, Self-Validation, and Entertaining Performances," *Deviant Behavior: An Interdisciplinary Journal* 24 (2003): 38.
3. Redmon, "The Liberation Thesis," 10–11.
4. Redmon, "Playful Deviance."

Mardi Gras: Made in China[5]

This longer view is from half a world away in the Fujian Special Economic Zone in Fuzhou, China, at the bead factory owned by the Hong Kong–based Tai Kuen Ornament Company. The company produces millions of pounds of the colorful plastic beads that have become synonymous with the Mardi Gras festivities and that function as a kind of currency in the sexual commerce practiced there in particular. The factory is more than a few manufacturing buildings, however; it is an enclosed compound that the North American head of the company that purchases its beads likens to "a concentration camp."[6] It has a gate and guards, the purpose of which is less to ward off outsiders than to keep the compound's residents in line and inside. It is laid out in a manner that enables the guards and supervisors to surveil the grounds twenty-four hours a day, seven days a week, to make sure that all is in keeping with the manifold rules and regulations that order every aspect of the lives of the young workers. These workers are almost entirely female and come from distressed rural areas, hoping to make a little money to send to their families. Among these rules is a ban on workers leaving the compound, except on Sundays, and then only if they are not required to work and have obtained permissions from several layers of supervisors and managers. The compound has a cafeteria, where all eat the same thing and clean their bowls in a communal sink before those starting the workday go to the factory floor. The workers are to be on station exactly eight minutes before their shift starts, lest they are subject to one of the numerous fines. They must also be prepared to work their ten- to eighteen-hour shifts in silence, or face another fine of a day's pay for talking, and work without extraneous thoughts, lest their concentration on their task falters and are therefore subject to more fines. Those finishing their work shift head to the communal washroom before returning to the dorm rooms. Each sixteen-by-twenty-four foot dorm room houses ten workers who share five beds, an awkward arrangement that is manageable by the round-the-clock production schedule at

5. What follows is drawn from *Mardi Gras: Made in China*, directed by David Redmon (2008), and David Redmon, "From the Festival to the Factory," Carnivalesque Films, 3, http://www.carnivalesquefilms.com. See also David Redmon, *Beads, Bodies, and Transformation* (forthcoming), chap. 3.
   6. Redmon, *Mardi Gras*, 19:37.

the factory, which ensures that no more than five workers are free to use the beds at any given time.

The work is monotonous, repetitive, and in some instances dangerous. The beads are made of materials that are toxic and carcinogenic when melted and inhaled. A girl with scarred fingers quickly brings two beads together so an electrically heated pin can melt them into a string, something she does thousands of times a day, year after year. Another girl pulls strings of beads out of a loud, hot machine—with a reputation for cutting off hands—three thousand times a day. Young girls paint miniature Mardi Gras masks, figurines of naked women, and penises. Boys dye the beads, sew trinkets, and stack the beads. All of this is done for as little as ten cents an hour, assuming the workers manage to avoid the ubiquitous fines and collective punishments that can range from a lower, piecemeal rate to the loss of a day's or even a month's pay. This latter fine is incurred for entering the dormitory area of the opposite gender.

The bead factory is clearly a discipline and a capitalist one at that. The factory itself is the product of the opportunity created by Deng Xiaoping's overturning Mao's "Cultural Revolution" and instituting free-market reforms in the late 1970s and early 1980s in an effort to plug China more readily into the globalized capitalist economy. As such, the factory in Fuzhou is just one end of a globalized capitalist commodity chain that links the revelers on the streets of New Orleans with peasants from the Fujian province of China. Furthermore, the disciplinary regime of the factory is clearly and consciously devised and implemented toward the end of constructing good capitalist workers—from the design of the compound, enhancing the surveillance and availability of the work force, to the manifold regulations governing not only the time on task but also the so-called leisure time and space. The factory owner, Mr. Wong, is up-front about, even proud of, the deliberate efforts to transform the young rural women in his factory into highly productive capitalist workers by means of a discipline he notes was devised with the help of his brother who learned it in graduate studies in England. He constantly denigrates their rural mores as he justifies the economic discipline of his factory while simultaneously projecting on to them a capitalist profit motive.

The connection between Mardi Gras, or at least the plastic trinkets that pass for currency on the streets of Mardi Gras, and capitalist discipline is readily apparent in Mr. Wong's bead factory in

Fuzhou. But the connection between capitalist discipline and the revelers on the streets of New Orleans is not yet clear. Granted, a capitalist discipline makes those beads available to the revelers, but one could argue that it is an incidental or accidental connection and not indicative of the basic character of Mardi Gras, which remains transgressive and escapist.

The Political Economy of Mardi Gras

In the documentary *Mardi Gras: Made in China*, there is a moving scene where the women in the bead factory are shown pictures of the beads they produce being used during the Mardi Gras festivities. As photos of the beads being exchanged for men and women removing their clothes and exposing various parts of the bodies circulate, ripples of embarrassed laughter and amazement sweep the tables. Several of the women express their disbelief and incomprehension, declaring that the folks in the pictures must be crazy. Others conclude that what they are seeing is simply a cultural difference between the Chinese and Americans.[7]

While one might justly wonder how long such purported cultural differences will endure when fourteen-year-olds spend as many as eighteen hours a day painting breasts and penises in factories like Mr. Wong's, the scene does highlight the fact that what is on display in New Orleans is not necessarily an expression of some natural, uninhibited desire. One does not naturally or instinctively expose oneself on camera or perform sex acts on strangers in the middle of a crowded street. As the factory workers recognize, such practices belong to a very particular culture or set of customs. The revelers display in their actions a specific understanding of themselves, their bodies, and their relations to other selves and bodies.

In other words, notwithstanding the declarations of those engaged in that "playful deviance," such acts are not an escape from discipline into a time and space of uninhibited, unrestrained freedom. The desire on display there is not as "wild" as its consumers proclaim. While such acts may indeed enact an escape from or transgression of certain forms of discipline and customs—the actors

7. *Mardi Gras*, 1:03.18. Redmon, "From the Festival to the Factory," 20–21. See also Redmon, *Beads, Bodies, and Transformation* (forthcoming), chap. 3.

mention disciplines and customs associated with family and marriage, religion, work, and social circles—they are not necessarily an
escape from all discipline. As the factory workers note, such acts of
"freedom" are not obviously acts of freedom so much as they are a
display of a different cultural logic or discipline. The workers call
it "American." The revelers themselves suggest that what they are
about is not so much freedom as opposition and defiance.

This chapter will suggest that the discipline is better named
"capitalism," for Mardi Gras, far from being a liberating space
where persons can give expression to their true selves and release
repressed desire, is a thoroughly capitalist experience. The actions
on display there are carefully nurtured and encouraged for the sake
of capitalist accumulation. The exhibitionism and voyeurism are
not spontaneous acts of freedom but another instance of capitalist
consumption.

There may have been a time when Mardi Gras was a primarily
indigenous celebration of local culture and heritage that existed
independent of or only on the borders of the political economy
of capitalism, but such is not now the case and has not been for
many decades.[8] Today Mardi Gras is a product, a spectacle, an
experience that is produced, packaged, and marketed year-round
for the purpose of enhancing both New Orleans's position in the
global economy as well as the capitalist accumulation of a host of
economic actors—local and national businesses, as well as multinational corporations. Tourism bureaus, chambers of commerce,
metropolitan planning councils, economic development agencies,
and municipal offices all work alongside a plethora of businesses
to market the Mardi Gras experience. As the documentary *Mardi
Gras: Made in China* suggests, the production of Mardi Gras para-
phernalia is no longer a local craft but a global industry on a mass
scale. Likewise, souvenirs and memorabilia are available year-round
in local shops as well as on the Internet. The "experience" itself is
even packaged and sold, not only in the form of tourist packages
promoting the actual carnival but in do-it-yourself kits for class-
rooms, teenagers, or adults-only parties that purport to make the
experience available to anyone (who can afford it) anywhere and

8. What follows draws from Kevin Fox Gotham, "Marketing Mardi Gras: Commodification, Spectacle and the Political Economy of Tourism in New Orleans," *Urban
Studies* 39, no. 10 (2002): 1735–56.

anytime. Likewise local businesses have sprung up that promise the Mardi Gras experience year-round, complete with the ability to dress up in carnival costumes and so forth.

National and multinational businesses have also appropriated the spectacle of Mardi Gras as a means of furthering capitalist accumulation on a national and even international level year-round by means of various brand-alignment and extension strategies, as well as a host of tie-ins. Las Vegas, Disney, and Universal Studios all promote the experience as they duplicate it. So do various media corporations through such avenues as MTV, the Discovery and Learning channels, as well as the Playboy channel. Perhaps unsurprisingly, alcohol and tobacco companies are major actors in selling Mardi Gras, as are the companies that are appearing with increasing frequency as sponsors of floats in the various Mardi Gras parades.

Although it may feel like a spontaneous outburst of freedom, of desire shorn of any and every discipline, it is in fact the product of a particular formation of desire. In this regard, it is worth noting that the sexual exhibitionism and voyeurism that distinguishes Mardi Gras in the contemporary popular imagination is not a long-standing part of Mardi Gras. To the contrary, the sexually transgressive dimension of the carnival rose to ascendancy at roughly the same time that Mardi Gras became "big business," all of which is to say that the Mardi Gras experience is the effect of a capitalist formation of desire. That it is experienced as freedom by the revelers is but a testimony to the spectacular magic of capitalist disciplining of desire. For a deeper appreciation of this capitalist discipline of desire we return to Deleuze and Foucault.

Capitalism, Desire, and the State

Describing Deleuze's work, Foucault suggests that it is a kind of "introduction to the non-fascist life." He writes that Deleuze is about the work of ferreting out "the fascism in us all, in our heads and in our everyday behavior, that fascism that causes us to love power, *to desire the very thing that dominates and exploits us.*"[9] This

9. Michel Foucault, preface to Gilles Deleuze and Félix Guattari, *Anti-Oedipus: Capitalism and Schizophrenia*, trans. Robert Hurley, Mark Seem, and Helen R. Lane (Minneapolis: University of Minnesota Press, 1983), xiii. Italics added.

is striking because it is commonplace to think of domination and exploitation as both obvious and abhorrent by those who experience them. Yet how often do we encounter folks who are addicted to something or who are suffering the consequences of some great injustice who seem oblivious to their bonds? The streets of Mardi Gras provide a glaring example. From the perspective of the classic Christian tradition, much of the behavior there is a bold display of human captivity to the madness that is sin. Yet that would be news to many of the revelers who insist they are experiencing and expressing freedom.

Building on the micropolitics of desire sketched in the last chapter, Deleuze and Foucault develop an account of human desire and its capture by capitalism that accounts for how we could be enslaved to the capitalist market in a way that we actually *want* or *desire* that captivity, all the while calling it and claiming ourselves to be "free." This chapter focuses on Deleuze's and Foucault's account of how capitalism is an economy of desire, how it disciplines desire for market ends.

With regard to capitalism's disciplining desire, Deleuze focuses in particular on the state and how it has disciplined the creative, productive power that is desire so that it is available to capitalism. His tale is of the state descending from sovereign heights above the economy, being submerged in the economy, before finally becoming utterly subservient to the economy, to global capitalism. It is also a tale of flows of desire in the form of labor and capital becoming more abstract, that is, less tied to particular, concrete forms and sites. Deleuze recounts this capitalist disciplining of desire by focusing on the history of three forms of the state: the imperial state-form, diverse state-forms, and the modern state-form.

His history of capitalism's capture of desire begins with the archaic imperial state. The archaic imperial state appeared against the backdrop of primitive agricultural communities.[10] According to Deleuze, these agricultural communities organized or disciplined desire by means of lineage and territory. Flows of goods, people, and privileges were coded according to kinship (filiation) and marriage (alliance). When the archaic imperial state arrived, these primitive

10. Deleuze draws on the anthropological work of Pierre Clastres. See Gilles Deleuze and Félix Guattari, *A Thousand Plateaus: Capitalism and Schizophrenia*, trans. Brian Massumi (Minneapolis: University of Minnesota Press, 1987), 429.

territorial codes were dismantled, or, as Deleuze says, "deterritorial-ized," by the despotic rule of the emperor. Yet at the same time that the imperial state *released* desire from the primitive social codes that had shaped and defined it, the imperial state also *recaptured* or "reterritorialized" desire. That is, the imperial state did not sim-ply set desire in the form of money, property, and labor free but instead replaced the older discipline with a new discipline—one that made the emperor the sole public-property owner, the master of the surplus or stock, the organizer of large-scale works, and the cornerstone of all public functions.[11] Thus the first state-form sought simply to control desire and subject desire to the state.

Yet recall from the preceding chapter that desire is a dynamic force that resists every organization. Thus even as the archaic im-perial state reterritorialized desire, its control of that desire was uncertain, unstable, contested. For this reason, writes Deleuze, the law of the state is *not* the law of all or nothing.[12] This is to say, state sovereignty or control is never total. While it may succeed in capturing and disciplining some flows of desire, the state does not succeed in capturing all desire, and even the control it succeeds in exerting is always tenuous, contingent. (Think, for example, of the impossibility of containing all "leaks" in a government or orga-nization.) At any moment, flows of desire may create or exploit cracks in the system of control and so escape.

So it is unsurprising that some flows of desire elude capture by the archaic imperial state.[13] As a consequence of this escape and efforts to recapture desire, the imperial state undergoes a mutation. Ex-tremely diverse states—evolved empires, autonomous cities, feudal systems, monarchies—now appear. This is the second state-form Deleuze considers.

For our purposes, what is important to note with regard to this state-form is how it forgoes the effort to *contain* desire. Instead, it seeks only to *regulate* flows of desire. Eschewing control, it opts for regulating relations between persons and things, between labor and capital. A crude analogy that might clarify this is the differ-ence between a dam or a dike, and a waterwheel or perhaps a lock.

11. Deleuze and Guattari, *A Thousand Plateaus*, 428; Deleuze and Guattari, *Anti-Oedipus*, 199.
12. Deleuze and Guattari, *A Thousand Plateaus*, 360.
13. Ibid., 449.

Whereas the first state-form is like a dam or a dike that tries to contain a flow of water, the second state-form is like a waterwheel or a lock that seeks only to harness or regulate a flow that exceeds containment.

The diverse state-form regulates flows of desire. It frees (or deterritorializes) desire from the archaic imperial state and then attempts to reterritorialize the flow of desire not by containing it but by regulating it. Thus all property is no longer the property of the state or emperor, but property is still associated with particular, concrete land, people, and things that the state can regulate and tax. Likewise, labor is no longer owned by the monarch, but it is still tied to individual workers' relations of dependence on particular owners (a condition that will change with the next mutation), which, again, could be regulated by the state.

Accompanying this shift in the goal of the state from containment to regulation is a reconfiguration of social space. Whereas the archaic imperial state attempted to assert complete and total sovereignty over social space, as if the state were the tip of a pyramid completely overseeing the base below, the diverse state surrenders such grandiose aspirations. The diverse state is no longer the container *of* the entire social field but rather is now only one player *within* a social field that is crisscrossed by flows of desire and other social formations. If the archaic imperial state functioned as the *transcendent* unity of the social field (i.e., the tip of the pyramid that is society), the new state-form has become *immanent* to the social field (i.e., the pyramid has collapsed into the base).

Yet, again, flows of desire escape this regulation, and the diverse state-form is overwhelmed. This happens as the flow of labor escapes determination as slavery or serfdom (which are concrete relations of personal dependency) and becomes naked, free labor, and as wealth is no longer merchants' or landed wealth (which, again, is tied to concrete land, people, and things) but becomes pure homogenous capital, a capital where money begets money and value begets surplus value.[14] Think of how contemporary capital has become

14. Ibid., 452–53; see also Deleuze and Guattari, *Anti-Oedipus*, 231. Herman Daly and John Cobb summarize this change well: "Land was abstracted from the totality of the natural world and treated as an exchangeable commodity. Work time or labor was abstracted out of life and treated as a commodity to be valued and exchanged according to supply and demand. Capital was abstracted out of the social inheritance, no longer to be treated as a collective patrimony or heirloom, but as an exchangeable source of

abstract, a matter of value, of electronic digits in the capitalist world's financial computers, that may be temporarily attached to particular concrete land, people, or things but can detach from any given concrete form or relation and move around the world with relative ease. Think of how, increasingly, labor is less a matter of a specific career or vocation and more of an abstract productivity attached temporarily to particular careers or jobs that may change many times over a life. History, argues Deleuze, is now on the brink of capitalism. Capitalism is born as flows of desire overwhelm the diverse state's ability to regulate desire and connect it to specific, concrete people, land, or things.

Thus the advent of capitalism is the crossing of a new threshold of deterritorialization.[15] Recall that as the various state-forms emerged, they deterritorialized desire, freeing land, labor, and money from the previous social formations' discipline. But such deterritorialization was always *relative*; it was not complete. Desire was always reterritorialized, reattached to the concrete territories under the state's relative or regulatory control.

Capitalism, however, is not territorial.[16] Capitalism, Deleuze writes, oversees an "enormous, so-called stateless, monetary mass that circulates through foreign exchange and across borders, eluding control by the States, forming a multinational ecumenical organization, constituting a de facto supranational power untouched by governmental decisions."[17] Examples of the nonterritorial character of capitalism include the transnational corporation, the internationalization of the division of labor, the advancement of flexible manufacturing systems, the expansion of a standardized market/global culture and consumption patterns, the growth of the informal sector of the economy, the introduction of complex systems of credit and exchange, and so forth.[18] Such developments reflect capitalism's abstract, deterritorializing character—capitalism is not constrained by any territory or tied to any organizing center.

---

unearned income to individuals" (*For the Common Good*, 2nd ed. [Boston: Beacon, 1994], 61). They are drawing on the work of Karl Polanyi, *The Great Transformation* (Boston: Beacon, 1957).

15. Deleuze and Guattari, *A Thousand Plateaus*, 453.

16. Ibid., 454.

17. Ibid., 453.

18. Kenneth Surin, "On Producing the Concept of a Global Culture," *The South Atlantic Quarterly* 94 (1995): 1185.

Instead, capitalism is a matter of the abstract, generalized flow of labor and capital. By "abstract" and "generalized," Deleuze means labor and capital that are not tied to specific economic activities and locations but can shift to any activity or location that is profitable. Think of the changes involved in the shift from "craft" and "trade" to wage labor and the ease with which capital can become liquid (financial) and then move to different economic sectors and sites. The central mechanism for this abstracting is money, which renders everything fungible, liquid.

In light of its abstract or nonterritorial character, Deleuze identifies capitalism as a general axiomatic of decoded flows. As an axiomatic, it concerns "purely functional elements and relations whose nature is not specified, and which are immediately realized in highly varied domains simultaneously," as opposed to dealing in codes, which "are relative to those domains and express specific relations between qualified elements."[19] The distinction Deleuze is making is not easily grasped. Simplified, we might say that codes are analogous to the specific rules that govern specific games, whereas a general axiomatic is the general rule that governs all games. For instance, "Do no harm and do good" might be called a general axiomatic of the moral life, whereas "Don't take the Lord's name in vain" and "Don't practice usury" are codes that specify what the axiomatic looks like in particular, concrete moral contexts.

This distinction should become clearer as we proceed, but a word is in order about why it is important for understanding the nature of contemporary global political economy, for there was a time when capitalism was defined in terms of a particular mode of production and was contrasted with socialist and even feudal modes of production that persist in some regions of the world. And people would argue that such and such a country or region was or was not capitalist based on the mode of production present there. Recognizing that capitalism is no longer a matter of a certain manner of production but is rather an axiomatic governing all modes of production clears the way for grasping how the contemporary global political economy might be described as capitalist even though noncapitalist forms or modes of production continue to persist. (Think, for example, of the way the factory in Fuzhou is capitalist even as it resides in and was enabled by a country whose

19. Deleuze and Guattari, *A Thousand Plateaus*, 453.

political economy is Communist.) These matters should become clearer as we continue with Deleuze's narrative of capitalism and the state-form.

At this point in the narrative, at the moment of the advent of capitalism and its infinitely superior forces of deterritorialization, one might wonder if the state-form is even necessary at all. Many argue today that the nation-state is an anachronism whose usefulness has been eclipsed. Deleuze is not one of them. Rather, he argues, in this situation the state-form undergoes yet another mutation.

As capitalism overwhelms the diverse state-form, the modern nation-state emerges. What is distinctive about this state-form is that it is completely subsumed by and thus subservient to capitalism. "Never before," writes Deleuze, "has a State lost so much of its power in order to enter with so much force into the service of the signs of economic power."[20] If the first state-form asserted its sovereignty over economy and the second state-form descended to regulate economy, the modern state-form now *serves* economy.

Specifically, the modern nation-state operates as a model of realization for the worldwide capitalist axiomatic. It serves capitalism by organizing desire, by organizing the social basis of production and preparing it for insertion into the worldwide capitalist machine. (Think, for example, of national government efforts on behalf of a host of "free trade" agreements and local government efforts on behalf of economic development.)

What is noteworthy is that this holds true for all states. All states serve capitalism, regardless of the particular modes of production present within their territory. Because capitalism is no longer simply a matter of an economic mode of production but is instead a generalized axiomatic of production for the market, capitalism is like a megapolis of which all the nations constitute neighborhoods.[21] And these neighborhoods need not look alike. As an international ecumenical organization, capitalism neither proceeds from an imperial center that imposes itself on and homogenizes an exterior, nor is it reducible to a relation between similar formations.[22] The neighborhoods need not be homogeneous because the capitalist axiomatic is capable of incorporating diverse social formations.

20. Deleuze and Guattari, *Anti-Oedipus*, 252.
21. Deleuze and Guattari, *A Thousand Plateaus*, 434–35.
22. Ibid., 435.

It is not wedded to any single mode of production or logic of accumulation. In other words, capitalism as an axiomatic can effect surplus value from a multitude of diverse political and economic formations. As Deleuze writes:

> To the extent that capitalism constitutes an axiomatic (production for the market), all States and all social formations tend to become *isomorphic* in their capacity as models of realization: there is but one centered world market, the capitalist one, in which even the so-called socialist countries participate. . . . Isomorphy allows, and even incites, a great heterogeneity among States (democratic, totalitarian, and especially "socialist" States are not facades).[23]

The recent history of the Labour Party's rule in Britain, of socialist France, or of García's Peru bears this out. The global capitalist order is able to take desire in whatever form it is organized locally and bend it according to the axiomatic of production for the market.

The unity or consistency of the capitalist axiomatic is in the relation of production for the market. How production for the market is effected is flexible, as long as desire produces for the market. There is a relative independence of capitalist axioms. They can be added, as was the case following the world wars—axioms for the working class, employment, union organization, social institutions, the environment, the role of the state, domestic and foreign markets, and so forth—or they can be subtracted, as was the case in Chile under Pinochet, NAFTA, and GATT, and as characterizes global capitalism generally. Capitalism is flexible—whatever it takes to ensure production for the market.

This flexibility ensures the integration of noncapitalist sectors and modes into the market. Take, for instance, much of the so-called Third World. Neoconservatives are not wrong when they point out that much of Latin America is not "capitalist" in the classic sense associated with the presence of capitalist modes of production. Where they err is in their failure to appreciate the flexibility of contemporary capitalism. Hence, capital acts as the relation of production even in the noncapitalist modes that predominate in the Third World. Thus underdeveloped sectors do not constitute a separate world but rather are integral components of the worldwide

23. Ibid., 436.

capitalist megapolis. It is as though capitalism has put a new twist on Augustine's famous dictum, "Love and do as you please." Now it is, "Produce for the market and do as you please."

This flexibility accounts for the productive typography of places like Brazil or North Carolina. In Brazil there is a broad spectrum of modes of production, from the Stone Age production of the indigenous peoples of the Amazon basin to the advanced computer technology of São Paolo. These very different modes of production coexist within the same national space and produce for the same market. Amazonian artifacts appear on the tourist markets of downtown São Paolo beside laptop computers and video cameras.[24] A similar situation, although perhaps not as pronounced in its extremes, exists in North Carolina, where the Research Triangle Park engages the most technologically advanced production, while, virtually in its shadow, migrants harvest tobacco in conditions approaching those of slavery.

As capitalism has enveloped the globe, all states serve capital. In the current era, the principal way this function is carried out is negative. States' reason for being is increasingly found in reterritorializing the flows of desire that capitalism unleashes. When capitalism advances, it deterritorializes desire, releasing it from prior social formations and codes. The modern state reterritorializes this desire so that it is available to capital. As is painfully clear to the countless so-called developing countries that have felt the state's wrath in response to their resisting capitalism's advance, and as is becoming increasingly clear to North Americans (on the streets of Seattle, for example), the "small-state, strong-state" of global capitalism exists to neutralize and crush resistance, to block the flow of desire that would escape the capitalist discipline.

To this point, Deleuze's narrative of the state-form and capitalism has accomplished three things. First, it has provided an explanation of how the global political economy can be capitalist even though not every state or mode of production is capitalist. Second, it accounts for the persistence and importance of the state-form in this global economic order, even as many continue to claim that the state is obsolete. Third, it tells this story in terms of the liberation and disciplining of the fundamental dynamic creative power that is desire.

24. I owe this example to Surin, "Concept of a Global Culture," 1191.

Unfortunately, Deleuze's work remains highly abstract and generalized. He does not get very specific on *how* desire is disciplined. For this reason, we turn to Michel Foucault and his work on technologies of the self and governmentality. Foucault reminds us that the state-form of which Deleuze wrote is much more than the ensemble of institutions called "the state." Rather, it is a project that includes a host of disciplines exercised through a variety of agents and institutions.

Governmentality

The previous chapter introduced Foucault's thought on the ubiquity of power through his memorable cry, "Behead the King." He asserts that power is exercised throughout the social body and not simply through the institutions and authority of the state. His term for this dispersed discipline is "governmentality."

Governmentality concerns "how to govern oneself, how to be governed, how to govern others, by whom the people will accept being governed, how to become the best possible governor."[25] Governmentality concerns the conduct of oneself and the conduct of others at the micro- and macropolitical levels. At the macro level, governmentality engages power in terms of political sovereignty— the state and society. At the micro level, it engages power in terms of individual conduct. This distinction between the two dimensions of governmentality is further clarified when Foucault distinguishes between four technologies of power:

> (1) technologies of production, which permit us to produce, transform, or manipulate things; (2) technologies of sign systems, which permit us to use signs, meanings, symbols, or signification; (3) technologies of power, which determine the conduct of individuals and submit them to certain ends or domination, an objectivizing of the subject; (4) technologies of the self, which permit individuals to effect by their own means or with the help of others a certain number of operations on their own bodies and souls, thoughts, conduct, and way of being, so as to transform themselves in order

25. Michel Foucault, "Governmentality," trans. Rosi Braidotti, rev. by Colin Gordon, in *The Foucault Effect: Studies in Governmentality*, ed. Graham Burchell, Colin Gordon, and Peter Miller (Chicago: University of Chicago Press, 1991), 87.

to attain a certain state of happiness, purity, wisdom, perfection, or immortality.[26]

Governmentality involves the convergence of technologies of domination and technologies of the self, totalizing power and individualizing power.[27] Governmentality encompasses the relation between the totalizing power that the state exercises as a framework for unity and the individualizing power that Foucault calls "pastoral," a power that aims at ensuring, sustaining, and improving the lives of each and every individual.[28]

Christianity and Pastoral Power

At this point, Foucault's account of governmentality takes the form of a genealogy, which commences with the emergence of pastoral power in ancient Oriental societies, particularly the Hebrews, and its adaptation by the early Christians. The term "pastoral power" is derived from the shepherd's practice of watching over sheep and is associated with the deity or king functioning as a shepherd of the people.[29] In contrast with more impersonal and collective forms of rule, pastoral power is characterized by immediate, direct, and sustained involvement with the flock in ways that are individualized and personal: the shepherd watches over each individual sheep and cares specifically for that one.[30]

Christianity developed and enhanced the use of pastoral power through the practices of examination of conscience and confession.

26. Michel Foucault, "Technologies of the Self," in *Technologies of the Self: A Seminar with Michel Foucault*, ed. Luther H. Martin, Huck Gutman, and Patrick H. Hutton (Amherst: University of Massachusetts Press, 1988), 18; see also Michel Foucault, "About the Beginning of the Hermeneutics of the Self: Two Lectures at Dartmouth," *Political Theory* 21 (1993): 203.

27. Ibid.,132; see also Michel Foucault, *Power/Knowledge: Selected Interviews and Other Writings 1972–1977*, ed. Colin Gordon (New York: Pantheon Books, 1980), 144; Gilles Deleuze, "What Is a *dispositif?*" in *Michel Foucault: Philosopher*, ed. and trans. Timothy J. Armstrong (New York: Routledge, 1992), 159–66; Michel Foucault, "The Subject and Power," *Critical Inquiry* 8 (1982): 782.

28. Michel Foucault, *Politics, Philosophy, and Culture: Interviews and Other Writings 1977–1984*, ed. Lawrence D. Kritzman (New York: Routledge, 1988), 67.

29. Ibid., 63.

30. Ibid., 61–63.

Foucault identifies several aspects of these practices that intensified this pastoral power. First, he notes, Christian practice involved *public* confession, which meant that the shepherd now acquired intimate knowledge of every detail of the sheep's life. Second, confession was cast as a kind of torture or death. Penance was a ritual martyrdom. It marked a rupture of the self with the self, the past, and the world. Hence, Christian pastoral power was oriented not so much toward the acquisition of truth and the establishment of a self as it was toward the renunciation and sacrifice of the self. "In the ostentatious gestures of maceration," Foucault observes, "self-revelation in [confession] is, at the same time, self-destruction."[31] Third, he notes that as confession developed in the monastic traditions of the fourth century, obedience or submission of the sheep to the shepherd became permanent and comprehensive.[32] Fourth, at this time self-examination became much more concerned with thoughts than with actions, with present thoughts rather than past actions.[33] Thus the pastoral power of the Christian technology became geared toward excavating guilt.

Foucault's point is that as Christianity refined the use of pastoral power, it did so in a manner that made the end or purpose of self-disclosure the renunciation and sacrifice of the self. Or, to put this in terms consonant with Deleuze, Christianity developed technologies of the self for the sake of renouncing and repressing desire.

The Sovereign State and the Disciplines

From the Christian expansion of pastoral power, Foucault's narrative jumps to the fifteenth and sixteenth centuries, for it is then, with the advent of the modern state, that individualizing pastoral power is coupled with the totalizing power of the state. This occurred as the doctrine of "reason of state" developed.

"Reason of state" embodied a novel understanding of the nature and purpose of the state. If the medieval Christian vision asserted that the state should serve supernatural ends, and the tradition of princely sovereignty associated with the likes of Machiavelli held

31. Foucault, "Hermeneutics of the Self," 215.
32. Foucault, "Technologies of the Self," 44.
33. Foucault, "Hermeneutics of the Self," 217.

that political power was primarily about preserving the person of the ruler or prince, reason of state insisted that the point of governing was to enhance the strength of the institutions that organize and preserve order within a particular domain. (Here we see "the state" used for the first time in the sense that we typically use it today.) Hence, the sixteenth-century Italian jurist Giovanni Botero defined the doctrine as a "perfect knowledge of the means through which states form, strengthen themselves, endure, and grow."[34]

Reason of state is concerned first and foremost with strengthening and perpetuating the state, but the state recognizes that its strength lies in the strength and prosperity of its subjects. Consequently, the state takes an abiding interest in the details of its subjects' lives. Thus was born what was then called political statistics, or political arithmetic, and the concept of "population." Each individual is now observed, measured, and recorded (birth and mortality rates, geographic distribution, etc.). Subjects are now addressed (measured by the new political statistics) in terms of how that individual's life may contribute to or detract from the state's strength. Thus did government expand to include pastoral power for the sake of, as Foucault puts it, administering life.

Here Foucault's treatment of governmentality incorporates his work on technologies of domination. In his well-known book *Discipline and Punish*, Foucault examines the ways in which governmental power forms and shapes its subjects, not merely by means of overt violence, but also through more subtle technologies of domination. Governing apparatuses form political subjects by weaving an intricate web of micropolitical forces, a "heterogeneous ensemble consisting of discourses, institutions, architectural forms, regulatory decisions, laws, administrative measures, scientific statements, philosophical, moral and philanthropic propositions."[35] This is to say that disciplinary power should not be identified simply with a single institution or cluster of institutions, nor with overt violence. The paradigmatic example of how this disciplinary power operates is Jeremy Bentham's Panopticon, which Foucault describes at length:

> We know the principle on which it was based: at the periphery, an annular building; at the centre, a tower; this tower is pierced

34. Cited by Foucault in *Politics, Philosophy, and Culture*, 74.
35. Foucault, *Power/Knowledge*, 194; see also Deleuze, "What Is a *dispositif*?" 159–66.

with wide windows that open onto the inner side of the ring; the peripheric building is divided into cells, each of which extends the whole width of the building; they have two windows, one on the inside, corresponding to the windows of the tower; the other, on the outside, allows the light to cross the cell from one end to the other. All that is needed, then, is to place a supervisor in a central tower and to shut up in each cell a madman, a patient, a condemned man, a worker or a schoolboy. By the effect of backlighting, one can observe from the tower, standing out precisely against the light, the small captive shadows in the cells of the periphery. They are like so many cages, so many small theatres, in which each actor is alone, perfectly individualized and constantly visible. . . . Each individual, in his place, is securely confined to a cell from which he is seen from the front by a supervisor; but the side walls prevent him from coming into contact with his companions. He is seen, but he does not see; he is the object of information, never a subject in communication.[36]

To perfect the Panopticon, Bentham suggested that the windows of the central tower be fitted with blinds, thereby concealing the presence or absence of the guard. In this situation, unable to verify the occupancy of the tower, it was asserted that inmates would internalize the surveillance and in effect become their own guards. The Panopticon is the model of a governing power that creates subjects who in the absence of direct force nevertheless police themselves.[37] Here we might recall Mr. Wong's comments regarding the intentionality behind the design of the bead factory in Fuzhou.

The Panopticon is a metaphor of sorts for a host of power relations—those operative not only in prisons, but in all sorts of enclosures, like hospitals, schools, armies, and factories, indeed, in the human sciences as a whole, with their constituent forms of observation, surveillance, and judgment enforcing and reinforcing what is deemed normal.

What happens in the seventeenth and eighteenth centuries is the convergence of technologies of domination (the disciplines) with the individualizing pastoral power (sciences of population). The result is the birth of the modern art of government: governmentality.

36. Foucault, *Discipline and Punish*, trans. Alan Sheridan (New York: Vintage, 1995), 200.
37. Ibid., 202–3.

The Rise of Economic Government

At this time, Foucault argues, governmentality was young and immature. It was so because it remained wedded to state sovereignty.[38] As we have seen, reason of state dictated that everything pass through the bottleneck of the state. Yet as the seventeenth and eighteenth centuries unfolded, as a result of political and economic crises, people began to lose confidence in the sovereign state.

Foucault argues that what finally doomed state sovereignty was the economy's escape from the state's control. This escape was linked to the problem of population. The new science of statistics gradually revealed that the population was subject to movements and forces (epidemics, mortality rates, spirals of labor and wealth, changing customs and activities, etc.) that the sovereign power of the state could not contain or control.[39]

Furthermore, the pastoral power exercised by the state also ironically undermined the state's sovereignty by fostering an individualism that made it impossible to unite the population under the state. The diverse ends and processes and interests of the population simply could not be correlated with the end of the state. As populations and commerce expanded, the state was unable to guide those currents through the bottleneck of the state.

In this situation, the eighteenth-century economic thinkers known as the Physiocrats argued that far from constituting a chaotic swamp that needs the state to order it, society and its economy generate their own order and prosperity. Individual interests do not need the state's control; rather, they naturally and spontaneously converge in the public interest. Thus was born the doctrine of laissez-faire, which holds that society is a self-regulating mechanism that is only harmed by excessive state regulation.

Adam Smith's famous "invisible hand" is part of this development.[40] Indeed, the invisibility of Smith's hand is of particular importance; the invisible hand functions precisely because it is

38. Graham Burchell, "Peculiar Interests: Civil Society and Governing 'The System of Natural Liberty,'" in *The Foucault Effect: Studies in Governmentality*, ed. Graham Burchell, Colin Gordon, and Peter Miller (Chicago: University of Chicago Press, 1991), 124.
39. Foucault, "Governmentality," 99.
40. Adam Smith, *An Inquiry into the Nature and Causes of the Wealth of Nations* (Chicago: University of Chicago Press, 1976), 1:477.

invisible. As such, it marks the dissolution of the state's economic sovereignty. The state cannot know how the individual pursuit of interests will conspire toward the public interest; the processes of the economy are opaque.[41]

Not only does economy escape the state, but it also returns to capture its former master. The state now finds itself immersed in a social field that it had previously sought to contain and control. According to the laissez-faire logic of the liberal state, flows of wealth and prosperity dry up when the state attempts to contain them. The state must therefore become immanent to the economic processes; that is, it must forgo the direct acquisition of wealth and instead reconfigure its mission as supporting the economic pursuit of individual interests. Hence, the liberal state is the state of liberty and freedom, with liberty and freedom understood in terms of bolstering the laissez-faire operation of the natural economic processes. The objective of liberal government is the securing of the optimal conditions for the autonomous functioning of the economic processes within society.[42]

As a consequence of this altered objective, the art of government undergoes a transformation. One might say that liberalism is economic government in a dual sense. First, it is government that is particularly attuned to the precepts of political economy. It is government that serves economy. Second, it is economic in the sense that it recognizes that government can at times be more effective and efficient when left in private hands. Liberalism severs the link between maximal governmental effectiveness and a maximal state.[43] This is to say, whereas reason of state equated government with state institutions and assumed that maximal government meant the growth of state programs and institutions, liberalism distinguishes between government apparatuses and the act of governing. It recognizes that government can be extended across society without necessarily extending or expanding state institutions. More to the point, with the arrival of liberalism, governmental control is exercised not only through the formal mechanisms of the state but now operates throughout civil society as well.

41. Ibid., 2:208.
42. Burchell, "Peculiar Interests," 139.
43. Michel Foucault, "Naissance de la biopolitique," in *Résumé des cours*, cited in Burchell, "Peculiar Interests," 138.

Civil Society and Government through Freedom

The liberal state's character as economic government in the dual sense returns us to the intersection of technologies of domination and technologies of the self. Liberalism still has use for technologies of power, but they undergo subtle alteration. They are dispersed beyond state into civil society.

The early liberals argued that society apart from the state was governed by natural economic processes and insisted that the state's job was to aid those economic processes. Thus the space apart from government—civil society—was not a space opposed to government. On the contrary, Foucault insists, even as liberalism restrains the state and champions civil society, it does not juxtapose government and freedom. Rather, liberal government is government *through* freedom. It is government exercised through nonstate apparatuses.

In this regard consider various privately led campaigns of moralization/normalization often associated with health, education, philanthropy, or religion that flourish in civil society. These private campaigns participate in the art of government as they promote specific techniques of the self. By encouraging practices of financial saving or the acquisition of insurance or particular parenting roles or the habits of cleanliness, sobriety, fidelity, self-improvement, responsibility, and so on, they exert a pastoral power, essential to government, that ensures that individual freedom is exercised in ways appropriate to the optimal functioning of the economy.[44] These are of a piece with the bead factory in Fuzhou, designed to alter the behavior of the young rural workers so that they conform to the needs of the machines, as well as the revelry of Mardi Gras, carefully marketed and commodified to consumers as "freedom."

Civil society and the realm of the "private" designate areas of the social field where, in the name of efficiency, government is the responsibility of apparatuses other than the state.

Societies of Control

There is one more turn in this tale of the economic governance of desire. Shortly before his death, Foucault suggested that the

44. I owe these examples to Graham Burchell, "Liberal Government and Techniques of the Self," *Economy and Society* 22 (1993): 272.

disciplinary society was entering into a crisis, prompting yet another mutation in the art of government:

> In the last few years society has changed and individuals have changed too; they are more and more diverse, different, independent. There are ever more categories of people who are not compelled by discipline . . . so that we are obliged to imagine the development of society without discipline. The ruling class is still impregnated with the old technique. But it is clear that in the future we must separate ourselves from the society of discipline of today.[45]

These remarks remained largely undeveloped until Deleuze turned his attention to what he called "societies of control."

Picking up from where Foucault left off, Deleuze notes that the disciplinary society consisted largely of vast spaces of enclosure, such as the school, hospital, prison, and factory. These enclosures ordered life by manipulating the timing and spacing of human activity.[46] Moreover, the force employed by disciplinary mechanisms to accomplish this was, according to Foucault, "heavy, ponderous, meticulous and constant."[47] By the 1960s, however, it was clear that such cumbersome forms of power were no longer efficient and effective. Just as the self-interested subject formed by the early modern state eventually escaped, by the mid-twentieth century the subject of discipline was mounting effective resistance. Whether in the school, the factory, or the family, the disciplined subject was showing itself less compelled by that discipline.

Consequently, in the late 1960s and early 1970s liberal governmentality underwent a mutation, and the society of control emerged, which was a neoliberal intensification of governmentality. Whereas early liberalism was characterized by a passive attitude, with government striving to minimize interference with the naturally occurring patterns and processes of economy, neoliberal governmentality aggressively advances the extension of economic reason into every fiber and cell of human life. As such, it is governmentality fit for a time in which capitalism has enveloped society, absorbing all the conditions of the production and reproduction of life.

---

45. Foucault quoted in Michael Hardt, "The Withering of Civil Society," *Social Text* 14 (1995): 41.

46. Gilles Deleuze, "Postscript on the Societies of Control," *October* 59 (1992): 5.

47. Foucault, *Power/Knowledge*, 58.

This neoliberal art of governmentality, however, is exercised in a manner quite different from that which characterized disciplinary societies. According to Deleuze, the time frame of the closed disciplinary system is collapsing, and we are increasingly subjected to ultrarapid forms of free-floating control.[48] In the disciplinary society, the docile body was formed as it was channeled through a series of enclosures—school, hospital, factory, army, prison—where it was molded in accord with a norm. As the society of control takes hold, those disciplinary enclosures are retreating. The hospital is giving way to neighborhood clinics, HMOs, hospice, and day care. The factory is giving way to the flexible productions of the corporation. The penal system is experimenting with electronic collars. Even school is being replaced by perpetual training.

In societies of control, the body is rendered pliable not by careful containment and conformity to a norm, but by a flexible, variable modulation that is ubiquitous. The corporation, homework, the Internet, cell phones, ATMs, and GPSs: structured passages are receding before the spread of a web of control. "The disciplinary man was a discontinuous producer of energy," writes Deleuze, "but the man of control is undulatory, in orbit, in a continuous network."[49] The human being is no longer enclosed but "wired" and in debt, and, unlike the enclosure, both the network and debt go everywhere, all the time. The credit card has surpassed the time card as the dominant mechanism of insertion into the economy.

No longer is it sufficient for individuals to accept their place beside their machines, in their cubicles, in the lines at the malls as producers and consumers; now they must submit every aspect of their lives to the logic of the economy; they must be entrepreneurs of themselves. Accordingly, the previous era's welfare state is dismantled in the name of reform, and bodies are delivered to the logic of the market. Churches are now run like businesses, with ministers proclaiming themselves "CEOs" and corporations offering contributions in exchange for advertising space. Schools are corporate-sponsored training camps for producers and consumers. Athletic events are saturated with corporate logos and viewed by the participants as merely a means to financial gain in the form of endorsements. Public media and public libraries face extinction. The

48. Deleuze, "Postscript," 4.
49. Ibid., 5–6.

body is just one more commodity—as the revelers of Mardi Gras remind us. Even marriage, children, and the elderly are subjected to the ruthless calculus of economic rationality.[50] In all these ways and more, pastoral power in service of economy has become virtually omnipresent, conforming desire to the capitalist axiomatic even as we proclaim that we are free.

Conclusion

Such is Deleuze's and Foucault's account of the economy of desire, of capitalism's disciplining of desire. Deleuze's history of capitalism and the state-form shows how the state slowly became subservient to capitalist ends and seeks to render desire available to those ends. Foucault's account of governmentality in turn clarifies how what Deleuze calls the state-form is rightly understood as an ensemble of technologies of desire that are not coterminous with the institutions of state but are dispersed throughout civil society. Accordingly, Foucault illuminates how desire is disciplined by capitalism and enslaved to the axiomatic of production for the market not merely by the disciplinary capacity of the state but also through the pastoral power operative in all dimensions of life, from the social and civil to the personal and familial. As a consequence, we are governed through freedom. Capitalism sets us free, deterritorializing desire, even as it sees to it that desire is reterritorialized and our freedom conforms to the needs of the market. So the workers in Fuzhou were set free from their backward rural ways and by means of various disciplines and technologies of the self were enabled to work in grueling conditions as wage earners who produce the beads that in turn are so central to the capitalist apparatuses that ensure we freely desire to spend and consume (to the tune of millions and millions of dollars) as voyeurs and exhibitionists of Mardi Gras.

Gesturing toward the work of later chapters, we might ponder the lessons there are in this for economic discipleship in a postmodern world. If it is commonplace to think about economy in terms of the allocation, production, and distribution of material resources, Deleuze and Foucault challenge the church to think more broadly

50. See chap. 3.

about economy, to consider how the globalized "total market" is neither concerned narrowly with material goods, nor does it merely respond to desire, but rather it is deeply implicated in forming and shaping human desire such that economy does not so much serve human ends as subdues and shapes human desire in service of capital ends.

This leads us to the next chapter, where we take up a moral-theological evaluation of capitalism. If capitalism is an economy of desire, what is wrong with the way that it disciplines desire? How is capitalism at odds with the good news proclaimed by Christianity?

3

What Is Wrong with Capitalism?

From its inception, capitalism has been a force of cataclysmic transformation in one country after another. Capitalism has radically changed every material, social, political, and cultural facet of the societies it has touched, and it continues to do so. Understanding this revolutionary impact of capitalism . . . is a formidable and important intellectual task.[1]

Are Our Hands Clean?

A story is told about a monk, St. Ignatius of Sardinia, who used to travel the streets adjacent to his monastery with a sack to beg. It was his habit to avoid begging from a certain merchant who had amassed his fortune by defrauding the poor. The merchant, concerned that this reflected poorly on him in the eyes of his neighbors, complained to Ignatius's superior, who then commanded Ignatius to solicit the merchant. To this order, Ignatius responded obediently, "Very well. If you wish it, Father, I will go,

1. Peter Berger, *The Capitalist Revolution* (New York: Basic Books, 1986), 3.

81

but I would not have the [monastery] dine on the blood of the poor." As expected, on being visited by the monk the next time he was out begging, the merchant received him with fanfare, gave generously, and insisted that he come again in the future. Ignatius departed with his sack of newly acquired alms over his shoulder, and turned down the street toward the monastery. Yet no sooner had he begun this journey than a dark stain appeared on the underside of his sack and large drops of blood began oozing from it. The drops splattered on the merchant's doorstep and continued to fall from the sack onto the street. Everywhere he went, a trickle of blood followed Ignatius. When he arrived at the monastery, he was met by his superior. Ignatius unshouldered the oozing sack and laid it at his superior's feet. His superior gasped and recoiled, asking, "What is this?" "This," said Ignatius, "is the blood of the poor."[2]

A contemporary version of this tale, suited to our globalized economy with its long commodity chains that simultaneously reveal and conceal that connection, might begin with a stop on our morning commute, under an electronic sign that reads "The Perfect Experience." Around a table, we are cheerily greeted by a barista gushing about the amazing experience of working there and about all the lives the company she works for touches, and are served one of the two billion cups of coffee that are poured daily, as retail coffee sales have exploded over the last two decades from $30 billion to over $80 billion. And the tale might end in Tilapa, Mexico, or Oromia, Ethiopia, where farmers like Burte Arba attempt to eke out a living producing coffee for sale on an international commodity market dominated by a handful of international brands that pit producers against one another so that the prices offered for their coffee sometimes fall significantly below the cost of production and never reach a level sufficient to lift them out of the grinding poverty that leaves their children malnourished, unschooled, and often in dire need of international emergency food aid.[3] This is a tale that could be told in countless settings, involving the misted

2. Dorothy Day, *Selected Writings*, ed. Robert Ellsberg (Maryknoll, NY: Orbis, 1993), 108–9.

3. See *Black Gold: Wake Up and Smell the Coffee*, directed by Marc Francis and Nick Francis (2006). See also *Coffee, Corn, and the Cost of Globalization*, by Mennonite Central Committee (2004), and *Life and Debt*, directed by Stephanie Black (2001).

fruits and vegetables in the produce section of the corner grocer, to the shirts and undergarments that cover our bodies, to the wood, oil, plastic, rubber, and silicon circuitry that empower our lives. However the tale is told, the questions remain the same: What is this? Are our hands clean?

What Is Wrong with Capitalism?

For Deleuze and Foucault, rejection of capitalism was simply taken for granted. Yet this will not do, for it is not at all clear that capitalism and Christianity are at odds to any significant degree. Indeed, evangelical Christians—precisely those Christians who most forthrightly proclaim their adherence to the classic Christian faith—are some of the most ardent advocates of capitalism and its advance.

Granted, insofar as capitalism was cast as the villain on the streets of Seattle, Mardi Gras, and on the shop floor in Fuzhou, we might surmise the shape of that critique. Likewise, the previous two chapters imply that Deleuze and Foucault perceive capitalism to be in some way repressive of the creative, productive power that is desire. In what follows, a moral and theological evaluation of capitalism is developed. This moral and theological evaluation, however, does not proceed in the usual way, which is precisely why Deleuze's and Foucault's account of capitalism as an economy of desire proves helpful. To sort all of this out, let us begin with the usual way of morally weighing capitalism.

What is this usual way of morally evaluating capitalism? Engage someone in a conversation about the morality of capitalism. Ask if it is good or bad, right or wrong. Invariably, the conversation will revolve around the issue of whether capitalism *works*. More specifically, the question will turn—in endless circles of undoubtedly escalating rhetoric, if not tempers as well—on whether it aids persons who are poor in escaping their poverty or abets the forces that perpetrate and perpetuate that poverty. Does capitalism reduce poverty and elevate the standard of living of persons who are poor, or does it perpetuate and exacerbate the suffering of the destitute and impoverished?

Furthermore, it is an argument that hinges on empirical evidence. So both advocates and opponents of capitalism appeal to facts, figures, numbers, and statistics, with perhaps a bit of anecdotal evidence thrown in for good measure, to support their claim that capitalism does or does not work. Reports of various economic institutes or nongovernmental organizations that track the welfare and development of peoples are appealed to. Income, economic growth, poverty, and mortality rates are bandied about in an effort to establish what is the case.

The empirical focus of these debates makes perfectly good sense because there is widespread agreement among Christians that concern for persons who are poor and alleviating the afflictions associated with poverty are indeed proper tasks of the economic order and so are rightly used to gauge the morality of an economic order.

While empirical debates about the efficacy of capitalism may be appropriate, unfortunately, they are as endless as they are fruitless. This is not to say that they do not have answers, only that the answers and evidences proffered in such discussions rarely, if ever, prove persuasive.

The problems with the typical empirical debate about the morality of capitalism, however, run deeper than the inability of empirical evidence to win the day. The more fundamental flaw to the debate concerns the nature of the question that is put to capitalism.

Does capitalism work? is the wrong question to put to capitalism. It is the wrong question because it is rather obvious that capitalism works. Indeed, although they reject capitalism, Foucault and Deleuze do not question that it works, that it is a profoundly productive force. No economic order to date has so obviously displayed such an enormous productive capacity as has capitalism. Hence, when the empirical question put to capitalism is, Does it work? there really is no debate; the obvious answer is yes.

What Work Does Capitalism Do?

Instead of asking, Does capitalism *work?* we ought to ask, *What* work does it do? This is the case because capitalism's moral problems do not reside merely in its failure to work but in the kind of work that it does when it works, where it succeeds. In this regard, the Christian philosopher Alasdair MacIntyre has noted, "Although Christian indictments of capitalism have justly focused attention upon the wrongs done to the poor and the exploited, Christianity has to view any social and economic order that treats being or becoming rich as highly desirable as doing wrong to those who must not only accept its goals, but succeed in achieving them. . . . Capitalism is bad for those who succeed by its standards as well as for those who fail by them, something that many preachers and theologians have failed to recognize."[4] In other words, even if capitalism is actually improving the situation of persons who are poor, as its defenders claim, it would still be wrong and therefore rightly resisted.

Why? Why would capitalism still be wrong even if it worked, in the commonplace sense of alleviating or reducing poverty? Why is it wrong not simply for what it fails to do, but for what it does? For an answer to this question, we need to step back for a moment—way back to the beginning—and ask the seemingly innocuous question, What are people for?

What Are People For?

Why are we here? What is our end or purpose? St. Augustine (354–430 CE) captured the Christian tradition's answer as well as anyone when he said that our hearts are restless until they rest in God. St. Thomas Aquinas (1225–74 CE) made the same point a bit differently when he said that our end is beatitude, or blessedness, which is nothing less than friendship with God. And the Calvinist divines who met at Westminster in 1647 made a similar claim when they declared that the chief end of the human being is to worship and enjoy God.

In other words, people are for desiring and delighting in God and reflecting God's glory. We are created for friendship, for communion, with God. The Trinity is a communion of love into which we are invited. Of course, this friendship is not merely a matter of me and God, of me and Jesus. After all, Scripture reminds us we cannot be friends of God if we hate our neighbors (1 John 3:17; 4:20–21) and that redemption involves breaking down the walls of hostility that divide peoples (Eph. 2; Gal. 3:28); hence, the commandments are succinctly summed up in the exhortation that we "love God and neighbor" (Matt. 22:35–40).

4. Alasdair MacIntyre, *Marxism and Christianity*, 2nd ed. (London: Duckworth, 1995), xiv.

More than this, the communion for which we were created involves the nonhuman creation as well. Thus Scripture casts redemption on a cosmic scale, speaking of a new heaven and a new earth, proclaiming Christ to be the communion of all in all, and painting a picture of the peaceable kingdom where humanity and critters exist in harmony and where critters join the heavenly host in praising God.

What, then, is the problem? If we were created to desire God and live in communion with one another in God, why are our hearts so clearly not at rest? Why can't we all just get along? If we are created for friendship, why do we have to pray for our enemies? Why do we live in fear of our neighbors and constantly look over our shoulder at the stranger? The Christian tradition accounts for this in terms of sin.

And what is sin at its heart? Not merely the breaking of rules or doing what we should not, although a full account of sin would certainly encompass those. Recalling both Augustine and the Calvinist divines, we might construe sin as fundamentally a matter of the corruption of our desire. We were created to desire God and the things of God, to delight in and enjoy God and to revel in God's glory; yet, in sin we no longer do so. We do not desire God and the things of God. Our desire is disordered. As the prophet Isaiah suggests (55:2), we desire things that do not satisfy. It would not be too strong to say that we are enslaved, held captive by, this disordered desire (see 1 Tim. 6:9). That is why our hearts are restless.

Furthermore, recalling Aquinas as well as Scripture, we might elaborate a bit more and describe sin in terms of a breach or rupture of communion. We were created for friendship with God and one another, yet, captive to our disordered desires, we struggle, fight, compete (see James 4:1–3; Gen. 4–11). As the early church taught, sin is a matter of division, of the breach or rupture of communion. For this reason, Origen (185–254 CE) declared that where there is sin, there is a multitude, and Maximus the Confessor (580–662 CE) observed that our post-fall condition is such that "now we rend each other like wild beasts."[5] Unfortunately, far too often this is a painfully accurate description of what we see displayed in the headlines day after day.

5. Cited in Henri de Lubac, *Catholicism* (San Francisco: Ignatius, 1988), 33–34.

Desire, Economy, and Communion

What has all this to do with economics, and with capitalism in particular? Everything. It has everything to do with economics because every economic system is about human desire. As Deleuze and Foucault suggest, economy has everything to do with the nature and character of human desire, with the end or purpose of human desire. Although it frequently goes unnoticed, that this is the case is reflected in what is widely regarded as a classic definition of economics: "Economics is the science which studies human behavior as a relationship between ends and *scarce* means which have alternative uses."[6] The reference to scarcity is frequently mistaken to refer principally to the material limits of a finite world, that is, the fact that there is just not enough stuff, but it is first and foremost a statement about human desire. Another common definition of economics makes this clearer when it notes that economics is "the social science that deals with the ways in which men and societies seek to satisfy their material needs and desires."[7] Modern economy is powered by human desire, by human desire exceeding the capacity to produce goods and services.[8] Economy is about the labor of human desire and how it makes use of the created order.

Not only does this have to do with economics in general, but it has everything to do with capitalism in particular. In the quotation that opened this chapter, the noted Christian thinker and advocate of capitalism Peter Berger observes that capitalism has effected a cataclysmic transformation of society not simply in the economic realm but in the social, political, and cultural realms as well.[9] His observation is seconded by other Christian advocates of capitalism who recognize that capitalism is much more than an economic system, that it involves moral and cultural forms as well.[10] All of this comports with what we have gleaned from Deleuze and Foucault.

6. Lionel Robbins, *An Essay on the Nature and Significance of Economic Science* (London: Macmillian, 1952), 16. Italics added.

7. Albert Rees, cited in Gary S. Becker, *The Economic Approach to Human Behavior* (Chicago: University of Chicago Press, 1976), 3. See also Edwin Mansfield, *Principles of Macroeconomics*, 7th ed. (New York: Norton, 1992), 5.

8. Mansfield, *Principles of Macroeconomics*, 7.

9. Berger, *Capitalist Revolution*, 3.

10. See, e.g., Michael Novak, *The Catholic Ethic and the Spirit of Capitalism* (New York: Free Press, 1993), 7–8.

As Deleuze and Foucault suggest, capitalism is not merely a particular economic mode of production, but is rather an economy of desire operative in and through various regimes of governmentality, like liberalism's government through freedom and societies of control. And this governmentality works not only in the economic and political but also in the cultural, social, and personal dimensions of life as well. In other words, capitalism as an economy of desire has everything to do with how life is ordered or organized toward particular ends or purposes.

More specifically, the question, What are people for? has everything to do with capitalism because capitalism embodies a very different answer to the question than the classic Christian tradition. Put a bit more pointedly, the capitalist economy of desire is a manifestation of sin because it both corrupts desire and obstructs communion. Capitalism is wrong because its discipline distorts human desire. It corrupts desire so that it no longer flows according to its proper, created end; it twists desire and in so doing obstructs our friendship with God, one another, and creation. In other words, the problem with capitalism is not simply that it may not work but that even if it does increase aggregate wealth, even if it made everyone on the planet a millionaire tomorrow, it is still wrong and is to be opposed because of what it does to human desire and human sociality. The problem with capitalism is not simply that it may not facilitate, in the words of John Paul II, the ordering of material goods to their universal destination[11]— the succoring of the needs of all and especially persons who are poor—but that it does not facilitate, and instead actively works against, the divine will for the renewal of communion with God and humanity. Which draws us close to the heart of the matter of the problem with capitalism.

Thus far I have argued that the problem with capitalism is not simply whether it works; rather, the problem is the work that it does. But even this reformulation of the question does not adequately articulate the essence of the moral problem with capitalism. In light of the preceding discussion of what people are for, the moral question that should be put to capitalism, and indeed to every economic order, would be better phrased, Does it enable and enhance humanity's chief end of glorifying and enjoying God

11. John Paul II, *Centesimus Annus* 4.30–31.

forever?[12] Does it aid or obstruct desire in its ascent to God? The fundamental question that should undergird all other questions we put to capitalism is, With our economic lives ordered by capitalism, are we able to worship God truly? Are we able to desire God and the gifts of God as we ought?

Putting the question this way, however, immediately raises a red flag, for does not this sound more than a little like expecting spiritual things from an economic order? And is not this to expect too much from any economic order? Isn't it the case, as one friend and parishioner angrily reminded me after a sermon one Sunday morning, that no economic order can or is meant to bear that burden?

The answer to this question depends on the burden that economy is being asked to bear. When I suggest that we can and should ask of every economic order whether it enables and enhances desire's attainment of its supernatural end, I am *not* suggesting that the economic order can save us. Even though, as we shall see shortly, some of capitalism's Christian defenders come dangerously close to anointing capitalism with such messianic expectations, I do not. To put this rather bluntly, I am not suggesting that we are saved by our economic labor. We do not earn salvation by getting our economics right; no economic order can justify us or open the gates of heaven to us.

Nevertheless, it is entirely appropriate to ask how our economic lives ought to be ordered in response to the gift and call of the One who does save, Jesus Christ. It is entirely appropriate to ask if our lives are ordered economically in such a way that they nurture rather than corrupt desire, enhance rather than hinder faithful discipleship, and foster rather than obstruct communion. After all, economy is not outside the sovereignty of God and so is not exempt from God's will and design for humanity and creation.

That we might find such theologically pointed questions about economy odd reflects only how far we may have moved away from our roots, where even one's pots and pans were expected to be holy (Zech. 14:20). And if Paul was not lying when he said that we should glorify God *in all that we do* (1 Cor. 10:31), then, notwithstanding

---

12. The point here is *not* that the impact of an economy on others is of no concern. Rather it is that the impact of an economy on persons and communities cannot be fully and accurately evaluated if it is not framed by the question of rightly worshiping God.

the division of modern life into neat compartments like "politics" and "religion," economy is not exempt from holiness and the expectation that all would reflect the glory of God. Whether we are on the clock, in the mall, or at church, our chief end or purpose is to glorify and worship God rightly.

Moreover, that a properly ordered economy ought to have a spiritual depth, which might be associated with what the Christian tradition calls a "means of grace" and so aids in the sanctification (being made holy) of humanity, is not that far-fetched; after all, capitalism's Christian defenders constantly proclaim the theological or spiritual density of capitalism. In other words, economy in general and capitalism in particular should not be divorced from theological investigation and expectation.

Capitalism as a Theological Revolution

Putting the moral question of capitalism in terms of the work it does with regard to our desire to love God and neighbor brings to the fore the way in which the question of economy is not merely material—concerning the production and circulation of goods and services—but, most important, theological—concerning the true nature and supernatural end of our desire. In this regard, Berger and those who share his opinion of capitalism are absolutely right: capitalism does indeed mark a cataclysmic change, a revolution, that reaches far beyond the narrowly economic. Indeed, capitalism is nothing less than a *theological* revolution, involving radical changes not only in the circulation of material things but also in the nature of desire and its relation to its supernatural (spiritual, theological) end.

If the suggestion above that economies ought to be subject to theological expectation raised concerns, certainly this additional claim that capitalism is itself a theological order will provoke even deeper suspicions. Such suspicions, however, are unfounded because, given a moment's reflection, its truthfulness is easy to discern and rather benign.

Just as every economy, by virtue of dealing with human behavior, necessarily embodies an understanding of the nature and end of desire, so too every economic system rests on either an implicit or explicit theology. This is the case because insofar as every economic order reflects a particular understanding of how reality hangs together—what the nature and end of the material world is, how that world operates, and the place of humans within it, including the nature of their behavior and interactions as well as their purpose and prospects—every economic order is implicitly making claims about God and humanity and how the two interact as humanity strives for the good life.

Capitalism is no exception. In fact, capitalism is often praised by its Christian proponents for its theological underpinnings. For example, it is lauded by many for being the most realistic economic order because it does not ignore human sin.[13] This realism sets it apart from socialism. Whereas socialism might be great if we were angels, the sad truth is that we are not. We are sinners; therefore, the argument goes, socialism expects too much and as a result is unrealistic or utopian. What is worse, this lack of realism results in a social order that, as history shows, is oppressive and deadly. In comparison, capitalism is an order that recognizes we are not angels; it recognizes humanity's persistent struggle with selfishness and greed and so avoids the oppressive and deadly results of naively trusting in the virtue of socialist planners. Likewise, capitalism is celebrated for the way it nurtures and harnesses our God-given freedom and entrepreneurial spirit—our ability to choose and make and create.

Conclusion

In this chapter, the benefit of working through Deleuze and Foucault for the sake of considering faithful discipleship in a postmodern world begins to come into focus more sharply. Conceiving of postmodern life in terms of desire, as they do, suggests a new way of morally evaluating capitalism. Recognizing capitalism as an economy of desire prompts us to move beyond asking *whether* it works and instead to consider the work that it does. Specifically, Deleuze and Foucault prompt us to inquire into what capitalism does to the fundamental human power that is desire.

13. Michael Novak, *The Spirit of Democratic Capitalism* (New York: Touchstone, 1982), 82–88. See also Ronald Preston, *Church and Society in the Late Twentieth Century: The Economic and Political Task* (London: SCM, 1983), 30–33.

This, finally, is a theological question, for human desire is rightly ordered toward a supernatural end, toward communion in God. Accordingly, in the next chapter we are going to examine the theological character of capitalism—what it says about desire's nature and end, and the relation between the two. At its most basic level, we will be asking, is the theological revolution that capitalism brings about faithful? Is it in harmony with the original revolution that is the good news of Jesus Christ? Specifically we will consider the assumptions regarding the nature of and relations between God, humanity, and the good life that are implicit in capitalist practice and on occasion made explicit by its Christian and secular theorists.

4

Capitalist Theology

The Agony of Capitalist Desire

Treating the theology implicit in capitalism serves two purposes. First, it is intended to flesh out the claim that capitalism is an economy of desire that works against the created end of humanity, which is to share in the communion of the divine life of the blessed Trinity. By looking at the theology implicit in capitalism, we will begin to see how capitalist practice works against desire's rest in God and communion with our neighbors. Second, this theological assessment is an important step in establishing capitalism and Christianity as conflicting economies of desire. The theological account of capitalism presented here serves as the foil for a later chapter where a Christian account of humanity, God, and the good life is developed, one that shows Christianity to be an economy of desire that does not *discipline* desire so that it is distracted and distorted from its true end but rather *heals* desire of its capitalist corruption, aiding desire in finding its true home in God, where it enjoys communion with all. Because the comparison with a Christian theological account of economy will not be completed until a later chapter, some of the points and claims made here will not attain full clarity until then. Likewise, the problematic nature of this capitalist theology may not be obvious until that comparison is complete.

Homo Economicus

Our theological exposition of capitalism begins with capitalist anthropology, that is, with how capitalism envisions and forms the human being. What does capitalism imply, and what do its defenders say about the nature of the human being and human desire? How do humans relate to others in the capitalist economy of desire?

As Deleuze and Foucault argued, capitalism does not simply act on a pregiven human subject; rather, it forms a particular kind of human subject, one that relates to its environment in a certain way, as both the Mardi Gras revelers and factory workers in Fuzhou suggest. Capitalism's Christian advocates often laud it for the kind of subject it fosters, describing that subject in terms of creativity, inventiveness, independence, cooperation, and the self-interested pursuit of personal happiness devoid of envy and greed, and so forth. This is a rosy portrait of what is widely acknowledged as the anthropological center of capitalism, namely, *homo economicus*. There are six aspects or marks of this capitalist subject that bear highlighting.

The Individual

Homo economicus is above all an individual. As one of the more prominent Christian advocates of capitalism observes, the individual rules the capitalist market system, and for this reason capitalism is properly identified with "the Age of the Individual."[1] Likewise, another Christian advocate notes that the moral case for the capitalist economy is tied to capitalism's commitment to the dignity of the individual.[2]

The prominence that capitalism grants the individual sets it apart from what are regarded as oppressive traditionalist and collectivist economies and societies. Capitalism's proponents celebrate the movement away from "collectivism" toward "individualism and private markets,"[3] a move characterized by one Christian advo-

---

1. Michael Novak, *The Catholic Ethic and the Spirit of Capitalism* (New York: Free Press, 1993), 27. See also Michael Novak, "God and Man in the Corporation," *Policy Review* 3 (Summer 1980): 22, 31.

2. Brian Griffiths, *The Creation of Wealth* (Downers Grove, IL: InterVarsity, 1984), 91.

3. Milton Friedman and Rose Friedman, *Free to Choose* (San Diego: Harcourt, Brace, 1980), ix.

cate as a shift from "organic, 'given' community" to "voluntary association built upon individual choice."[4] Or, as another Christian advocate puts it, in more down-to-earth terms, "A free life is not the life of a hive, herd, or flock. Each person is on the spot."[5] As Milton Friedman puts it, competitive capitalism is "a collection of Robinson Crusoes."[6]

In its most extreme form, the individualistic nature of capitalism is thought to do away with society altogether, as one head of state famously declared.[7] More frequently, capitalism is thought not to abolish but alter the nature of society. Capitalism is thought to render society "thinner" in the sense that it is no longer a community that could be united by a common good; instead it is simply a conglomeration of individuals and "super-individual structures."[8]

The capitalist individual has several attributes worth noting. First, a fundamental marker of the individual's humanity is autonomy—the ability to rule oneself without being subject to the authority, coercion, or will of others. As one prominent economist says, "One important thing that is distinctive about the way economists approach the world is their great emphasis on respect for individuals—and the needs, tastes, choices and judgment *they make for themselves.*"[9] Whereas traditional societies hold that the community is prior to the individual, such that the individual is always already born with communal ties and responsibilities, capitalism severs those ties and asserts that the individual has no innate or involuntary ties to community. As a leading capitalist economist put it, mere existence does not confer on anyone a right or claim against any other.[10] Individuals are endowed with an integrity and

4. Robert Benne, *The Ethic of Democratic Capitalism* (Philadelphia: Fortress, 1981), 13.

5. Michael Novak, *Will It Liberate?* (Lanham, MD: Madison Books, 1986), 47.

6. Milton Friedman, *Capitalism and Freedom* (Chicago: University of Chicago Press, 1982), 13.

7. Margaret Thatcher, cited in Ronald Preston, *Religion and the Ambiguities of Capitalism* (Cleveland: Pilgrim Press, 1993), 25.

8. Friedrich A. von Hayek, *The Fatal Conceit* (Chicago: University of Chicago Press, 1988), 75. See also *idem, Law, Legislation, and Liberty*, vol. 2, *The Mirage of Social Justice* (Chicago: University of Chicago Press, 1976), 102–3, 147.

9. Lawrence H. Summers, "Morning Prayers Address," Harvard University, September 15, 2003, accessed July 22, 2010, www.hks.harvard.edu/fs/lsummer/speeches/2003/prayer.html. Italics added. See also Friedrich A. von Hayek, *The Road to Serfdom* (Chicago: University of Chicago Press, 1972), 14.

10. Hayek, *Fatal Conceit*, 152.

a standing apart from and against every collectivity.[11] The capitalist individual is sovereign in the sense that she is not dependent on or subject to others *except* to the extent that she *voluntarily* enters into relations with a view to her own interests.

It follows, second, that the capitalist individual is essentially self-made. Under capitalism, the independent, self-made individual is lauded and held up for emulation. Thus capitalism encourages creativity and self-expression over obedience.[12] Individuals are charged with making themselves—using their property (bodies, skills, labor) to build themselves. We all become entrepreneurs of ourselves; we are about the endless work of self-construction, ceaselessly producing our identity through production and consumption. One might even say that in a sense we all become "small business owners," and the small business that we are about is the production of our self. "We are CEOs of our own companies: Me, Inc.," declares one popular author. "To be in business today, our most important job is head marketer for the brand called you."[13] A capitalist life is basically a matter of drawing up a business plan of what we want to be and then setting forth acquiring, producing, consuming, and marketing ourselves in accord with that plan.

Third, a corollary of being independent and self-made, is the proprietary or possessive character of the capitalist individual. Insofar as individuals are autonomous entrepreneurs of themselves, they are fundamentally owners of the body and its capacities, of which they are free to dispose and use without an obligation to society.

Before moving to the next characteristic of *homo economicus*, it is worth noting that some Christian proponents of capitalism recognize that individualism can be problematic and so attempt to articulate a qualified or reformed individualism that recognizes the necessity of community for the individual person.[14] One prominent Christian advocate of capitalism goes so far as to argue that capitalism, far from fostering individualism, encourages a "communitarian

11. Peter Berger, *The Capitalist Revolution* (New York: Basic Books, 1986), 91.

12. Peter H. Sedgwick, *The Market Economy and Christian Ethics* (New York: Cambridge University Press, 1999), 87, 100–101; Colin Campbell, *The Romantic Ethic and the Spirit of Modern Consumerism* (Great Britain: Alcuin Academics, 2005).

13. Tom Peters, "The Brand Called You," *Fast Company* 10 (August/September 1997): 83.

14. Ronald Preston, *Religion and the Persistence of Capitalism* (London: SCM, 1979), 70, 73; Berger, *Capitalist Revolution*, 16.

personality."[15] Michael Novak argues that the capitalist subject is deeply immersed in community, in relationships with others. From the civic association and the corporation to the market and the globalized economy, capitalism connects more people in more ways than any previous social and economic order.

Novak's point is helpful for further understanding the individualistic character of the capitalist subject. Novak is right that even as capitalism forms individuals, it does not form them to withdraw from contact with others. When capitalism forms individuals, it is not producing isolated hermits but rather subjects who relate to others *in a particular way*. This is what Novak fails to recognize. "Individualism" is not about *isolation* but about a particular way of relating to others. As one leading economist notes, individualism is a theory of society.[16]

Specifically, capitalism produces persons who relate to others as independent, autonomous individuals who neither owe nor properly expect anything from others beyond that to which each individual voluntarily commits. The character of these relations as something less than most would recognize as "communal" comes through clearly in Novak's own rather bleak description of the capitalist individual as alienated or detached from all things. Capitalism produces individuals, he says, who are "oddly alone" in the midst of society. "Individuals wander alone, in some confusion, amid many casualties" on the "wasteland at the heart of democratic capitalism [that] is like a field of battle."[17] More will be said about this battle and its casualties shortly.

Free to Choose

The second mark of capitalist anthropology is that the individual is, in the words of a famous capitalist text, free to choose.[18]

15. Novak, *Will It Liberate?* 42; Novak, *Catholic Ethic*, 27–29. Many economists suggest that corporations are not about community but efficiency and economizing on transactional costs. See, e.g., the work of Douglass North and the New Institutionalists. See Robert H. Nelson, *Economics as Religion: From Samuelson to Chicago and Beyond* (University Park, PA: Penn State University Press, 2001), 63.

16. Friedrich A. von Hayek, *Individualism and Economic Order* (Chicago: University of Chicago Press, 1948), 6.

17. Michael Novak, *The Spirit of Democratic Capitalism* (New York: Touchstone, 1982), 54.

18. Friedman and Friedman, *Free to Choose*.

Capitalism is said to be liberating precisely because it sets the autonomous individual free to choose.[19] Whether it is between two hundred channels on TV, one hundred brands of toilet paper, the condiments on my burger, whom I can have sex with, or what I want to be when I grow up, capitalism celebrates freedom as the freedom of the individual to make one's own choices without external interference. "It is the absence of prescribed common ends," writes an economist, "which makes a society of free men all that it has come to mean to us."[20] The freedom of the capitalist individual "cannot be reconciled with the supremacy of one single purpose to which the whole of society must be entirely and permanently subordinated."[21] Indeed, our dignity as human beings is related to the individual's unfettered ability to choose, to be self-determining and self-governing.[22] Furthermore, the exercise of free choice is the fundamental opportunity and expression of the individual's efforts at self-construction.[23] Hence, the expansion of choice is a virtue in and of itself.[24]

However, this freedom to choose is decidedly formal and negative. It is *formal* in the sense that what we are free to choose is left undefined, indeterminate. The freedom of the capitalist individual is associated with no particular object, end, or purpose. Moreover, this freedom entails no assurance that any goal will actually be attained. For this reason, this freedom is also first and foremost a *negative* freedom. By this I mean that capitalist freedom is "freedom from" instead of "freedom for." It is freedom from interference, from authority, from others imposing their will on me, from others deciding for me. It is freedom as a kind of private space where the individual can act (or not act, as the case may be) without the intervention of any authority, other wills, or coercion. Thus a well-known economist writes, "Freedom requires that the individual be allowed to pursue *his own* ends: one who is free is . . . no longer bound by the common concrete ends of his community.

19. Berger, *Capitalist Revolution*, 86–7.

20. Hayek, *Mirage of Social Justice*, 111.

21. Hayek, *Road to Serfdom*, 206.

22. Michael Novak, *Business as a Calling* (New York: Free Press, 1996), 104.

23. Vincent J. Miller, *Consuming Religion* (New York: Continuum, 2004), 142–44, 225.

24. Amartya Sen, *Development as Freedom* (New York: Anchor, 2000), xii, 109; W. Arthur Lewis, *The Theory of Economic Growth* (London: George Allen & Unwin, 1955), 421.

Such freedom of individual decision is made possible by delimiting distinct individual rights (the rights of property, for example) and designating domains within which each can dispose over means known to him for his own ends."[25]

It is important to note that the negative character of this freedom cannot be supplemented by a substantial account of "freedom for," as some Christian advocates would wish, for, as we shall see shortly, the market *requires* that freedom remain negative in order for the invisible hand to work. Subordinating capitalism to a positive, substantive account of freedom associated with a particular vision of the good would dispel the magic of the free market. Moreover, such an imposition would constitute an assault on the dignity of the individual, tied as it is to freedom from prescribed common ends. As one economist puts it, "Individual freedom cannot be reconciled with the supremacy of one single purpose to which the whole of society must be entirely and permanently subordinated."[26] In other words, capitalist freedom is inherently and intrinsically formal and negative.

Interest Maximizer

The third mark of capitalist anthropology concerns the way in which *homo economicus* is quintessentially an interest maximizer,[27] with interest referring specifically to self-interest.[28] Thus in a capitalist culture we are constantly reminded to look out for number

25. Hayek, *Fatal Conceit*, 63. Italics in original.

26. Hayek, *Road to Serfdom*, 206; see Hayek, *Mirage of Social Justice*, 110–11.

27. See Albert Hirschman, *The Passions and the Interests: Political Arguments for Capitalism before Its Triumph* (Princeton, NJ: Princeton University Press, 1981); and Milton L. Myers, *The Soul of Modern Economic Man* (Chicago: University of Chicago Press, 1983). See also Samuel Gregg, *Economic Thinking for the Theologically Minded* (Lanham, MD: University Press of America, 2001), 12–13.

28. That the pure interest maximizer may be an ideal rarely attained is beside the point. As Deleuze and Foucault suggest, this only points to the contested nature of capitalism's discipline. In defense of the interest-maximizing presumption, see Milton Friedman's essay, "The Methodology of Positive Economics," in *Essays in Positive Economics* (Chicago: University of Chicago Press, 1953), 3–43. See also George J. Stigler, "Economics or Ethics?" The Tanner Lectures on Human Values, Harvard University, April 1980, 176, accessed July 20, 2010, http://bbs.cenet.org.cn/uploadimages/200442020285010025.pdf. See also Gary S. Becker, *The Economic Approach to Human Behavior* (Chicago: University of Chicago Press, 1976), 3–14.

one, businesses are increasingly run with an eye not toward public service but toward increasing the value of stockholdings, our youth respond to queries about why they want to do what they want to do with the mantra "to make money," and worship is planned and marketed in terms of how it can meet my needs and what I get out of it. Here we might recall the well-known line from Adam Smith: "It is not from the benevolence of the butcher, the brewer, or the baker, that we expect our dinner, but from their regard to their own interest. We address ourselves, not to their humanity but to their self-love."[29] For Smith, the dominant force in human life was "the uniform, constant and uninterrupted effort of every man to better his own condition,"[30] a sentiment echoed by a contemporary economist as he writes, "I do not know the fruit salesman personally; and I have no particular interest in his well-being. He reciprocates this attitude. I do not know, and I have no need to know whether he is in direst poverty, extremely wealthy, or somewhere in between. . . . Yet the two of us are able to . . . transact exchanges efficiently."[31]

What is noteworthy is that capitalism's promotion of self-interest is not a matter of making a virtue of necessity, as if it would be better if humanity were not self-interested, but since it is, the best must be made of it. Rather, capitalism holds that self-interest is a positive good. Thus a prominent architect of the current economic order declares, "One of the strongest and most creative forces known to man [is] the attempt by millions of individuals to promote their

29. Adam Smith, *An Inquiry into the Nature and Causes of the Wealth of Nations* (Chicago: University of Chicago Press, 1976), 1:18. See also *idem, The Theory of Moral Sentiments* (Indianapolis: Liberty Fund, 1984), 184. It should be noted that there is an ongoing debate regarding how to read Smith on economic motivations. Some, such as Kathryn Blanchard, argue that Smith's economic vision was not fundamentally selfish but altruistic, concerned with the well-being of others. While such defenses of Smith are correct in absolving him of the rank egoism and selfishness with which he is some- times equated, they go too far in absolving him of the fundamentally self-interested character of his work. Blanchard, for example, misunderstands what Smith means by "sympathy." See Kathryn Blanchard, *The Protestant Ethic or the Spirit of Capitalism* (Eugene, OR: Cascade, 2010). For an accessible treatment of this question in Smith and a cogent account of what he means by sympathy, see Kelly S. Johnson, *The Fear of Beggars* (Grand Rapids: Eerdmans, 2007), 102–13.

30. Smith, *Wealth of Nations*, 1:364, cf. 1:367. See also Smith, *Theory of Moral Sentiments*, 304.

31. James Buchanan, quoted in Samuel Bowles, "Endogenous Preferences: The Cultural Consequences of Markets and Other Economic Institutions," *Journal of Economic Literature* 36 (March 1998): 78.

own interests, to live their lives by their own values."[32] Self-interest is not simply a fact that we must deal with; rather it is one of the strongest and most creative forces there is.

The emphasis on self-interest entails a rejection of any substantive notion of a shared purpose or common good that unites humanity. Already we have seen how the capitalist individual and capitalist freedom are set over against communal ends and collective purposes. Some Christian economists defend this rejection of a shared purpose on the grounds that such is simply not possible in large societies.[33] Other economists suggest that "as commendable as the goals of friendship, charity, and fairness are, it is naive to expect people to behave in a way that they will be realized."[34] This is echoed by one of the leading lights of the neoliberal economic vision when he notes that love is simply not possible as an economic motive,[35] and it is further reinforced by other economists who strive to show how self-interest can explain decisions in all realms of life, from theft to governance to marriage.[36] Perhaps the most famous expression of this rejection of any notion of a common good comes from Milton Friedman, when he dismissed the idea that businesses have a "social responsibility," saying, "Few trends could so thoroughly undermine the very foundations of our free society as the acceptance by corporate officials of a social responsibility other than to make as much money for their stockholders as possible."[37] This is echoed today in resistance to the notion

32. Friedman, *Capitalism and Freedom*, 200.

33. Peter J. Hill and John Lunn, "Markets and Morality," *Journal of Religious Ethics* 35, no. 4 (2007): 640.

34. Nancy Ruth Fox in D. Stephen Long and Nancy Ruth Fox, *Calculated Futures* (Waco: Baylor University Press, 2007), 44.

35. Frank Knight quoted in Nelson, *Economics as Religion*, 122.

36. See, in particular, the work of Gary Becker, a leading light of the third generation of the Chicago School. See also note 57 in this chapter.

37. Friedman, *Capitalism and Freedom*, 133. See also Willa Johnson, "Freedom and Philanthropy: An Interview with Milton Friedman," *Business and Society Review* 11 (1989): 11–18. On the dominance of "shareholder value," see David Nussbaum, "Does Shareholder Value Drive the World?" in *Christianity and the Culture of Economics*, ed. Donald A. Hay and Alan Kreider (Cardiff: University of Wales, 2001), 33–52. Following this logic to its conclusion, Judge Frank Easterbrook and Professor Daniel Fischel have famously argued that firms should obey the law only so long as it is profitable to do so, but when breaking regulatory law can be done profitably, it should be. See Frank H. Easterbrook and Daniel R. Fischel, "Antitrust Suits by Targets of Tender Offers," *Michigan Law Review* 80 (1982): 1155–78.

that enterprise should broaden its concern from shareholders to stakeholders as well.

As Friedman suggests, it is not simply that a common good does not exist, but that even if it did, it should be resisted on the grounds that it is destructive of freedom. Thus a social order organized around a common good or shared love is likened to a state of savagery.[38] At best, capitalism is compatible with only the thinnest notion of a general interest, understood as securing the conditions whereby individuals are free to pursue their disparate private goods.[39]

Capitalism not only fosters self-interested individuals, but it also encourages the maximization of those interests.[40] The capitalist individual is one who always acts to maximize self-interest, whether that is profit on what I produce, utility in what I purchase and use, or the satisfaction and advancement of my interests through interactions with others. Another name for this maximizing quality is efficiency. The capitalist market is said to be efficient because it maximizes the yield from society's resources. The self-interested individual mirrors the market's efficiency insofar as *homo economicus* is an interest maximizer.

Insatiable Desire

The interest-maximizing character of the capitalist individual is closely related to the way in which human desire is construed by capitalism as fundamentally insatiable, which is the fourth mark of capitalist anthropology. The problem that drives the entire economic enterprise is rooted in the unquenchable, infinite nature of

38. Hayek, *Fatal Conceit*, 65.
39. Hayek, *Mirage of Social Justice*, 1–2.
40. Gary S. Becker, *The Economic Approach to Human Behavior* (Chicago: University of Chicago Press, 1976), 284; Rebecca M. Blank, "Market Behavior and Christian Behavior," in *Faithful Economics*, ed. James W. Henderson and John Pisciotta (Waco: Baylor University Press, 2005), 37. Note that while this vision of humanity as an interest maximizer has faced sustained critique, even within the discipline of economics—particularly by feminist economists and perhaps most famously by Amartya Sen ("Rational Fools: A Critique of the Behavioral Foundations of Economic Theory," *Philosophy and Public Affairs* 6 [1977]: 317–44), it remains the dominant paradigm. See Donald A. Hay, "On Being a Christian Economist," in Hay and Kreider, *Christianity and the Culture of Economics*, 170.

human desire. Thus Adam Smith speaks of that desire in humanity "which cannot be satisfied, but seem[s] to be altogether endless."[41] *Homo economicus* is a being of unlimited wants.[42] Because human desires are unlimited, economics, as the allocation of limited material resources, is necessary.

In this regard, consider how the health of the economy is measured. When we listen to the daily business news, what are we told is a sign of economic health? Growth. When retail companies evaluate the health of a particular store, what do they look at? Growth over the same period last year. When a labor force is evaluated, what is the standard? Increased productivity. When politicians want us to vote for them, what do they ask us? Are we better off (i.e., do we have more) now than before? Growth is the benchmark of well-being, the measure of good and evil.[43] More is better.[44] Consider, as well, the notion of "opportunity cost." In teaching us to weigh not just the out-of-pocket cost of a choice but to consider as well the "cost" of all the opportunities foregone by making that particular choice, we are in effect being taught that we rightly desire everything. After all, one must desire everything for not choosing something to be regarded as a cost.[45]

All of this is to say that capitalism deforms and corrupts human desire into an insatiable drive for more that today is celebrated as the aggressive, creative, entrepreneurial energy that distinguishes *homo economicus.*

The Agony of Competition

The previous marks concerned primarily how the self is constructed by capitalism; now we consider how the capitalist self relates to others. How does the capitalist discipline of desire fashion human relations?

41. Smith, *Wealth of Nations*, 1:183.

42. Benne, *Ethic of Democratic Capitalism*, 71.

43. William J. Baumol and Alan S. Blinder, *Macroeconomics: Principles and Policies*, 5th ed. (San Diego: Harcourt Brace Jovanich, 1991), 7; Robert Nelson, "The Theology of Economics," in Henderson and Pisciotta, eds., *Faithful Economics*, 92.

44. Blank, "Market Behavior and Christian Behavior," 38; Blank, "Viewing the Market Economy through the Lens of Faith," in *Is the Market Moral?* by Rebecca M. Blank and William McGurn (Washington, DC: Brookings Institute Press, 2004), 19.

45. D. Stephen Long in Long and Fox, *Calculated Futures*, 41.

It is not difficult to imagine the interaction of interest-maximizing capitalist individuals quickly degenerating into a war of all against all. As one Christian proponent of capitalism notes, "If freedom is defined solely as individuals being able to maximize their happiness though expanding choices, everyone else, far from being considered essential to their happiness, quickly becomes a potential threat to individual freedom."[46] Here the oft-repeated boast of capitalism's advocates that economy tames bellicose passions is pertinent. While one would be hard-pressed to make a convincing empirical case that capitalism has reduced either the frequency or ferocity of war,[47] it is true that capitalism does redirect the clashing interests of *homo economicus* by means of the competitive agony that is the "free" market. This is to say, capitalism does not promise an end to the agony of conflict but rather diverts the clash of self-interested individuals in accord with the golden rule of production for the market. As one economist puts it, the peace that capitalism offers is, like its freedom, essentially negative; it is not the peace of genuine solidarity but of the absence of open conflict.[48] Hence, it is at best akin to a wary and guarded truce or cease-fire. At worst, it is, to play on Clausewitz's well-known aphorism, war by other means. Capitalism, we might say, is commercial war.

Thus the fifth mark of capitalist anthropology is competition. Capitalism orders human relations as struggle and conflict.[49] In the absence of a shared end or common good, individuals are left to struggle to secure private goods and interests against other individuals, who must now be viewed as a threat. All of us, winners and losers, First-World consumers and Fourth-World excluded, compete for resources, for market share, for a living wage, for a job, for the time for friendship and family, for inclusion in the market, and so forth.

Granted, under the sign of utopian capitalism—capitalism with a human face that at least gave lip service to promoting the common good of human development—it was perhaps possible to overlook

46. William McGurn, "Creative Virtues of the Economy," in Blank and McGurn, *Is the Market Moral?* 40.

47. See Ellen Meiksins Wood, *Empire of Capital* (New York: Verso, 2003).

48. Friedrich A. von Hayek, *The Constitution of Liberty* (Chicago: University of Chicago Press, 1960), 19; Hayek, *Fatal Conceit*, 19, 36.

49. Julio de Santa Ana, *La Práctica Económica Como Religión* (San José: DEI, 1991), 44.

this global conflict as it slowly engulfed the world. Yet with the advent of nihilistic capitalism, of capitalism shorn of its human face, this commercial war is ever more evident. We are now submerged in an economy that is no longer concerned with the fiction of a mutually beneficial comparative advantage; instead, we seek competitive advantage.[50] All that matters is winning the war.

One of the clearer indications of the capitalist distortion of human relations is how everything and everyone increasingly is treated like a commodity and subject to the cost/benefit logic of efficiency. Everything and everyone are increasingly treated as fungible goods valued only in terms of how and how long they satisfy my desires and serve my interests. As one economist put it, it is one of the positive aspects of capitalism that we are "only impersonal means to our fellows."[51] Or as one Christian proponent of capitalism (approvingly) notes, consider the dehumanizing force of the not uncommon question, "What is he worth?"—a question that reflects the power of capitalism to reduce the human to a thing, to a monetary equivalent, to "human capital," and consequently subsume us in a network of relations that are coldly calculating, superficial, and transient.[52] A prime example of this kind of calculation is provided by a prominent economist at the World Bank who suggested that some less developed countries were "vastly under-polluted" and that "the economic logic behind dumping a load of toxic waste in the lowest-wage country is impeccable."[53] This logic asserts it is better that lower-wage-earning persons suffer the health-impairing effects of pollution than higher-wage earners.

Under capitalism people exist for one another in an instrumental fashion; capitalism encourages us to view others in terms of how they can serve our self-interested projects. In the worst case, people are reified and so become commodities themselves—mere bodies to be exploited or consumed and then discarded; think of slavery, organ mining, or the sex trade, for example. In a less extreme case, we stand before one another merely as representations or owners

50. See Michael Porter's work, *The Competitive Advantage of Nations* (New York: Free Press, 1990) and *On Competition* (Cambridge, MA: Harvard University Press, 1998).

51. Hayek, *Constitution of Liberty*, 141.

52. Berger, *Capitalist Revolution*, 110, 113.

53. Editorial Board, "Let Them Eat Pollution," *The Economist*, February 2, 1992, 66.

of commodities that we seek to acquire.[54] The capitalist market is nothing less than a Darwinian calculus of human lives, with the highly productive regarded as more valuable than others, who are esteemed less and hence may be sacrificed or abandoned.[55] In a world dominated by commodities, persons come to be valued by the same criteria as commodities—marketability, profitability, and consumability.[56]

As a consequence, marriages are viewed as (short-term) contracts subject to a cost/benefit analysis, children become consumer goods or accessories, family bonds are weakened, and our bodies are treated like so many raw materials to be mined and exploited for manufacture and pleasure.[57] Those individuals rendered worthless as producers and commodities by obsolescence—the old and infirm—are discarded (warehoused or euthanized) and the nonproductive poor (the homeless, the unemployed, the irresponsible, the incompetent) are viewed as a threat.[58]

Related to the agonistic and brutally efficient character of human relations under capitalism is their contractual nature. Already we have seen capitalism's aversion to traditional, communitarian forms of social organization in the name of the freedom of the individual to compete. Within this competitive environment, individuals will form cooperative relations. What distinguishes capitalist cooperative relations is that they are decidedly contractual—limited, temporary, and voluntary. They are limited in the sense that under capitalism, individuals gain "from *not* treating one another as neighbors, and

54. I owe this insight to Graham Ward, "The Commodification of Religion or the Consummation of Capitalism," in *Idolatry*, ed. Stephen C. Barton (New York: T&T Clark, 2007), 308; and Jung Mo Sung, *Neoliberalism y Pobreza: Una Economía sin Corazón* (San José: DEI, 1993), 91.

55. Sung, *Neoliberalism y Pobreza*, 91. See Hayek, *Fatal Conceit*, 131–32.

56. M. Douglass Meeks, *God the Economist* (Minneapolis: Fortress, 1989), 170.

57. On marriage, see Becker, *Economic Approach to Human Behavior*, 205–50. On children as consumer goods, see Friedman, *Capitalism and Freedom*, 33; and Juliet Schor, *Born to Buy: The Commercialized Child and the New Consumer Culture* (New York: Scribner, 2004). On the weakening of familial bonds, see Smith, *Theory of Moral Sentiments*, 223. See also Bowles, "Endogenous Preferences," 100. For a powerful analysis of how the cost/benefit calculus aids insertion into the market, see Elizabeth Anderson, *Value in Ethics and Economics* (Cambridge, MA: Harvard University Press, 1993), 190–216.

58. Richard John Neuhaus, *Doing Well and Doing Good* (New York: Doubleday, 1992), 212.

by applying in their interactions rules of the [capitalist] order—such as those of [private] property and contract—instead of the rules of solidarity and altruism."[59] This is to say, capitalist relations are first and foremost relations among strangers and entail a reduction of the duties we owe to one another.[60] One's responsibilities and obligations toward others extend only as far as one is contractually obligated. If one has not entered into a contract that imposes an obligation or responsibility, then as far as the capitalist order is concerned, no obligation exists. Likewise, contractual relations are temporary insofar as contractually assumed obligations endure only so long as the terms of the contract stipulate. (One might think here of how marriage vows are rewritten, changing "till death do us part" to "so long as our love shall last.") Finally, they are voluntary in that the only obligations and responsibilities that are morally binding are those that have been entered into freely and without coercion. Indeed, to be subject to responsibilities one did not freely choose is to descend into serfdom, savagery, and slavery.

The distortion of human relations is further manifest in how the capitalist market produces and trades in commodities. Adam Smith thought that one of the central components of the astonishing productivity of capitalism was the division of labor. The division of labor refers to the increasingly fragmented and specialized character of the production of goods for the market. Today it is seen, for example, in how the production of a shirt or an automobile may be dispersed around the world.

The benefits (to some) of such an arrangement are obvious; what is less obvious are the effects of the capitalist division of labor on persons and their relations with others. Smith himself noted its brutal effects on some, in an image that might call to mind the workers in the bead factory in Fuzhou:

> The man whose life is spent performing a few simple operations, of which the effects too are, perhaps, always the same, or very nearly the same, has no occasion to exert his understanding, or to exercise his invention in finding out expedients for removing difficulties which never occur. He naturally loses, therefore, the habit of such exertion, and generally becomes stupid and ignorant as it is possible for a human creature to become. The torpor of his mind renders him not

59. Hayek, *Fatal Conceit*, 12.
60. Hayek, *Mirage of Social Justice*, 90.

only incapable of relishing or bearing a part in any rational conversation, but of conceiving any generous, noble or tender sentiment.[61]

Beyond its detrimental effects on the individual, its degradation of family life and humanity's interaction with creation have also been extensively noted.[62] Of the former, Smith was also not unaware, observing:

> In commercial countries . . . the descendants of the same family, having no such motive for keeping together, naturally separate and disperse, as interest or inclination may direct. They soon cease to be of importance to one another; and in a few generations, not only lose all care about one another, but all remembrance of their common origin, and of the connection which took place among their ancestors.[63]

Once production is taken out of the realm of the household by the capitalist division of labor, the family becomes primarily an association of consumption and is subject to the centrifugal forces that pull persons outside and away from the family—whether due to the necessity of traveling to the factory or simply the pursuit of maximizing self-interested desire.

Not only the manner in which commodities are produced but also the manner in which they are circulated is detrimental to human relations. The capitalist division of labor renders goods, and frequently services offered, abstract and impersonal. The connections that global capitalism makes among people could hardly be called relationships in any normal and meaningful sense of the term.[64] After all, the production and assembly of goods is so fragmented and global commodity chains so complex that it is not easy to know the conditions under which products are produced and services provided.[65] The global division of labor renders it difficult to know the needs of the persons involved in the commodity chains and exchanges that sustain our lives. Hence the things we consume appear to us like capitalist manna, miraculously and without any discernable connection to the

---

61. Smith, *Wealth of Nations*, 2:302–3.
62. See Miller, *Consuming Religion*, 41–50. See also the work of Wendell Berry.
63. Smith, *Theory of Moral Sentiments*, 223.   −
64. Blank, "Market Behavior and Christian Behavior," 44–45.
65. See Tom Beaudoin's account of his efforts in this regard in his *Consuming Faith* (Lanham, MD: Sheed & Ward, 2003).

social factors of their production. In this regard, economist Samuel Bowles calls the market a "powerful cognitive simplifier."[66]

This is reinforced by the way such commodities are valued. Capitalism reduces value to exchange value, or what is popularly called market value. The value of something is strictly a matter of what it garners on the market. Any assessment of value in accord with an order or purpose external to the market falls by the wayside. Thus notions of a just price or just wage all but disappear. After all, given the way the capitalist division of labor obscures the connection between producers and consumers, as well as the plethora of individual conceptions of value, how could anyone really know what persons on the other end of the commodity chain need or what the standard of justice should be if it is not simply market value?

Awash in a sea of commodities, we are all like the child who declares that milk comes from supermarkets. The abstraction of commodities and the veil of ignorance that conceals their conditions of production and consumption encourages moral insulation and passivity.[67] Like the abbot in the story of St. Ignatius, we can honestly declare our ignorance when confronted with the conditions the market conceals. When we learn that the children of the persons who caught the seafood we see in the supermarket case died of malnutrition, we can protest sincerely, "I did not know."

Commutative Justice

The sixth and final mark of capitalist anthropology to be considered here concerns the nature of justice under the free market. Under capitalism, justice is strictly personal or "commutative."[68] This is to say, justice is solely a matter of enforcing the terms of voluntary, contractual exchanges. Justice does not mandate that those exchanges result in a particular outcome or even that exchanges be made in the first place. All justice entails is the maintenance of the space for the possibility of voluntary (i.e., noncoercive) exchanges, which it does by enforcing the rules of contracts and property. Indeed, the dominance of Pareto optimality (which insists exchanges do not result in a loss of utility) to measure efficiency rules out any

66. Bowles, "Endogenous Preferences," 90.
67. Miller, *Consuming Religion*, 132–34.
68. What follows is drawn from Hayek, *Mirage of Social Justice*.

notion of justice-as-redistribution that might require the wealthy to surrender some utility for the sake of the impoverished.[69]

In this regard, capitalist justice, like its freedom, is essentially negative. It imposes no positive duties or obligations on individuals or communities. It is not concerned with livelihood, only exchange.[70] It insists only on noninterference in the free choices of others and on adherence to the strictures of contracts into which one has freely entered.

Indeed, the effort by individuals or governments to coerce one into redistributing wealth is itself regarded as an act of injustice. In this way, persons—like, for example, beggars and persons who are poor—become a threat. Not only are they a threat insofar as they might steal what I have accumulated, but they are a more insidious threat insofar as they may divert resources from the circulation of the market, thereby reducing the productivity of the market and threatening my prospects for prosperity.

In other words, under the capitalist order, there is no such thing as social justice. This was alluded to earlier when the common good and social responsibility were challenged. Capitalism recognizes no obligation or responsibility to manage outcomes of voluntary exchanges or redistribute goods and services under the guise of what is often called social or distributive justice. Indeed, the outcomes of the capitalist market are said to be "beyond justice" in the sense that justice does not even apply to the market. Beyond the commutative justice of voluntary exchanges, justice is meaningless when applied to the capitalist market. That some succeed and others fail through no merits of their own, that some flourish and others perish under the capitalist order, may be tragic but it is not unjust.[71]

Deus Abscondus: The Hidden God of the Free Market

The second step in our theological interrogation of capitalism considers the nature of the God that underwrites the capitalist economy of desire. What does the capitalist order of things imply

69. Paula England, "Separative and Soluble Selves: Dichotomous Thinking in Economics," in *Feminist Economics Today*, ed. Marianne A. Ferber and Julie A. Nelson (Chicago: University of Chicago Press, 2003), 40–41.

70. Meeks, *God the Economist*, 52.

71. Hayek, *Mirage of Social Justice*, 69.

about God's way with the world? What do capitalism's defenders say about God? Here we consider four points.

The Invisible Hand

One of the best-known features of the capitalist order is the way in which the market is said to work by means of an invisible hand, which operates as a surrogate for divine providence. Thus Adam Smith, who is explicit in linking the invisible hand with divine Providence,[72] writes of one who enters into capitalist-market relations, "He generally, indeed, neither intends to promote the public interest, nor knows how much he is promoting it. . . . He intends only his own gain, and he is in this . . . led by an invisible hand to promote an end which was no part of his intention."[73] The capitalist market providentially functions so that individuals' pursuit of their self-interest works out for the good of the whole. One might say that the invisible hand of the market functions sacramentally to transform private vice into public virtue, to borrow a turn of phrase from an early capitalist thinker.[74] Or, as a critic has noted, under capitalism sin acquires a brilliant and beneficial side, and capitalism's God makes use of sin to advance the kingdom.[75]

It should be noted that the working of this invisible hand is not a matter of a safety net that comes into play on occasion when individuals fail to care for their neighbors but rather is thought to be the normal and even optimal manner of conducting business. This providential ordering of self-interested behavior is said to work as good as or even better than any intentional altruistic effort to serve others. In other words, it is better that we pursue self-interest and leave caring for others to the invisible hand of providence. Society is not worse off for the individual neglecting the public good, Smith writes; rather, "by pursuing his own interest he frequently promotes that of the society *more effectually* than when he really intends to

72. Smith, *Theory of Moral Sentiments*, 185.
73. Smith, *Wealth of Nations*, 1:477–78.
74. Bernard Mandeville, *The Fable of the Bees and Other Writings*, abridged and edited by E. J. Hundert (Indianapolis: Hackett, 1997), 27, 149. See also Hayek, *Fatal Conceit*, 13.
75. Sung, *Neoliberalism y Pobreza*, 92.

promote it."[76] A contemporary capitalist theorist clarifies this point even more sharply when he writes:

> In fact we generally are doing most good by pursuing gain. It was somewhat misleading, and did his cause harm, when Adam Smith gave the impression as if the significant difference were between the egoistic striving for gains and the altruistic endeavour to meet known needs. The aim for which a successful entrepreneur wants to use his profits may well be to provide a hospital or an art gallery for his home town. But quite apart from the question of what he wants to do with his profits after he has earned them, he is led to benefit more people by aiming at the largest gain than he could if he concentrated on the satisfaction of known persons.[77]

Put simply, life is providentially ordered such that the most good is produced by individuals pursuing their own, maximal gain.

This is the case because providence has ordered the world according to a logic of unintended consequences. Just as the invisible hand of the market sees to it that the neglect of the common good actually works through the magic of the market to benefit the whole, so when the attempt is made to harness or guide the economy toward a perceived common good, the inevitable and unintentional result is more harm than good. Whereas the invisible hand of the market ensures that private vice unintentionally leads to public virtue, the same hand sees to it that intentionally aiming at public benefit unintentionally results in public harm, hence the generalized resistance to governmental intervention in the economy.

God Is Not Redeeming

The second mark of the capitalist God is that God is not active now in redeeming humanity from sin. This follows directly from both capitalist anthropology and the association of divine providence with the invisible hand of the market.

As noted previously, capitalist anthropology begins from the premise that human beings are fundamentally interest maximizers. Even as Christian proponents of capitalism may attempt to

76. Smith, *Wealth of Nations*, 1:477–78. Italics added.
77. Hayek, *Mirage of Social Justice*, 145.

mitigate this in various ways, they agree that humans are, at least for the time being, inescapably self-interested. Indeed, they are united in the conviction that it is unrealistic and utopian to think that economic life can be ordered otherwise. The kingdom of God is not of this world, they assert, and by this they mean that prior to Jesus's return, we cannot expect to live our economic life in any other way. Because we are stuck in the ambiguities of history and cannot know what the future kingdom will bring, our economic decisions here and now cannot be based on the kingdom.[78] The complete submission of everything to the divine rule is not a present expectation but an eschatological (future/eternal) promise.[79] Sin is an "ineradicable given."[80]

At its most extreme, the conviction that sin is inescapably part of our economic life is not limited to the assertion that it is inescapable in this time before Christ returns. Rather, it becomes a claim that we will *never* be free of sin. Thus writes one Christian proponent of capitalism: "The point of the Incarnation is to respect the world as it is, . . . and to disbelieve any promises that the world is now or ever will be transformed into the city of God. . . . The world is not going to become—ever—a kingdom of justice and love. . . . The single greatest temptation for Christians is to imagine that the salvation won by Jesus has altered the human condition."[81]

What these claims amount to is a denial that God is active here and now redeeming us from sin, sanctifying us, making us better than we otherwise would be. They are claims that at least for the time being, we are stuck in our sin, that the best we can hope for is that sin can be managed in a way that minimizes its harm. And this is precisely what divine providence in the form of the invisible hand of the market does—it manages sin. It is a system under which "bad men can do least harm."[82] It is a system that "does not depend for its functioning on our finding good men for running it, or on all men becoming better than they are now."[83] Indeed, it is thought to be a virtue of capitalism that it *reduces*

78. Preston, *Religion and the Ambiguities of Capitalism*, 131–32.
79. Neuhaus, *Doing Well and Doing Good*, 173.
80. Novak, *Spirit of Democratic Capitalism*, 82.
81. Ibid., 341–43.
82. Hayek, *Individualism and the Economic Order*, 11.
83. Ibid., 12.

the need for compassion, fraternal love, and solidarity.[84] As economist Charles Schultze writes, "Market-like arrangements reduce the need for compassion, patriotism, brotherly love, and cultural solidarity,"[85] and as Dennis Robertson famously noted, if economists assist in rightly arranging the economic order, they can "contribute mightily to the economizing . . . of that scarce resource Love."[86]

Taken together, the invisible hand, the denial of sanctification now, and the disincentive to holiness suggest that capitalism is founded on an idolatrous vision of God, a vision of God that is atheistic, deistic, or Stoic. It is atheistic in the sense that some of capitalism's leading proponents see these qualities as part and parcel of an entirely naturalistic order, requiring no God.[87] It is deistic in the sense that Smith's vision was rooted in an image of God as a kind of great architect or engineer, who set the machinery of the universe in motion and then withdrew, like an absentee landlord, leaving it to run according to its natural order and processes.[88] It is Stoic in the sense that it is a vision of the movement of the universe that is deeply indebted to the ancient Stoic vision of sovereign individuals, proprietors of their own bodies, who move through the trials and tribulations of this life, making the most of their capacities and endowments, hoping thereby only to endure, to survive, expecting no redemption.[89]

84. Benne, *Ethic of Democratic Capitalism*, 143; see also 154. Herman E. Daly and John B. Cobb Jr. make this observation as well in *For the Common Good*, 2nd ed. (Boston: Beacon, 1994), 50–51, 89, 92.

85. Charles Schultze, cited in Bowles, "Endogenous Preferences," 92.

86. Dennis H. Robertson, *Economic Commentaries* (Westport, CT: Greenwood, 1978), 152, 154. See also Summers, "Morning Prayers Addresses."

87. Hayek, *Fatal Conceit*, 72–73. See also 139.

88. See Griffiths, *Creation of Wealth*, 107, 53. See also Novak, *Business as a Calling*, 38–39. On Smith's religiosity, see the editors' introduction to *Theory of Moral Sentiments*, 5–6, 19, 20. See also Peter Minowitz, *Profits, Priests, and Princes: Adam Smith's Emancipation of Economics from Politics and Religion* (Stanford, CA: Stanford University Press, 1993); Samuel Fleischacker, *On Adam Smith's "Wealth of Nations"* (Princeton, NJ: Princeton University Press, 2004), 45. For a defense of Smith that suggests his work was not outside what passed for "orthodoxy" in his day, especially as found in the likes of Bishop Joseph Butler and Rev. Josiah Tucker, see A. M. C. Waterman, "The Beginning of Boundaries: The Sudden Separation of Economics from Christian Theology," in *Economics and Interdisciplinary Exchange*, ed. Guido Erreygers (New York: Routledge, 2001), 43–47.

89. See Griffiths, *Creation of Wealth*, 81; Berger, *Capitalist Revolution*, 223–24.

Scarcity: God Did Not Create Enough

The third mark of the capitalist God involves the fundamental premise of modern economics: there is not enough. This was alluded to already insofar as it is taken as a given that the desires of the individual exceed available resources. Likewise, recall the definition of economics: "Economics is the science which studies human behavior as a relationship between ends and *scarce* means which have alternative uses."[90] God's failure to provide enough is the starting point for the economic task of allocating the resources we have; God's afflicting creation with scarcity is the beginning of the commercial war that is capitalism.

This, however, is not a bad thing according to one prominent Christian defense of capitalism, for it is precisely the condition of scarcity that prods individuals to exercise their creativity, that stimulates productivity and the entrepreneurial spirit. Scarcity is the "law" that drives us to the gospel of creativity and productivity. "Creation left to itself is incomplete, and humans are called to be co-creators with God, bringing forth the potentialities the Creator has hidden. Creation is full of secrets waiting to be discovered, riddles which human intelligence is expected by the Creator to unlock. The world did not spring from the hand of God as wealthy as humans might make it."[91]

In other words, the created order calls forth the agony that is capitalist relations. Humanity is created with desires that cannot be sated, and then humanity is set in a natural order that is incomplete and lacking. The result is desire driven by fear of loss into a frenetic search for security in the face of both a hostile environment and other humans who are likewise scrambling to secure what they can under conditions of scarcity.

90. Lionel Robbins, *An Essay on the Nature and Significance of Economic Science* (London: Macmillan, 1952), 16. Italics added. See also Preston, *Religion and the Persistence of Capitalism*, 24; idem, *Church and Society in the Late Twentieth Century: The Economic and Political Task* (London: SCM, 1983), 24.

91. Novak, *Spirit of Democratic Capitalism*, 39. See also idem, *Business as a Calling*, 176–77. Michael Novak, "Wealth and Virtue: The Moral Case for Capitalism," *Word & World* 12, no. 4 (Fall 1992): 324; Novak, "God and Man in the Corporation," 32. See also Brian Griffiths, "The Culture of the Market," in Hay and Kreider, *Christianity and the Culture of Economics*, 23.

In this way, God is cast as a kind of sadistic cosmic Easter bunny, hiding stuff from humanity so that in the conflict and competition to find it, individuals will develop various traits and capacities. This is a sadist's game because not everyone succeeds in developing and finding.

Moreover, even where those traits are stimulated, there is no guarantee one will succeed or even survive. This is the case because there is no necessary connection between the development of the capitalist virtues and success in the capitalist market. "It is almost never possible to determine what part of a successful career has been due to superior knowledge, ability, or effort and what part to fortunate accidents."[92] One who develops the aforementioned traits may nevertheless be subject to unmerited failure just as one who does not develop such traits may flourish.[93] As mentioned before, "The effects on the different individuals and groups of the economic processes of a [capitalist] society are not distributed according to some recognizable principle of justice."[94]

The ways of capitalism's God are not just, although they may well be tragic. As one Christian advocate puts it, "The future may not have an upward slant, except as Golgotha had: So be it."[95] In other words, we may serve this God well, striving, asserting, creating, producing, and competing, and yet still be crucified—with no hope of any kind of resurrection.

The Corporation as Savior and Smith as Its Prophet

The fourth and final mark of the capitalist God concerns the mediating role that the corporation, as well as Adam Smith, plays in this capitalist providence. Some Christian theologians award the corporation a salvific or messianic role in this world. For example, rejecting the hostility and suspicion that characterize the approach of some toward the corporation, they suggest that the modern business corporation be compared to God's Suffering Servant of Isaiah 53 and recognized as "a much despised incarnation of God's presence in the world today" that has a religious vocation

92. Hayek, *Constitution of Liberty*, 82.
93. See Hayek, *Mirage of Social Justice*, 68–80.
94. See ibid., 83.
95. Novak, *Spirit of Democratic Capitalism*, 73.

as "instruments of redemption."[96] Others suggest that the corporation is best regarded as a "worldly ecclesia [church]" that we should love as we love our churches as they go about their mission of capitalization and profit seeking.[97]

Accompanying the elevation of the corporation as a mediator of God on par with the church is the elevation of Adam Smith, and modern economists in general, as heralds of the good news of material redemption above and beyond what Jesus envisioned. Thus it is not uncommon to find the economic history of humanity divided into two periods: Before Smith and After Smith. Before Smith, it is said, the world was locked in a "zero-sum" logic where the gain of the few could come only at the loss of the many. "In those days, wealth implied a zero-sum game. If one person had all, others had zero. . . . No one knew how to create wealth, only how to take it."[98] Prosperity was strictly a matter of distribution and money was inert; this is to say, it was regarded as immoral to use money to make money by means of interest and investment. "In premodern times, money was almost entirely a medium of exchange. It had very little role as investment capital, that is, as a social instrument for the creation of new wealth."[99] Trapped as he was in this zero-sum vision of the world, Jesus, it is said, thought that nothing could be done to alter the permanent condition of persons who are poor; all one could do was offer charity.

But then Adam Smith appeared, and with him came the knowledge of the causes of wealth. This new knowledge shattered the zero-sum vision that focused on redistribution. Now creativity and productivity became central, and capitalists could dream of lifting every last person on earth out of poverty.[100] So Smith surpasses Jesus as the prophet of God's economic ordering of creation.

96. Michael Novak, "A Theology of the Corporation," in *The Corporation: A Theological Inquiry*, ed. Michael Novak and John W. Cooper (Washington, DC: AEI, 1981), 203, 224; Novak, "God and Man in the Corporation," 23.

97. Max Stackhouse and Dennis P. McCann, "A Postcommunist Manifesto," in *From Christ to the World*, ed. Wayne G. Boulton, Thomas Kennedy, and Allen Verhay (Grand Rapids: Eerdmans, 1994), 487.

98. Michael Novak, "Root of All Evil No More," Beliefnet, accessed May 22, 2000, http://www.beliefnet.com/Faiths/2000/05/Root-Of-All-Evil-No-More.aspx. See also Neuhaus, *Doing Well and Doing Good*, 172–73.

99. Novak, "Root of All Evil No More."

100. Ibid.

A Higher Standard of Living: The Capitalist Good Life

The third and final step in our theological overview of capitalism concerns its vision of the good life. What are the characteristics of a life well lived, and how is that life attained? For the most part what follows is drawn from what has already been said: the nature of the good capitalist life is implicit in how it forms human desire and envisions God. From this can be discerned two distinct but related dimensions of the good capitalist life. On the one hand, there is the constant threat of scarcity that drives us into the agony of the capitalist market. Thus the good life is a matter of survival, of self-preservation that is secured by means of the market's blessing. On the other hand, there is the exercise of freedom as autonomy, independence, and self-interest by means of distinguishing oneself in the market. We begin with the latter.

Justification by Distinction

Already we noted that the measurement of the value and meaning of an individual's life is determined by one's position in the market. In 1899 Thorsten Veblen coined the famous term "conspicuous consumption" to refer to the ways people consume in order to impress others: "Since the consumption of these more excellent goods is an evidence of wealth, it [the consumption of these goods] becomes honorific. . . . Conspicuous consumption of valuable goods is a means of reputability. . . . The only practical means of impressing one's pecuniary ability on these unsympathetic observers of one's everyday life is an unremitting demonstration of ability to pay."[101] Veblen identified the class imitation and competitive consumption that characterized capitalist society. The term and analysis are still useful, although the nature of capitalist justification today does not correspond so neatly to Veblen's original vision where the highest income bracket in society sat atop a social hierarchy to which it was thought all aspired.[102]

101. Thorstein Veblen, *The Theory of the Leisure Class* (Rockville, MD: Arc Manor, 2008), 48–49, 55.
102. See Juliet B. Schor, *The Overspent American* (New York: Harper, 1998). For a critique of Veblen, see Sedgwick, *Market Economy and Christian Ethics*, 92–96; Miller, *Consuming Religion*, 149.

To begin with, the theory of conspicuous consumption assumes that imitation and emulation are the fundamental means by which persons seek to justify themselves in capitalist society. While what is called the "bandwagon effect"[103] certainly plays a significant role in contemporary capitalist consumption patterns, at least as significant is the "snob effect," that is, the effort to set oneself apart from others, to distinguish oneself by means of consumption choices.[104] In other words, persons establish themselves through market choices in more complex ways than the theory of "conspicuous consumption" suggests.

Furthermore, the directionality of the emulation or imitation is more diverse than Veblen suggests. It is not only the denizens of the lower-income brackets who aspire to the summits of wealthy styles and behaviors. Rather, everyone is immersed in an effort to achieve distinction. Consider, for example, the phenomenon of affluent white youth emulating the dress and behavioral styles of black urban culture in North America.

Moreover, the directionality is not simply one of moving in both directions on the economic ladder. Rather, distinction is established not merely by one's position on the hierarchical register of economic capital but also on the much "flatter" or dispersed register of cultural capital as well. We might say that distinction is a three-dimensional struggle. Thus, as Vincent Miller writes, "There is more going on than elites establishing their status thorough ostentatious displays of wealth and the lower strata of society parroting those above. Culture is a constant play of groups withholding, appropriating, and innovating in competition for social status."[105] This is perhaps nowhere more obvious than in the constantly changing iterations of what is the latest "hot" item or fad in popular culture and how the market moves to convert that cultural capital into profits, even as the ever-shifting cultural trendsetters elude the corporate "cool-hunters" in an effort to maintain the distinction that their newly created cultural capital grants them, however fleeting it may be.[106]

Finally, it is important to note that what is happening in this quest for distinction is not a stereotypical crass materialism or hedonism.

103. Harvey Leibenstein, "Bandwagon, Snob, and Veblen Effect in the Theory of Consumers' Demand," *Quarterly Journal of Economics* 62 (1948): 165–201.

104. Ibid.

105. Miller, *Consuming Religion*, 150.

106. Naomi Klein, *No Logo* (New York: Picador, 2002).

Rather, this effort at justification by distinction is a matter of identity or recognition. Adam Smith acknowledges this when he raises the question, "To what purpose is all the toil and bustle of this world?" He observes that it is not merely supplying the needs of nature, since those can be met by "the wages of the meanest labourer," and yet we are greatly adverse to that laborer's situation. Rather, he deduces that the motive is recognition: "To be observed, to be attended to, to be taken notice of with sympathy, complacency, and approbation, are all the advantages which we can propose to derive from it. It is the vanity, not the ease, or the pleasure, which interests us. But vanity is always founded upon the belief of our being the object of attention and approbation."[107]

Recall that the capitalist individual has the task of making herself. This is reflected well in contemporary consumerism.[108] In this construction, material goods and services are less about possession in the sense of "having" or hoarding and more about the constant and endless acquisition of novelties for the sake of distinguishing oneself, for the sake of appearance, of being recognized as valuable in the eyes of the market and, hence, in the eyes of others.[109] We live in an age of expressive individualism, which Guy Debord famously called, "the society of the spectacle," where image is among the most valuable of commodities.[110]

Salvation by Production and Accumulation

The second side of capitalist salvation involves the problem of scarcity. Given that scarcity is the fundamental problem of economic life, it follows that "more" is the solution. There are three dimensions to this salvific striving for more that bear noting. The first concerns the human condition considered globally. In the face of

107. Smith, *Theory of Moral Sentiments*, 50. See also Marglin, *Dismal Science*, 209–10; Luigino Bruni, "Common Good and Economics," trans. Michael Brennen, 4, accessed July 13, 2010, http://michaelbrennen.com/common-good-and-economics/; Luigino Bruni and Stefano Zamagni, *Civil Economy: Efficiency, Equity, Public Happiness* (New York: Peter Lang, 2007), 102, 208.

108. Sedgwick, *Market Economy and Christian Ethics*, 89; Miller, *Consuming Religion*, 115–16; Joseph E. Davis, "The Commodification of Self," *The Hedgehog Review* 5, no. 2 (Summer 2003): 41–49.

109. Sedgwick, *Market Economy and Christian Ethics*, 107–9.

110. Guy Debord, *The Society of the Spectacle* (New York: Zone, 1994).

the afflictions of scarcity, our only hope lies not in redistribution
of what we currently have but in the production of more. "The history of the modern age," economist Robert Nelson writes, "reveals
a widely held belief that economic progress will solve not only
practical but also spiritual problems of mankind."[111] Thus noted
economist John Maynard Keynes could write of a day soon coming
when capitalism's solution to our economic needs would release
humanity to revel in religion and virtue,[112] or a more recent Nobel
laureate in economics could declare that the majority of the social
problems of the twentieth century were attributable to economic
mismanagement. Indeed, he suggested, had the economic policies been better, "there would have been no Great Depression, no
Nazi revolution, and no World War II."[113] Or as another economist
notes, "Our only chance of building a decent world is that we can
continue to improve the general level of wealth."[114] Capitalism is
the engine on which modern civilization depends for both its origin
and its preservation.[115] Only capitalism's ability to generate more
can sustain the population of the world.[116]

The second side of capitalism's messianic provision concerns the
individual. The individual is saved by acquiring more. More income
results in more choices, which leads to greater satisfaction.[117] For this
reason one enters the competition of the market. The entrepreneur
takes a leap of faith, risks, in the hope of attaining more, thereby
securing one's life against the vicissitudes of scarcity and want. Thus,
we are told, the kingdom of God is like a commodity that can be
purchased by an entrepreneur who takes a risk in trade, negotiating the best price he can, in order to acquire a pearl of great price.[118]

Finally, the third dimension of the salvific quest for more concerns the corporate or class dimension. Already we noted that the

111. Robert Nelson, *Reaching for Heaven on Earth* (Savage, MD: Rowman &
Littlefield, 1991), xxi–ii, 6–7. See also Robert Nelson, "The Theological Meaning of
Economics," *Christian Century* 110, no. 23 (August 1993): 777.

112. See John Maynard Keynes, *Essays in Persuasion* (New York: Norton, 1963),
358–73.

113. Robert Mundell, quoted in Nelson, *Economics as Religion*, 78.

114. Hayek, *Road to Serfdom*, 210.

115. Hayek, *Constitution of Liberty*, 6.

116. Ibid., 85, 121–24.

117. Blank, "Market Behavior and Christian Behavior," 38.

118. Robert Sirico, "Bible Supports the Role of Entrepreneurs," *The Detroit News*,
July 30, 2005.

corporation is recognized as the sacred instrument of the search for more. Related to this, it is held that the wealthy play a privileged role in the redemptive creation of wealth. Together, the wealthy and the corporation function as a kind of means of grace, generating and then spreading wealth. As such, the rich are cast as a vanguard whose expenditures and extravagances pay for the experimentation with new things that later can be made available to persons who are poor.[119] "What today may seem an extravagance or even waste, because it is enjoyed by the few and even undreamed of by the masses, is payment for the experimentation with a style of living that will eventually be available to many. . . . Even the poorest today owe their relative material well-being to the results of past inequality."[120] So the wealthy classes join the corporation in its salvific work of creating more.

Conclusion

The first two chapters drew on Deleuze and Foucault to argue that capitalism is about more than the production and distribution of material goods and services, that it is in fact an economy of desire. The next two chapters suggested what is wrong with the capitalist economy of desire—it deforms human desire such that we neither desire the things of God nor relate to God and one another as we ought.

The question is, What is the alternative? Is another world, another economy possible? Is there a balm that can heal desire of its capitalist deformations? To these questions we now turn.

119. Hayek, Constitution of Liberty, 53, 130.
120. Ibid., 44.

5

Is Another Economy Possible?

The Church as an Economy of Desire

The Beauty of Friendship

It is a sunny summer day, and a middle-aged man and woman sit side by side on a bench outside a strip mall. They are dressed in worn T-shirts, and the woman has on brightly patterned pants that, if this were a beach or a small town on a Caribbean island instead of a city in northern Scotland, would suggest they are tourists on holiday. They are holding hands, and the man has his arm around the woman's neck, leaning in to her in an embrace that has drawn them cheek to cheek. They are smiling in an awkward sort of way that expresses affection and joy. The awkwardness of their expressions suggests as well that they are "different," as polite Southerners might say; this is to say, they are persons with Down syndrome. Their difference is highlighted by the poster of a female model, dressed in high fashion and impeccably coiffed, whose smoldering eyes stare intensely at the viewer just over and above the man's shoulder, beckoning from the window of the salon behind the seated friends.

A friend sent me this photograph several years ago, when she was an assistant at a L'Arche community.[1] I was struck immediately by the stark juxtaposition of desires present in the looming image of the model in the advertisement and the smiles of the friends—including my unseen friend—sharing a joyful moment together.

It is a suitable introduction to this chapter for three reasons. First, the existence of communities like L'Arche in the midst of the capitalist economy of desire suggests that God is about the business of renewing human desire and human relations according to a logic other than the agony of the capitalist market. Second, the photograph hints at the truth that capitalism will not be resisted by moralizing diatribes against materialism but at the deeper level of desire and its (re)formation. As Deleuze and Foucault suggest, capitalism is not driven by a crass materialism but is a matter of the spirit, of the highest aspirations of human desire. Third, the photograph reminds us that the struggle between capitalism and Christianity is not finally a matter of competing ideas circulating in universities and think tanks, but of the practices of and lives produced by Christian communities as they are about the work of God's economy.

The present chapter considers the church as a Spirit-empowered economy of desire, one that functions as a kind of therapy, healing desire of its capitalist distortions and enacting the divine gift economy. It begins by addressing two commonplace obstacles to this claim.

Is Another World Possible?

The previous chapter concluded by asking, What is the alternative to capitalism? From a Christian point of view the answer is rather straightforward. The alternative to capitalism is the kingdom of God, where those who build, inhabit; where those who plant, harvest; and where all are filled, and the agony that currently besets us ceases (Isa. 65:17–25). Few Christian theologians would dispute this. Furthermore, none would disagree with the observation that capitalism is not synonymous with Christianity. Michael Novak is not atypical in this regard when he writes, "Capitalism itself is not even close to being the kingdom of God. . . . The presuppositions,

1. For an introduction to L'Arche, see http://www.larcheusa.org/.

ethos, moral habits, and way of life required for the smooth functioning of democratic and capitalist institutions are not a full expression of Christian or Jewish faith, and are indeed partially in
conflict with the full transcendent demands of Christian and Jewish
faith."[2] Capitalism's Christian defenders do not presume capitalism
is perfect. Rather, it is, in the words of one economist, "a system
under which bad men can do least harm."[3]

The dispute, then, regarding capitalism is over whether a better
alternative is possible here and now. Christian proponents of capitalism argue that given the alternatives, capitalism is the best that
we can do, while for a long time Christian opponents of capitalism
were bold in asserting that socialism was the alternative.[4] In recent
decades, however, the cogency of the latter claim has faltered, as
actually existing socialism has proven neither particularly successful nor paradisiacal.

Does this mean that we are left with capitalism? It depends on
what we are given. Christian endorsements of capitalism are typically qualified, "*Given* the alternatives . . ." Here we get to the heart
of the matter. What does God give here and now? Is the divine
economy that is the kingdom possible now? Christian proponents
of capitalism argue that the divine economy is not possible now.[5]
Whatever effect the kingdom has now, it does not make possible
an alternative to capitalism.

Said in theological terms, Christian defenses of capitalism release
the tension between the "already" and "not yet" that properly characterizes Christian faith. The Christian faith does not rest solely
on promises that are *not yet* fulfilled. Rather, the faith rests as well
on promises that *already* have been fulfilled—such as the coming
of the Holy Spirit (John 14:26) to sustain, nurture, and guide the
faithful in discipleship in this world.

2. Michael Novak, *The Catholic Ethic and the Spirit of Capitalism* (New York:
Free Press, 1993), 227–28.

3. Friedrich A. von Hayek, *Individualism and Economic Order* (Chicago: University
of Chicago Press, 1948), 11.

4. It should be noted that many offer suggestions for reforming capitalism, although
the more substantial reforms—those that do more than suggest a social safety net—are
of dubious merit insofar as they would significantly undercut capitalism's celebrated
productivity and efficiency.

5. See, e.g., Michael Novak, "God and Man in the Corporation," *Policy Review*
3 (Summer 1980): 27.

Christian proponents of capitalism inevitably release this tension by emptying the "already" of any immediate material (social-political-economic) content, with the result that we are left with the capitalist status quo as the lesser evil, as the best we can expect until at some future point God decides to act. The kingdom is pushed entirely into the future. There is but one age, even as we look forward to the age to come. There is no overlap, no transformation or redemption here and now, beyond the comfort and assurance offered the economic winners of this age that they can be forgiven and the consolation offered to the impoverished that in the age to come things will be different.

This is the fundamental theological problem with Christian arguments for capitalism. They rest on the claim that God is *not* active here and now (and in the case of at least one prominent Christian advocate of capitalism, *ever*) *redeeming* us from sin, that the most that can be said about God's involvement in this world now is that God is *managing* sin through the mechanism of the market and perhaps motivating or inspiring us to work to reform the system and/or clean up after it (i.e., address market failures) with acts of charity that are "outside the market."[6] In other words, Christian defenses of capitalism presuppose that the economic shape of discipleship is limited to what *we* can do, to what we can accomplish under our own limited power and with our limited resources to reform and restrain capitalism, to curtail its worst excesses.

But the gospel is that we are not alone—or left for the time being with a Stoic or deistic God who at best only manages sin. Against the Christian defenses of capitalism that relegate the divine economy entirely to the future, the Christian tradition proclaims that the kingdom of God is at hand (Matt. 4:17). At the heart of the Christian faith is the confession that in Christ the kingdom has come near, which means that God's economy is a real, genuine possibility here and now.

The question, Is another world possible? is finally a theological question. It is not a question of what *we* can do, of what we are

6. Novak suggests that society should find ways to compensate for the injustices of the market. He does not suggest intervention in the market to prevent the injustice in the first place. See Michael Novak, *The Spirit of Democratic Capitalism* (New York: Touchstone, 1982), 212. In this regard, he echoes Friedrich A. von Hayek, *Law, Legislation, and Liberty*, vol. 2, *The Mirage of Social Justice* (Chicago: University of Chicago Press, 1976), 87, 136.

smart enough or strong enough or good enough to construct. Rather, it is a question of what God has and continues to give in Jesus Christ. It is a question of what the blessed Trinity has and continues to do in the world here and now.

Accordingly, the question of alternatives is not a matter of economic theory and human imagination, but of confession. This is so because the kingdom is not something we build; it is something we receive. The divine economy is not a product of our labor but is, instead, a gift. All of this is to say that the alternative to capitalism is not something that we construct; rather, it is something we confess that God is doing here and now. Thus the argument about "the best we can do" is moot. The interesting question never was, What can we do? but rather, What is God doing?

Against capitalism and its chaplains, the church confesses that the alternative to capitalism has *already* appeared, even if it is *not yet* present in its fullness. The ages are not juxtaposed, with one following the other, as capitalism's Christian proponents suggest; rather, they overlap (1 Cor. 10:11). God has given and continues to give here and now more than capitalism's chaplains can see.

And what is it that they fail to see? For one thing, it is the way that God has and continues to gather persons together into a body called the church where, by means of the divine things in our midst—Word and sacrament, catechesis, orders, and discipline—human desire is being healed of its capitalist distortions and set free to partake of a different economic ordering. Christian proponents fail to discern the divine economy that is already taking form in our midst as persons enter into new economic relations, producing and exchanging, not according to the rhythm of capital's axiom of production for the market, but in a way animated by the Spirit of faith, hope, and love. What there is to see that is not being seen, we will return to in later chapters.

Christianity and Desire

It is, however, not just capitalism's proponents who do not see what God is doing to heal desire of its capitalist distortions, which brings us to the second obstacle to envisioning Christianity as an economy of desire. Recall that even as Deleuze and Foucault argued that Christianity functions as an economy of desire, they were critical of it for the way it represses desire. Foucault, in particular, addressed the Christian economy of desire in his treatment of pastoral power—that governing power that is individualized and personal. Recall as well that Foucault highlighted the practice of confession and penance as an example of this pastoral power being exercised on desire. Confession, he said, was a kind of public exposure and renunciation of one's innermost thoughts and desires, a self-revelation that amounted to ritual martyrdom and self-destruction for the sake of reshaping desire in obedience to a transcendent ruler.

Not only do secular thinkers like Deleuze and Foucault believe Christianity is fundamentally antagonistic toward and so repressive of desire. Much of modern Christianity too approaches desire with suspicion as something that must be controlled and suppressed. Indeed, with the division of the Western church on the eve of modernity into Roman Catholic and Protestant denominations, Christianity became much more rationalist in orientation, placing a new emphasis on "beliefs" and doctrines and intellectual assent to true propositions while simultaneously displacing the significance of holiness enacted in character, action, and social unity.[7]

But Christianity has not always been so negatively inclined toward desire. Whether we turn to Scriptures like "As a deer longs for flowing streams, so my soul longs for you, O God" (Ps. 42:1) or consider voices of the early church—several of whom we have already mentioned, like Augustine, Thomas Aquinas, or the Calvinist divines at Westminster—Christianity has a rich history of engaging and even embracing desire. As C. S. Lewis has observed:

> If there lurks in most modern minds the notion that to desire our own good and to earnestly hope for the enjoyment of it is a bad thing, I suggest that this notion has crept in from Kant and the Stoics and is no part of the Christian faith. Indeed, if we consider the unblushing promises of reward and the staggering nature of the rewards promised in the Gospels, it would seem that Our Lord finds our desires, not too strong, but too weak. We are half-hearted creatures, fooling about with drink and sex and ambition when infinite joy is offered us, like an ignorant child who wants

7. For more on these developments, see John Bossy, *Christianity in the West: 1400–1700* (New York: Oxford University Press, 1985), and Ephraim Radner, *The End of the Church* (Grand Rapids: Eerdmans, 1998).

to go on making mud pies in a slum because he cannot imagine what is meant by the offer of a holiday at the sea. We are far too easily pleased.[8]

Indeed, for much of its history, the church was understood as a workshop of desire, a hospital where desire that had been disordered by sin recovered its true direction toward God and the things of God. It was in Deleuze's and Foucault's sense, an economy of desire—an ensemble of disciplines and practices and institutions that (re)shapes desire to flow in particular ways. It was also an economy of desire in the sense that it dealt directly and at length with desire as it was involved in what we typically mean when we speak of economy. For example, from its very birth the church has been concerned with reshaping or redirecting desire that has been distorted into avarice or greed, with avarice being understood broadly to encompass not merely the commonplace understanding of an immoderate desire for money and wealth but also intangible things like honor, knowledge, and even life itself.[9] In short, avarice was the name given desire that had been warped into a craving for more than what is sufficient.

Broadly speaking, the church's economy of desire enacted two distinct but interrelated disciplines, or asceticisms, for the sake of healing desire of its economic disorder. The first discipline, drawing from the example and teaching of Jesus (e.g., Mark 10:21), could be summarized as renunciation, and it is perhaps best associated with the monastic life, which is fitting since the traditional monastic vows—poverty, chastity, and obedience—express the sense of renunciation well. The second discipline focused on sharing and is associated with what I shall call "the parish." It might be captured under the heading of "almsgiving" or what would later be called "stewardship."

These disciplines were distinct because of the sites of their practice and the forms they took. The life of a monastic was different from that of secular clergy and laity. Yet they were nevertheless

8. C. S. Lewis, *The Weight of Glory and Other Addresses* (New York: Harper-Collins, 1976), 26. See also C. S. Lewis, *The Screwtape Letters* (New York: Touchstone, 1996), 83.

9. In what follows I am indebted to Richard Newhauser, *The Early History of Greed: The Sin of Avarice in Early Medieval Thought and Literature* (New York: Cambridge University Press, 2000).

interrelated because, on the one hand, monastic renunciation was rarely complete—a reality that was the source of great conflict and at times hypocrisy and embarrassment[10]—and the practices associated with the discipline of almsgiving were a significant part of monasticism. For example, even as members of monastic orders renounced possessions, some going so far as to become beggars or even to refuse to touch currency, they also extended hospitality to travelers and the needy; cared for the ill and the wayward, such as lepers and prostitutes; and provided food (feasts even!) for persons who were poor.[11] On the other hand, the discipline of almsgiving or stewardship that characterized parish life did not preclude the possibility of renunciation.

Medieval Monasticism as an Economy of Desire

One of the great examples of premodern Christianity's functioning as an economy of desire is provided by Bernard of Clairvaux and the monastic order he led. His work, as well as that of the Cistercian order, was geared, as Bernard put it, "to teach thirsting souls how to seek the one by whom they are themselves sought."[12] In this regard Bernard and the Cistercians fit in well with the rich tradition that stretches from the biblical writers through Augustine to C. S. Lewis of characterizing humanity in terms of a desire for God. This desire, however, should not be confused with a feeling or an instinctual reaction to an external stimulus that needs to be suppressed by the rational will. According to premodern Christians like Bernard, humanity was created in motion, and desire is this movement toward a goal, or *telos*.

Moreover, this desire is not properly understood as a lack or an absence, a void or vacuum, that is pulled forward in search of something to fill what is missing. Rather, according to Bernard, humanity is constituted not by a lack or absence but by a fullness, a presence, an excess. This fullness is God. Human desire is a gift of God, the consequence of God's presence. It is God's desire that creates human

10. See Lester K. Little, *Religious Poverty and the Profit Economy in Medieval Europe* (Ithaca, NY: Cornell University Press, 1978).

11. See ibid.

12. Bernard of Clairvaux, quoted in Michael Casey, *A Thirst for God* (Kalamazoo, MI: Cistercian Publications, 1988), 53.

desire.[13] Thus, Bernard writes, "No one has the strength to seek you unless he has first already found you. For it is a fact that you will to be found in order that you may be sought and you will to be sought in order that you may be found. It is possible, therefore, to seek you and to find you, but it is not possible to anticipate you."[14] In other words, God's presence, God's desire, God's love, evokes our desire. Thus for Bernard, like much of the tradition before and after him, desire is synonymous with love, and as such it is not so much an acquisitive drive, which is characteristic of a lack, but a generosity and giving expressed in the many forms of charity.

Humanity is constituted by a positive movement of desire called love; at least this desire was positive charity under the pristine conditions of creation. Since the fall, Bernard recognizes, desire has been corrupted, love has been disordered, by sin. As a consequence, human desire is no longer in harmony with the desire from whence it came. Desire no longer conforms to God but rather conforms to the world.[15] Drawing on the references to the image and likeness of God in Genesis 1:26, Bernard says that insofar as humanity was created in the image and likeness of God, it was "upright," that is, without iniquity.[16] Desire moved or flowed freely as it was created to do. With the advent of sin, however, humanity was deformed, bent from its true path. Desire was captured and enslaved to alien powers. As a consequence, desire now finds pleasure in what debases it; it is attracted to that which defaces the image. Desire is still a positive, productive power, only now it finds joy in the wrong productions; it takes pleasure in the wrong goods; it serves the wrong ends or purposes.

Of course, Bernard proclaims, humanity has not been left to languish in this condition. God in God's grace has acted to redeem desire. Indeed, says Bernard, the Word has come to heal desire.[17] Jesus is our medicine.[18] Jesus restores our desire, leading it on the path of virtue, wisdom, justice, holiness of life, and fruitfulness[19]— which leads nicely to how the monastic discipline functioned as a gracious economy given to heal desire.

13. Bernard of Clairvaux, On the Song of Songs, 4 vols., trans. Kilian Walsh (Kalamazoo, MI: Cistercian Publications, 1971–80), sermon 57.6.
14. Bernard of Clairvaux, quoted in Casey, Thirst for God, 85.
15. Bernard, On the Song of Songs, sermon 21.6.
16. Ibid., sermon 24.6.
17. Ibid., sermon 83.
18. Ibid., sermon 15.
19. Ibid., sermons 13, 22, 48.

Contrary to some popular misconceptions, the monastery was not a compound to which the pure withdrew, safe and secure from the vicissitudes of sin and temptations that batter life in the world. Neither was it a means by which those who sought holiness could squelch desire. Rather, the monastery was a school of charity, where desire was redeemed and love redirected. The monastery was the site of a divine pedagogy whereby desire underwent not annihilation but rehabilitation. The monastic life was not about the suppression of desire but the healing or transforming of desire that had been bent, distorted, deformed. "Far from being a constraint upon nature or a restraint in due freedom," writes Michael Casey, Cistercian life "works for the liberation of nature from the alien bondage of sin."[20] Far from being a place where desire was repressed and renounced, as Foucault suggested, monastic Christianity was about the liberation of desire.

The Cistercians are a particularly clear example of this because of their distinctive manner of recruitment. In particular, they drew heavily from the aristocracy—the knights and nobles. The significance of this lies in that these recruits had participated fully in a secular order that bent desire in ways that celebrated violence, pride, vanity, and sensuality.[21] And it was precisely this distorted desire that was the material for exercising virtue.[22] Jean Leclercq describes the sublimation of distorted desire among Bernard and the Cistercians this way:

> Thus, anger, when controlled, becomes the vehicle of good zeal; pride brought low can be pressed into service in defence of justice. . . . If a strong sexuality is brought under control and disciplined by the practice of works of mercy, the very quarter whence people are exposed to the darts of wickedness becomes itself an incitement to solicitude for others.[23]

The disordered impulses that monks had acquired in their previous lives as knights and nobles were redirected or rechanneled into a

---

20. Casey, *Thirst for God*, 143.
21. Jean Leclercq, *Monks and Love in Twelfth-Century France* (Oxford: Clarendon, 1979), 21, 88–89. What follows draws from Leclercq.
22. Talal Asad, *Genealogies of Religion: Discipline and Reasons of Power in Christianity and Islam* (Baltimore: Johns Hopkins University Press, 1993), 142.
23. Leclercq, *Monks and Love*, 16–17.

spiritual engagement: doing battle and winning glory for the sake of divine love.[24] Desire that had strayed from its created purpose and been bound by violence, pride, and sensuality was enlisted in the service of Christ and given a new direction.

A vast matrix of technologies, including both those of the self and of others, were involved in bringing about this transformation of desire. According to the *Rule of St. Benedict*, which was the cornerstone of Cistercian life, chief among the various rites and tasks that shaped monastic life was the liturgy. The liturgy was integral to the rehabilitation of desire.[25] Through the hearing of the Word, the bodily performance of the liturgy in speech, song, and silence as well as in kneeling and standing, the reception of the sacraments, and so forth, the monks' desire was redirected toward heaven and renewed in the likeness of God. The divine office, however, did not stand alone as the sole instrument of the restoration of desire. It was but one strand in the fabric of monastic life out of which the divine pedagogy was woven. The liturgy was embedded within the wider network of relationships, daily disciplines, and institutional configurations that constituted Cistercian Christianity. The entire spectrum of monastic rituals and rites, from meditation and obedience to manual labor and hospitality, functioned as technologies of desire.

Chief among these other rituals and rites was the sacrament of penance, which, as we have already seen, Foucault singled out for particular scrutiny as a repressive technique of the self. Yet, as we have suggested, the practice of confession and penance was not a matter of the repression and sacrifice of desire. While confession is clearly part of a process whereby sinful desire is renounced—as is the entire monastic economy of desire—the renunciation of sinful desire should not be equated simply with the denial or repression of desire *in toto*. Granted, Foucault's analysis is correct insofar as he places the sacrament of penance at the heart of the monastic program of the rehabilitation of desire and as he identifies confession as crucial to that technology. However, this confession is not the sacrifice of authentic desire under the imposition of another, artificial desire by a repressive faith. The practice of confession is not concerned with the control and repression of a primordial or

24. Ibid., 92–93.
25. Asad, *Genealogies of Religion*, 136–37.

natural desire. On the contrary, it is part of a process of recognizing that desire has already been captured and corrupted, that desire's sinful orientation is not its natural, created, God-given direction.

According to Bernard, the recognition that desire has been captured is crucial to its renewal. Thus he writes in his reflection on the Song of Songs:

> There must be no dissimulation, no attempt at self-deception, but a facing up to one's real self without flinching and turning aside. When a man thus takes stock of himself in the clear light of truth, he will discover that he lives in a region where likeness to God has been forfeited, and groaning from the depths of a misery to which he can no longer remain blind, will he not cry out to the Lord as the Prophet did: "In your truth you have humbled me"?[26]

Once persons see that they are oppressed, they will cry out to God, and the divine likeness begins to be renewed and restored. Recognition of the bondage of desire is a prerequisite to the many other disciplines such as repentance, prayer, and works of mercy whereby desire is graciously redeemed and renewed:

> You therefore have sown righteousness for yourself if by means of true self-knowledge you have learned to fear God, to humble yourself, to shed tears, to distribute alms and participate in other works of charity; if you have disciplined your body with fastings and prayers, if you have wearied your heart with acts of penance and heaven with your petitions. This is what it means to sow righteousness.[27]

Bernard and the Cistercians are helpful as an example of how Christianity is amenable to display as an economy of desire, as a gracious discipline intentionally directed at healing desire that is corrupted by sin. They are, however, not as helpful as an example of resistance to contemporary capitalism. This is the case in part because monastic forms no longer play as significant a role as they once did in Christianity. The vast majority of Christians today find their lives ordered not by a monastic rule but by parish/congregational life. More than this, however, the eleventh-century Cistercians are not as helpful because they did not prove to be particularly

26. Bernard, *On the Song of Songs*, sermon 35.6.
27. Ibid., sermon 37.2.

successful at negotiating the birth of the money/profit economy in the late eleventh century. This is not to suggest that the Cistercian order did not take the vow of poverty seriously; far from it. Rather, it is simply to recognize that in the eleventh century, as Europe underwent a commercial revolution and a nascent profit economy developed, the understanding of poverty underwent significant change, and the Cistercians found themselves not as well situated as others to address the emergent economy.

Put simply, prior to the second half of the eleventh century, as monastic orders embraced poverty as part of their renunciations, what it meant to be poor was determined primarily in relation not to material wealth—of which there was neither a great deal of concentration nor extensive destitution—but to social power. Thus when monastics saw themselves as the "poor of Christ," it was as much a matter of being "weak," of being vulnerable and defenseless in a violent age, as it was a matter of being materially deprived.[28] We might say it was a matter of being "poor *in spirit*," which was opposed principally to the sin of pride. Yet as the profit economy began to emerge in earnest in the latter part of the eleventh century, material poverty became much more prominent as both great discrepancies of wealth became more apparent and many slipped from subsistence to destitution.[29]

All of this is to say that economies of desire like those of Bernard and the order he led were well situated to reform the desire of warriors and knights that had been corrupted by the violence of a feudal order,[30] but they were not optimally suited for sublimating the desires of newly prominent merchants and bankers.

In this context, another order emerged, one that was no less an economy of desire yet was deliberately focused on the challenge presented by the emergent commercial/profit economy. In 1208, Francis, the son of a wealthy cloth merchant, heard the call of Christ to a life of itinerant preaching and begging and soon gathered around him a following that would become the Friars Minor, or Franciscans.

28. Little, *Religious Poverty*, 68.
29. Christopher Franks, *He Became Poor: The Poverty of Christ and Aquinas's Economic Teachings* (Grand Rapids: Eerdmans, 2009), 138; see also Michel Mollat, *The Poor in the Middle Ages* (New Haven: Yale University Press, 1986).
30. This is not to suggest that Bernard and the Cistercians are not rightly subject to criticisms for their failures even with regard to the feudal economy of violence. Bernard, after all, was a supporter of the Second Crusade.

As this order took shape, it involved a total renunciation of the newly emergent commercial economy, even as the Friars lived and worked in the midst of it, by means of such practices as begging, the prohibition of ownership, and a refusal even to handle money.[31] Although Francis did not leave theological treatises comparable to those of Bernard from which one could as easily excavate how the order functioned as an economy of desire, the opposition it aroused suggests that it did indeed function as a counterformation of desire that threatened the emergent commercial economy by proclaiming and enacting a different economy, the divine economy, about which more will be said shortly.[32]

Christianity, Desire, and Capitalism

Not only do Deleuze and Foucault hold that Christianity represses desire, they also implicate Christianity in the advent of capitalism insofar as they credit Christianity with advancing a pastoral power that prefigures capitalism's own deterritorializing and reterritorializing power and that is integral to capitalist governmentality; that is to say, they argue Christianity captures desire and then subjects it to a transcendent order or authority, not unlike the way capitalism captures and subjects desire to the transcendent order of production for the market.

There is truth to Deleuze's and Foucault's charge; however, it is not the truth that they perceive. Christianity did indeed have much to do with the rise of the capitalist economy of desire, but not in the manner that Deleuze and Foucault suggest.

Recall that Deleuze narrates the advent of capitalism in terms of desire's capture and escape from various social forms. Various state-forms attempt to capture and harness the productive power that is desire, but flows of desire always create lines of flight and escape, prompting the state-form to mutate. Eventually, the state-form is no longer able to capture desire and so begins only to regulate the flows of desire in accord with capitalism's rule of production for the market.

31. Malcolm D. Lambert, *Franciscan Poverty* (St. Bonaventure, NY: Franciscan Institute, 1998), 33–72.

32. For the history of the Franciscan struggles regarding poverty, see Lambert, *Franciscan Poverty*, and David Burr, *Olivi and Franciscan Poverty: The Origins of the Usus Pauper Controversy* (Philadelphia: University of Pennsylvania Press, 1989).

Recall as well Foucault's genealogy of pastoral power and how it was intended to help the state harness the power of its subjects for the purposes or reasons of the state. Yet here too the movement of desire exceeded the regulatory capacity of the state. This reality gave birth to economic government, that is, government that no longer sought to contain the economic interests of the populace but instead served those interests and economic processes.

In addition to these two ways of telling the story of capitalism's emergence, there is a third way, this time as a kind of *moral* history of desire. As previously suggested, Christianity has long held that humanity was created to desire God and that sin is a matter of the disordering of our desire such that we do not desire God and the things of God. The solution to this predicament, however, is not simply the repression of desire. Rather, the church confesses that God in God's grace has given us Christ, who heals our desire as we are graciously gathered by the Spirit into Christ's body and partake of the various means of grace that constitute the church as an economy of desire that sanctifies desire. Christ's healing presence is graciously mediated through material objects, such as bread, wine, and water; material, bodily practices, such as worship, fasting, and almsgiving; and material relations, such as neighborliness, friendship, and marriage. This is the theology that underwrites the discipleship of the likes of Augustine, the Cistercians, and the Franciscans.

This vision of discipleship as the redemption of desire, this faith and hope that desire can be healed, did not hold, and eventually capitalism's Christian advocates began to argue that at best sin can be managed only by the free market. How did we get from the conviction that desire could indeed be healed of its sinful corruption to the situation where it was thought that humanity's best hope was the management of sin by harnessing self-interest to the market?

Concurrent with the growth and spread of the money/profit economy, there began to circulate in learned circles the belief that religion could not be counted on to restrain the destructive passions and disordered desires of humanity.[33] Instead, it was suggested, disordered desires must be harnessed in the name of an overarching or all-consuming aspiration or interest. Eventually "interest" was

33. Albert Hirschman, *The Passions and the Interests: Political Arguments for Capitalism before Its Triumph* (Princeton, NJ: Princeton University Press, 1981), 14–15.

identified specifically with economic interests. Before long, even theologians were agreeing, arguing that perhaps instead of resisting those disordered desires, we should use them in the hope that, by means of some invisible hand, they might produce the greatest good for the greatest number.[34]

During this time, as the church was adapting to a culture whose center was less the feudal lord, the warrior, and chivalry, and more the merchant, the banker, and the city market, it was still immersed in a thousand-year-old struggle with the secular rulers regarding the exercise of social and political authority. For a millennium at least, the church had been engaged in a battle with various secular rulers regarding the exercise of governing authority in society. This is the element of the story that is missing from Deleuze's and Foucault's narratives. They fail to acknowledge that the foil for the emergence of the modern state was not *only* an economy that eluded the previous state-form's grasp. The other pressure point was the church. The modern state emerged out of this long struggle with the church for authority over bodies and communities.[35]

Thus the concepts "reason of state" and "interests" were, in the words of one scholar, "meant to do battle on two fronts":[36] the ecclesial (churchly) as well as the economic. As Foucault noted, when the state asserted its interests in the form of reason of state, it was attempting to reorder the lives and desires of its subjects for the sake of the strength of the state. This effort to contain desire and direct it for the benefit of the prince/state, however, was simultaneously a move to direct the population's desire *away from* the church, which insofar as it exerted moral authority in this world and not just spiritual authority over the next stood in the way of the state's aspiration to unchallenged, sovereign authority over material life.

The state was only partly successful. While the church did ultimately concede governing authority to the state and retreat to the apolitical, spiritual realm of beliefs and values, the state was not as successful in reterritorializing the desire that had been freed from the moral discipline of the church. As Deleuze and Foucault point out, the state's efforts to capture desire under "reason of state"

34. Ibid., 16.
35. William T. Cavanaugh, "A Fire Strong Enough to Consume the House: The Wars of Religion and the Rise of the State," *Modern Theology* 11, no. 4 (October 1995): 397–420.
36. Hirschman, *Passions and the Interests*, 33.

ended up fracturing desire into the untamable and irreconcilably diverse self-interests of *homo economicus*.

Addressing this omission in the story matters because while Deleuze and Foucault imply Christianity aided and abetted this capture, the fuller picture of Christianity's relation to the emergence of capitalism is more complex. Indeed, it would be more accurate to suggest that capitalism emerged on the back of the church's defeat. This is to say, in order for capitalism to emerge, not only did the state have to be overrun by economy but the church had to be as well. That this is what happened is attested to by no less than Adam Smith, when he observed that initially the church was a great obstacle to the emergence of the capitalist economic order. He noted that the hospitality and charity of the church were very great, maintaining the poor of every kingdom, and he lamented that those practices "not only gave [the church] the command of a great temporal force, but increased very much the weight of their spiritual weapons." Indeed, he goes on to observe that the church constituted the most formidable obstacle to the civil order, liberty, and happiness that the free market could provide. But, alas, he is glad to report that eventually improvements in "arts, manufactures, and commerce" not only conquered the great barons but undercut the church as well, weakening both its spiritual and temporal authority by rendering its charity merely economic, that is, more sparing and restrained.[37]

This defeat took shape in several ways. First, as previously suggested, church leaders themselves lost faith in the means of grace available in and through the life of the church to heal desire of its avarice, its economic distortion. Second, monastic orders like the Cistercians were unprepared for the changes and challenges of the new profit economy, and even the formidable resistance of the Franciscans was eventually undermined through a series of internal and external problems. Third, the church's political retreat before the modern state as it yielded governance of this world to the secular lords contributed to the spiritualization of the faith, to the faith becoming increasingly a matter of the head or heart—of doctrine and feeling, to the detriment of bodily discipline and material practice, and of justification (pardon and forgiveness),

37. Adam Smith, *An Inquiry into the Nature and Causes of the Wealth of Nations* (Chicago: University of Chicago Press, 1976), 2:323-6.

to the eclipse of sanctification (healing and holiness). Fourth, the division of the church and subsequent flourishing of denominations slowly diminished the power of the church's economy of desire by rendering the constitutive disciplines more voluntary or optional as persons increasingly felt "free to choose" their faith in the marketplace of religions.

In the aftermath of this defeat, the productive, creative power that is human desire did not sink into a crass materialism. Instead, as Augustine noted long ago and as modern economics reminds us, desire remains unsatisfied. Indeed, it is condemned to restlessness as capitalism continuously entices or seduces it with novel distractions, all for the sake of harnessing its productive power to the market. For this reason, capitalism's Christian defenders are right. Capitalism is not a materialistic order but has everything to do with the spirit. Capitalism does not deny the spirit by grounding desire in the material but instead effects a horizontal displacement of desire by constantly misdirecting desire from its true (vertical) home in God, by means of the enchantments of consumerism,[38] perhaps not unlike the way capitalist desire is drawn from the embrace of friendship toward the seductive gaze of the model in the scene from the photograph that opened this chapter.

Is desire destined to be trapped forever in this economy that depends not on enjoyment and rest but on endless dissatisfaction and toil? This brings us to a critique of Deleuze and Foucault.

Madness and Beyond: The Failure of Deleuze and Foucault

Thus far we have responded to Deleuze's and Foucault's critique of Christianity by affirming it in part and rejecting it in part. They are right when they argue that Christianity is indeed an economy of desire. Yet they err in suggesting that it is repressive, that it calls for a destruction or sacrifice of desire. Drawing in particular from medieval monasticism, I have argued that Christianity is an economy of desire that is not destructive but therapeutic, healing.

38. Vincent J. Miller, *Consuming Religion* (New York: Continuum, 2004), 127–28. See also Eugene McCarraher, "The Enchanted City of Man: The State and the Market in Augustinian Perspective," in *Augustine and Politics*, ed. John Doody, Kevin Hughes, and Kim Paffenroth (Lanham, MD: Lexington Books, 2005), 280–89.

And by pointing toward Francis and the order he founded, I have at least gestured toward the possibility that it is an economy of desire that resists the capitalist economy of desire. Before continuing to explore this possibility, however, it is time to turn the critical eye back on Deleuze and Foucault.

Deleuze and Foucault envision their project as a contribution to a revolutionary effort to liberate desire from the coils of the capitalist serpent that have enveloped the globe. While many thought their account of desire's capture through governmentality and societies of control was a pessimistic one that snuffed out hope, they rejected such claims and insisted that the productive power that is desire is always capable of escaping. That power is ubiquitous and not the sole possession of the state and its (para)military units and security apparatuses is reason for hope. That desire is fundamentally restless, anarchic, and creative means that every capture of desire is always tentative, contingent. No victory by any state-form is ever guaranteed; indeed, such victories are always already unstable, for desire is never finally tamed and so can escape at any moment.

Accordingly, the revolution is a matter of nurturing the flow of desire.[39] Escape from capitalism is not a matter of destruction but of creation, addition, intensification. It is a matter of overwhelming capitalism's ability to adapt desire to the market. In other words, the path beyond capitalism for Deleuze and Foucault is not one that destroys capitalism but exceeds it. Revolution is a matter of achieving absolute deterritorialization—that condition where desire is not subject to any transcendent end or external discipline but instead is free to flow in the creative, anarchic sociality of love. Recall that capitalism is characterized by a profound power of deterritorialization, which is the power to release desire from social formations and codes and the purposes such impose on desire. But even as capitalism deterritorializes desire, it simultaneously reterritorializes desire by adapting it to the rule of production for the market. Hence, capitalist desire never attains the genuine freedom that is the anarchic, experimental desire Deleuze labels "schizophrenia."

Capitalism, observes Deleuze, in its voracious deterritorializing, is a form a madness, and as a way beyond this madness, Deleuze

---

39. Gilles Deleuze and Félix Guattari, *Anti-Oedipus: Capitalism and Schizophrenia*, trans. Robert Hurley, Mark Seem, and Helen R. Lane (Minneapolis: University of Minnesota Press, 1983), 246 and passim.

proposes intensifying the madness, continuing the process of deterritorialization until desire is free of all order.

Here it is worthwhile to return to the scenes that opened the first two chapters. Seattle and Mardi Gras both display a postmodern economy of desire, and although the Multitude in Seattle is celebrated as an oppositional assembly of desire by participants, as well as by political philosophers such as Hardt and Negri, Mardi Gras suggests that desire gone wild is amenable to capitalist reterritorialization. As the worker in the bead factory noted on viewing the revelry in New Orleans made possible by the long commodity chain of global capitalism, that is crazy, madness. Deleuze's madness is not a break with capitalism but an intensification of it. Indeed, even before the tear gas had cleared from the streets of Seattle, street venders were hawking souvenirs and memorabilia of the event.

We must ask, however, is madness the way beyond the madness that is capitalism? Or does madness intensified finally collapse in the black hole of nihilism, where life becomes death and an absolute violence is unleashed? Even granting for the sake of argument Deleuze's conviction that capitalism can be overwhelmed by flows of desire that exceed the market's ability to commodify (a claim that is by no means self-evidently true), from whence do Deleuze and Foucault generate the hope that such absolutely deterritorialized desire would result in a joyous sociality of love?

Reason to suspect their vision in this regard arises on account of the way they understand the sameness of being. Recall the discussion of the "univocity of being" in chapter 1 and how, according to that theory, desire is generic, the same, and that what differentiates beings one from another is a matter of intensity or degrees of desire. The appeal for Deleuze of this way of understanding being or desire is that it abolishes transcendence. There is no purpose or end attached to desire like there is for the Christian tradition, which says that the end or purpose of desire is to rest in and enjoy communion with God.

This creates two problems for their vision of freedom in madness beyond the madness of capitalism. First, insofar as being or desire is the same, individuals cannot draw too close to one another lest their identity as persons is lost in the melding together of their sameness. According to the univocity or sameness of being, identity requires a certain distance, a certain reservation in relating to others, lest in giving ourselves fully we are lost in the fusion of the same, undifferentiated being that constitutes us all. Because at our core all being or desire is the same, we must keep a distance from one another in order to preserve our selves. A self so constituted is intrinsically possessive—carefully preserving oneself lest one is lost in the sameness of being—instead of generous.

Furthermore, relations between such selves must be either a matter of conquest, where one intensity of desire consumes another, or contract, where the necessary distance between beings is maintained through the impersonal, formal boundaries of the contract. This suggests that Deleuze does not escape capitalist discipline, for capitalism has so construed the market that it too mediates all relations of desire agonistically. Capitalist discipline distorts desire into a competitive force—competing for resources, for market share, for a living wage, for the time for friendship and family, for inclusion in the market, and so forth—and so does Deleuze's univocal vision of desire.

The second difficulty is perhaps easier to appreciate. It concerns the way in which desire is shorn of any given end or purpose in favor of its own self-generated experimental expressiveness. Given this anarchic character of desire, on what grounds does he assert that when this self-creating, self-asserting desire is released from every organization, the flows of liberated desire will enter into joyful, harmonious relations? From where comes the confidence that the flows of desire, deprived of any shared end and restricted to relations of conquest or contract, will not simply collide in pure war? As was perhaps most famously pointed out by the early modern political philosopher Thomas Hobbes, the sort of vision of desire that Deleuze advocates requires a teleology (an account of given ends or purposes), be it divinely given or imposed by a secular state, to avoid a state of *bellum omnis contra omnem*—war of all against all. Lacking a shared end and incapable of entering into nonpossessive relations, Deleuze's schizoid desire does indeed resemble a "war-machine" (to echo one of his own concepts).

As a consequence of these two problems, Deleuze's assertion that desire overwhelming capitalism will result in a proliferation of joyous social relations akin to love is really a plea for the miraculous. This is to say, it cannot happen given the strictures of his thought. Moreover, it is a plea for the miraculous that must go unanswered because, having banished transcendence, the heavens are empty. Thus Deleuze's championing of assertive, creative desire looks more like the advancement of arbitrariness and portends not the proliferation of joy and harmony but the endless spilling of blood and shedding of tears.

Conclusion

The question that began this chapter was, Is another economy possible? Whether one considers the arguments of Christian advocates of capitalism or Deleuze and Foucault, the answer finally is theological. What is God doing to redeem us from sin, from the travail of disordered desire? What is God making possible here and now?

The church has long proclaimed that God in God's grace has provided certain means of grace in and through Christ and his body, the church, for the sake of healing our desire so that we might rest in and enjoy God. In this chapter we considered medieval monasticism as an example of one form that the sanctifying economy of desire has taken. We now turn more directly to the economic shape that desire takes in this divine economy.

6

The Economy of Salvation

The Economic Trinity

The previous chapter began with a snapshot that reflected two very different formations of desire and human relationships. Yet because few of us participate in the kinds of intentional Christian communities that movements like L'Arche represent, we may be tempted to dismiss such examples as oddities and exceptions rather than the norm. For many of us, the consumer culture represented by the poster of the fashion model is much closer to the normative or determinative flow of our lives, and the claim that "we are all capitalists now" rings all too true and all too deep. This is to say, we may be tempted to believe that the kinds of counterformation or healing of desire that I suggested happens in the church requires precisely a medieval, monastic church.

The remaining chapters constitute a response to this suspicion. Following Deleuze and Foucault, the response begins from the recognition that capitalism, by means of its governmentality and various disciplines, so forms us that we come to believe that the relations of desire constitutive of the agony of capitalism (involving ourselves, others, the rest of creation, and God) are not contingent practices that could be otherwise but rather are veritable laws of nature.

In the Gospel of Mark, the story is told of Jesus's encounter with a blind man at Bethsaida. Jesus touches the man's eyes, and as a result the man begins to see. However, his sight is not fully recovered. He can see people, but they look like walking trees. So Jesus lays hands on him a second time, and the man is able to see clearly (Mark 8:22–25).

The economy of desire that is capitalism produces a kind of virtual reality, and as a result we do not see what is really going on around us. Just as the capitalist division of labor conceals from us the conditions of commodity production, so we do not see the divine economy that is taking shape and already active all around us, even in the church. We may see a little; we may see walking trees. We may recognize that capitalism is not "the end of history," as one pundit has claimed. But our vision is corrupted; we do not recognize the things God has given and is doing now to heal desire of its capitalist distortions.

What exactly is God doing to heal desire of its capitalist distortions? What does this divine economy of desire look like? In Christian theology a distinction is sometimes drawn between the immanent Trinity, referring to the life of the Trinity in itself, and the economic Trinity, referring to how the Trinity is at work in this world. The remaining chapters consider the economic Trinity—what God is doing to overcome the capitalist economy of desire. In this chapter we consider the economy of salvation, that is, Christ's work of atonement and its effect on human desire, as well as the role or purpose of material goods within that economy of salvation.

The Divine Gift Economy: Christ's Work of Atonement

With the reference to "gift economy" one might be tempted to think that this is an effort to recover a traditional, premodern, or non-Western form of economy. Although non-Western gift economies have received renewed attention in theological circles of late, they are not the starting point for what follows, and this not merely because they are amenable to capitalist incorporation among other deficiencies.[1]

Instead, the alternative economy of desire is rooted in the Christian theological vision introduced previously. That theological vision

1. See Kathryn Tanner, *Economy of Grace* (Minneapolis: Fortress, 2005), 49–56. See also John Milbank, "Can a Gift Be Given? Prolegomena to a Future Trinitarian Metaphysic," *Modern Theology* 11, no. 1 (January 1995): 119–61.

is in fact an economic vision. The word "economics" is derived from terms for "rule or order" and "household." Economics is about the ordering of the household, and when we talk about a theological economics, we are talking about God's ordering of God's household, which is none other than creation. Thus far, appealing to the likes of Augustine, Aquinas, and the Calvinist divines of Westminster, we have described the divine economy in terms of the blessed Trinity giving the gift of life for the sake of incorporating all desire into the communion of divine love. Furthermore, following the tradition, we attributed the fact that not all enjoy this communion to the reality of sin, of which capitalism is a species. At the heart of the Christian gospel is a claim about how the economy of salvation rectifies this situation; namely, God sent the Son to take away the sin of the world (John 1:29). This is our starting point for unpacking the divine economy of desire.

Moreover, by starting here, with Christ's work, it should be clear that the question of Christian economics is *not* a matter of picking and choosing from among the world's options, as if all God in Christ did was supply us with abstract values or principles like "love" or "justice" that we have to correlate with an economic order established on other, secular terms. As suggested previously, the alternative economy of desire is first and foremost a question of what God is doing in the world here and now. And God is doing more than inspiring us to be good neoliberal free marketers or Keynesians or socialists.

Our consideration of what God is doing now to heal desire of its economic distortions begins with the Christian doctrine of atonement, of Christ's work on the cross. In particular, it begins with what is commonly called the satisfaction or substitutionary account of Christ's work on the cross that is frequently attributed to Paul, typically identified with the early chapters of his Epistle to the Romans, and developed most notably by the medieval theologian St. Anselm (1033–1109), whose interpretation of Christ's work on the cross in his classic treatise *Cur Deus Homo* has become widely influential in Western Christianity and is particularly well suited for highlighting the economic character of God's incarnation in the world to overcome sin.

Typically the satisfaction or substitutionary understanding of the cross holds that Christ's death on the cross satisfied the debt to God humanity incurred on account of sin, that Christ is the sinners' substitute on the cross, paying the penalty of that sin. Anselm's argument can be summarized as follows: in the face of human sin, which is an offense against God's honor, God, as one who must uphold justice, cannot simply forgive sin but must enforce a strict accounting of what is due. However, because humanity already owes God everything, it has no surplus with which to repay its debt. In this situation, the God-man, Christ, steps forward and fulfills justice, renders what is due, and pays the debt through his substitutionary death on the cross. In this way, redemption is the result of the payment of a debt incurred through sin by means of a compensatory death that satisfies divine justice.

At first glance, this account of Christ's work on the cross might not seem particularly relevant either to the matter of economics in general or to liberating desire from the distortions of capitalism. On the one hand, it appears to have little to do directly with economics, with the circulation and use of scarce resources; on the other hand, insofar as it might have some indirect relevance, it does not appear to present a serious challenge of any sort to the capitalist economy of desire. Indeed, to the extent that Christ's work of redemption on the cross seems to work entirely within a logic of scarcity and debt, commutative exchange, equity, and strict accounting of what is due, it would appear to reinforce the material logic that underwrites the capitalist economy of desire. Divine accounting, it seems, is not that different from capitalist accounting. Just as capitalism functions according to a contractual logic of debt, equality/equivalence (via the dollar and dominance of exchange value), retribution (as in an exact accounting and rendering what is due), and finally death (for it is death that gives scarcity its power), so too, apparently, does the atonement. Redemption requires a full settling of accounts, commutative justice. Christ's death is an exchange accounted equivalent to our debt that settles the divine-human balance sheet.

Yet, notwithstanding its widespread popularity, this reading of Paul and Anselm is a profound misreading. It reflects not the divine economy of salvation revealed in Scripture, expounded in the tradition, and lived out by the church, but rather reflects the way that our imaginations have been so disciplined by the capitalist economy of desire that was beginning to emerge during Anselm's time. As a result, we have blurred vision (like the blind man at

Bethsaida) and so misinterpret the work the crucified (and resurrected) Christ was doing; we misconstrue the character of God's economy that heals desire of its sin.

When understood rightly, the atonement is neither irrelevant to economy nor a tacit endorsement of the logic of the capitalist economic order. Rather, rightly understood, the cross reveals the gift of Christ as the incarnation of a divine economy that turns the capitalist order on its head. In particular, Anselm discloses how Christ's work on the cross cannot be correlated with a capitalist economic logic that revolves around scarcity, with its calculi of debt, equity, and death, but instead illuminates a divine economy of charity, an economic order characterized by plenitude and generosity that exceeds the strictures of capitalism as surely as Christ burst the bonds of death.

Anselm provides the first hint that a different kind of economic order is operating in Christ's work of atonement when he observes, in keeping with the teaching of the church, that God needs nothing and that no necessity compels God to act as God does in redeeming us from sin.[2] Already the standard interpretation of the cross is in trouble, insofar as it asserts that some necessity compels God to exact compensatory suffering as the penalty for sin. Anselm then goes on to say that God does not demand bloodshed,[3] that divine justice is not in conflict with divine mercy,[4] and that God's power and dignity cannot be diminished by human insurrection.[5] All of which is to say that whatever is happening on the cross, it is not about a strict settling of accounts and a rigid enforcing of commutative justice. Indeed, as Anselm argues, in the work of atonement, God in Christ both dismisses every debt[6] and gives a gift that far *exceeds* any settling of accounts, since in Christ we are renewed even more wonderfully than we were created.[7]

---

2. Anselm, "Why God Became Man," in *A Scholastic Miscellany: Anselm to Ockham*, ed. Eugene R. Fairweather (Philadelphia: Westminster, 1956), 2.5; see also 2.17, 19; Hans Urs von Balthasar, *The Glory of the Lord* (San Francisco: Ignatius Press, 1984), 2:240, 245, 250, 246.

3. Anselm, "Why God Became Man," 1.9–10.

4. Anselm, "Proslogion," in *Anselm of Canterbury: The Major Works*, ed. Brian Davies and G. R. Evans (New York: Oxford University Press, 1998), sec. 9–11. See also Anselm, "Why God Became Man," 1.24, 2.20.

5. Anselm, "Why God Became Man," 1.15.

6. Ibid., 2.19–20.

7. Ibid., 2.26.

What is going on, Anselm says, is not God collecting on accounts receivable but rather making good on God's intention in creating humanity. This is the key to understanding the claim that sin is an offense against God's honor. Anselm argues that sin is indeed an offense against God's honor in the particular sense that it is not fitting that God's will or intention for humanity be thwarted. To put this in the idiom of Augustine, Aquinas, and Westminster, sin is an offense against God because it is the thwarting of God's desire that humanity enjoy, find its rest or communion, in God. The injury to God's honor that is effected by sin is a matter of the absence of humanity from full communion with its Creator. Thus, rightly understood, God's honor is not a barrier to humanity's reconciliation with God—as though God were an aristocrat in a Hollywood movie whose pride was offended. As such, honor is the origin of God's free act to provide humanity with a path to renewed communion. God's honor demands not that one *pay* for thwarting God's intentions but that God's intentions for humanity *not* be thwarted.

Accordingly, Christ's work on the cross is a display of the plenitude of divine charity (John 3:16), of God's giving and giving again. The atonement is not a settling of accounts, an exaction of payment, or the calling in of a debt. Rather it is a matter of God's ceaseless generosity, of God's graceful prodigality. It is a matter of donation, of divine donation for our sake. Thus Christ is not our offering to God but God's offering to us (Rom. 5:8). God has always given to humanity in the form of love, and when humanity rejected that gift, God forgave and gave again in the form of love incarnate, which is the Son. Christ's work is that of giving again, of communicating God's prodigious love and grace (which has never ceased to flow) to humanity again (and again). The work of atonement is God in Christ forgiving, bearing human rejection, and extending the offer of grace again, thereby opening a path for humanity to recover beatitude, communion. In Christ, God reconciled the world (2 Cor. 5:18–19). In Christ, God has refused to render to humanity what is due sin, but instead graciously endures humanity's rejection and extends the gift/offer of redemption and reconciliation in Christ (Rom. 3:25).

(This, not incidentally, is entirely in keeping with Paul's argument in Romans, where Jesus is put forward as the justice [righteousness] of God because Jesus is the incarnation of God's faithfulness to the redemptive promise made to Abraham for the sake of Jew and gentile alike.)

This is the context for rightly understanding Anselm's claim that it is not fitting for God to simply forgive sin.[8] Contrary to the first impression such a statement makes, that it is unseemly for God simply to forgive sin without satisfaction, Anselm's claim is not a rejection of the entirely gratuitous nature of Christ's atonement in favor of a strict accounting of what is due. Rather, what Anselm rejects as "not fitting" is a construal of redemption as sheer negative pardon. By this I mean conceiving Christ's atonement as simply letting sinners off the hook, as God simply ignoring our sin as we are left otherwise unchanged.

The problem for Anselm with casting redemption in this way is that it would be both untruthful and unjust.[9] It would be untruthful because it would elevate or equate (pardoned) sinful humanity with sinless humanity. But this is falsehood because sinful humanity is not the same as sinless humanity. Sinful humanity is constitutionally incapable of enjoying blessedness, and a purely negative pardon, whatever it might accomplish, would not change this. This is the logic behind Anselm's striking claim that he would prefer to be in hell without sin than in heaven with sin.[10] Redemption construed as sheer negative pardon would result in humanity gaining entrance to heaven but still in need and thus devoid of blessedness. As a result, heaven would be hell.

Such an act of pardon would, likewise, be unjust because it would fail to accomplish God's desire for humanity. If, as we have seen, the point of the atonement is fulfilling God's intentions for humanity, a sheer negative pardon is insufficient; it does not restore or renew human nature. Here we might draw on the analogy Anselm develops of a pearl fallen into the mud.[11] Would it be wise, he asks, for one to pluck that pearl from the mud and store it, dirty and unwashed, in some clean and costly receptacle? "Of course not," is the reply. It would be far better to preserve the pearl clean rather than polluted. So it is with humanity. A sheer negative pardon would be equivalent to placing humanity, stained and corrupted by sin, in a clean and costly receptacle.

This is the meaning of "satisfaction" that runs through Anselm's argument. Thus, in contrast with the dominant modern reading,

8. Ibid., 1.12.

9. Ibid., 1.12, 19.

10. See Eadmer, *The Life of Saint Anselm* (New York: Oxford, 1972), 84; Von Balthasar, *Glory of the Lord*, 2:249.

11. Anselm, "Why God Became Man," 1.19.

which tends to render satisfaction the equivalent of a strict settling of accounts by means of punishment and retribution, Anselm consistently posits satisfaction as a gracious alternative to retributive punishment and a strict settling of accounts. Satisfaction is a matter of God's desire for humanity being accomplished. In this sense, Christ's faithfulness even to the point of death on the cross marks not a divine demand for retribution but a divine refusal to hold our rebellion against us. The Father's love and the Son's faithfulness to the desire to redeem us is such that God will even go to the cross rather than withdraw the offer of reconciliation. As such, the atonement is not a propitiation offered to appease an angry God but an expiation—a removal of the obstacle to communion that is sin—effected by the Father in the Son through the Spirit for us in our sinful obstinacy.

There is a sacrifice involved in this atoning work, and there is a substitution. But the nature and end of these are not rightly grasped when they are accounted movements in a "commercial drama,"[12] that is, the due processes of an economic order that disciplines exchange according to a strict calculus of equivalence and retribution. Rather, Christ's sacrifice is the donation of obedience and praise (the return of love) offered by the Son to the Father, and his role is substitutionary in that the Son offers the worship we cannot.

This is all to say that Christ's substitutionary sacrifice is an instantiation of the divine plenitude and superabundance that created, sustains, and now enables us to return to our source, to participate in the divine life, in the reciprocity that is the Triune circle of love that is our true end and for which we were created.

So understood, the atoning work of Christ is indeed an economic act. It is a movement of the divine economy of plenitude, ceaseless generosity, and superabundance. As such it runs counter to every economy that operates on the basis of scarcity, debt, desert, and a strict accounting of what is due.

Desire Renewed: Eternal Generosity

It follows from this that Christ's work of atonement renews desire in its true modality of gift, donation, and unending generosity. In this

12. The phrase belongs to A. M. Fairbairn, *The Place of Christ in Modern Theology* (New York: Scribner, 1903), 124.

regard, Anselm's account of the atonement is particularly helpful because he makes it clear that redemption entails our participation in the divine economy of ceaseless generosity and superabundance. The economy of salvation is about the healing of desire—the creative, filiative power of love—as it is taken up into the communion of charity that is the divine life (2 Pet. 1:4). Christ does not redeem by satisfying the strictures of an economy of debt, equity, and a strict accounting of what is due. Rather he redeems by pouring forth the divine plenitude in the giving of his body, the reception of which renews, transforms, and sanctifies our desire so that it recovers its created modality of ceaseless donation, of relentless generosity, of endlessly receiving and giving the gift of charity that is the presence of God and, in God, the neighbor as well.

This redemptive incorporation of our desire in the divine economy of eternal generosity is reflected in the worship of many churches when at the conclusion of the Communion service the congregation prays something like, "Eternal God, we give you thanks for this holy mystery in which you have given yourself to us. Grant that we may go into the world in the strength of your Spirit, to give ourselves for others, in the name of Jesus Christ our Lord. Amen."[13] The Christian's incorporation into this divine gift economy is also powerfully expressed in one of the more striking passages of Martin Luther, where he writes: "We should devote all our works to the welfare of others, since each has such abundant riches in his faith that all his other works and his whole life are a surplus with which [the Christian] can . . . serve and do good to his neighbor." Luther even goes so far as to suggest that having received Christ, we should in turn "be Christ to one another."[14] Likewise, Aquinas writes, "Divine love makes one ecstatic," by which he means that love places a person outside herself, not suffering her to belong to herself but to that which is loved.[15] As we receive the self-giving love of God in Christ, our love, our desire, is healed and so turned outward in eternal generosity toward others. And this self-offering is our true

13. "Word and Table: Service I," in *The United Methodist Hymnal* (Nashville: United Methodist Publishing House, 1989), 10.

14. Martin Luther, "The Freedom of a Christian," in *Luther's Works*, vol. 31, ed. Harold J. Grimm (Philadelphia: Muhlenberg, 1957), 364–68.

15. Aquinas is citing Dionysius the Areopagite. Quoted in Christopher Franks, *He Became Poor: The Poverty of Christ and Aquinas's Economic Teachings* (Grand Rapids: Eerdmans, 2009), 181.

nature; it is the joyous work desire was created to do. It is desire in the form of the virtues such as charity, justice, and generosity.

In this regard, Paul prefaces one of the most important passages in Scripture for understanding Christ's redeeming work, Philippians 2:5–11, with the exhortation that those who are in Christ are to imitate him in giving themselves to and for others. When Paul appeals to the atonement, it is not to point out that the cross changes God, either by means of a cathartic venting of God's anger or by precipitating an act of self-deception whereby God pretends we sinners are really righteous. Quite the opposite. Paul sees the cross as the ultimate sign of God's unwavering constancy. Christ's humble obedience, his fidelity even to the point of death on the cross, is the paradigmatic display of God's unchanging, long-suffering love of humanity and fidelity to the promise to redeem. The change that Paul sees effected by the cross is the change that Christ works in fallen humanity's desire. It is the change that comes about as sinners are joined to Christ as his body. In Christ, desire is healed of its self-absorption, of its obsession with its own interests, and turned outward as it is renewed as humble vulnerability in generous service to and with others.

Care must be taken, however, not to confuse this generous desire with noblesse oblige. The generosity of which Paul speaks may bear some resemblance to the ancient tradition of noblesse oblige, but the resemblance is only superficial. The age-old tradition of noblesse oblige expected that the noble, the rich and powerful, would do good and give to others out of their abundance.[16] Over the years, this sense of an obligation to give has migrated beyond the boundaries of nobility and class to take racial and national forms as well. For example, consider what was once called the "white man's burden," some contemporary North American missionary or developmental assistance efforts, where the powerful and privileged patronize others with their spiritual and/or material largess.

The resemblance between this tradition of noblesse oblige and the divine economy into which we are incorporated in Christ is more apparent than real for at least two reasons. First, Christian giving is rooted in the humble vulnerability that is open to receiving. Being vulnerable to receiving is a prerequisite of Christian giving. As Paul reminds the church at Corinth, its giving to others

16. See the discussion by Franks, *He Became Poor*, 164–65.

is made possible only by a prior act of receptivity on its part. Thus, he writes, "What do you have that you did not receive? And if you received it, why do you boast as if it were not a gift?" (1 Cor. 4:7). Or as Augustine says, we are all beggars before God.[17] Christian giving is always premised on the reception of the prior gift of God's gracious providence. Accordingly, it is the sharing or passing on of a gift that has already been given (by God) and is not the act of an individual or community creating a gift out of its own will and goodness. We do not give what we have earned or made, for our earning and our making are gifts made possible by the gifts of God that first created, then sustained, and finally redeem us. This is to say, Christians are neither the creator nor the source of the gifts they give; their giving is but the passing on of the gifts given by God for that purpose. About this more will be said shortly.

Receiving is not merely the precondition of giving but an ongoing reality as well. Thus even as we are called to give, even as it is the nature of redeemed desire in this divine economy to move outside itself toward the neighbor in charity, that movement remains a movement of humble vulnerability in that even as it gives it remains open to receive from those it aids. Perhaps the clearest scriptural signpost of this is Matthew 25:31–45, where disciples of Christ actually receive Christ when they serve the lowly and marginalized.

Christian giving is part of a cycle of gift-exchange; it is, after all, a practice meant to renew communion. Thus, even as those of material means give to those without, those without nevertheless have much to give. In this case, people who are poor may pray for the wealthy; that is indeed a great gift, for, as Scripture points out, God hears the cry of the poor and needy (Isa. 41:17). Giving to those in need becomes an opportunity to receive true riches (Luke 16:11).[18]

In contrast, giving born of noblesse oblige is not an expression of humble vulnerability and so is not receptive. Rather, it is anchored in a sense of self-sufficiency. There is no reciprocity or mutuality. It is not a giving meant to renew and restore communion; it is, rather, an expression of independence and invulnerability. Accordingly, it is not the giving to which Christians are called as they participate in the divine economy.

17. Quoted in Boniface Ramsey, "Almsgiving in the Latin Church: The Fourth and Early Fifth Centuries," *Theological Studies* 43 (1982): 239.

18. Kelly Johnson, *The Fear of Beggars* (Grand Rapids: Eerdmans, 2007), 38.

The second difference between giving as an expression of noblesse oblige and the giving that characterizes the divine economy
is that the former is limited. Insofar as it is born of self-sufficiency,
noblesse oblige is limited by the requirements of autonomy and
self-sufficiency. These limits are expressed in comments such as, "We
cannot be expected to give to the point of impoverishing ourselves."
Again we can compare this to Paul's exhortation to the church—
"You know the generous act of our Lord Jesus Christ, that though
he was rich, for your sakes he became poor" (2 Cor. 8:9)—and
Christ's exhortation to give all to the poor (Matt. 19:21). This is
a giving that knows no limits because its fount is the generosity of
the God who has given more than we could ever ask or imagine,
who creates out of nothing, who can raise from the dead, who did
not withhold even the Son.

The Universal Destination of Material Goods

The question of the limits of generosity provides a salutary lead
into the last aspect of the economy of salvation considered here,
namely, the role of material goods in this economy. If Christ is
given for the sake of the renewal of communion, and if having been
received into Christ's body, desire is renewed as eternal generosity
such that we are called to give ourselves without reserve to others
for the sake of the extension of communion, what role do material
goods have in this work, in the economy of salvation?

Consider how material goods are typically addressed in many
churches. The use of material goods is treated as a matter of stewardship, and stewardship is reduced to a matter of money. Granted,
most churches at least nod toward a notion of stewardship that is
more than financial, involving one's time and talents; a few have
begun to consider care of creation as part of stewardship; and many
will collect material donations for philanthropic purposes. But the
primary focus of stewardship in the church remains money. And
good stewardship is characterized as giving money to the church,
the amount of which is set ideally at a tithe, 10 percent. Granted,
some churches speak of tithes and offerings, but often the offering is instead of a tithe and, if the various studies and polls can
be trusted, giving amounts to somewhere around 2 or 3 percent of
one's income, with even what constitutes "tithable income" subject

to various qualifications and caveats such as equating it with net instead of gross income, or even "disposable" income. The point is that frequently the way giving and material goods are discussed in church, generosity could hardly be confused with the fundamental orientation of the church's life, and material goods appear peripheral to the spiritual life of faith. While giving is a part of the life of the church, it is not obviously at its heart, and material goods appear, at best, incidental to that life, as blessings and perhaps occasionally as temptations for misplaced trust, but not integral to the life of discipleship. Giving comes across more like paying a tax with God (or the church) in the role of a cosmic IRS agent. And material goods are, at best, of secondary importance to the spiritual things that really matter.

This understanding of giving and the use of material goods is foreign to much of the Christian tradition. Much of the tradition has followed Judaism in asserting that not merely 10 percent of our financial resources but *all* that we are and *all* that we have is to be used, offered, given in service to our Lord for the sake of our neighbors. Hence, Jesus tells us to give to anyone who asks and to give all that we have; Luther reminds us that having received Christ our life becomes a surplus with which to serve our neighbors; and in worship we pray that the Spirit will move us to give ourselves for others.

This is to say, all that we have and all that we are has a social mortgage or function. There is a "universal destination of material goods," in the language of Pope John Paul II.[19] All that we have and all that we are is meant to serve the common good, which, ultimately, is communion in the Triune life. This vision of a life driven entirely by a desire to give itself to and for others finds expression across the Christian tradition. Thus John Chrysostom (d. 407) could preach:

> For our money is the Lord's, however we may have gathered it. If we provide for those in need, we shall obtain great plenty. This is why God has allowed you to have more: not for you to waste on prostitutes, drink, or fancy food, expensive clothes, and all the other kinds of indolence, but for you to distribute to those in need. . . . The rich man is a kind of steward of the money which is owed for distribution to the poor. He is directed to distribute it to his fellow servants who are in want. So if he spends more on himself than his

19. John Paul II, *Centesimus Annus* 4.30–31.

need requires, he will pay the harshest penalty hereafter. For his own goods are not his own, but belong to his fellow servants. . . . For you have obtained more than others have, and you have received it, not to spend it on yourself, but to become a good steward for others as well.[20]

Likewise, the early church leader Basil (329–79) could write: "The bread you are holding back is for the hungry, the clothes you keep put away are for the naked, the shoes that are rotting away with disuse are for those who have none, the silver you keep buried in the earth is for the needy. You are thus guilty of injustice toward as many as you might have aided, and did not."[21]

Within the economy of salvation, the material goods with which God gifts us are given for the sake of meeting our needs—our needs and the needs of our near and distant neighbors (2 Cor. 9:8–10). Specifically, the purpose of material goods within the divine economy is that of nurturing communion. What God has given us is not intended solely for our *private* good. Indeed, as the great theologian St. Augustine argued, sin can be defined in terms of the pursuit of one's own private good instead of the common good.[22] And Aquinas can argue that the failure to use private property to foster life-giving relations with others constitutes theft:

Whatever certain people have in superabundance is due, by natural law, to the purpose of succoring the poor. . . . Each one is entrusted with the stewardship of his own things, so that out of them he may come to the aid of those who are in need. Nevertheless, if the need be so manifest and urgent . . . then it is lawful for a man to succor his own need by means of another's property, by taking it either openly or secretly: nor is this properly speaking theft or robbery.[23]

The church's practice of offering is a recognition of this. Offering is not about giving God God's "cut." After all, by virtue of

20. John Chrysostom, *On Wealth and Poverty*, trans. Catherine P. Roth (Crestwood, NY: St. Vladimir's Seminary Press, 1999), 49–50.

21. Basil the Great, *On Social Justice*, trans. C. Paul Schroeder (Crestwood, NY: St. Vladimir's Seminary Press, 2009), 70.

22. Augustine, "On Free Will," in *Augustine: Earlier Writings*, ed. J. H. S. Burleigh (Philadelphia: Westminster, 1953), 2.53. See 1 Cor. 12:7.

23. Thomas Aquinas, *Summa Theologiae* (Westminster, MD: Christian Classics, 1981), 2-2.66.7.

our creation and redemption, all that we have and all that we are belongs to God. As Scripture reminds us, "Do not say to yourself, 'My power and the might of my own hand have gotten me this wealth.' But remember the LORD your God for it is he who gives you power to get wealth" (Deut. 8:17–18; cf. 1 Cor. 4:7). Rather, offering is about receiving and returning the gifts that God gives us, that is, about seeing to it that material goods are put to their proper, divinely intended use as part of the economy of salvation that seeks to renew the communion of all in God. This is why in many churches the offering is linked to Communion. We are given and in turn give material goods for the sake of nurturing communion. And receiving Christ, being joined to his body, we become part of his offering, giving gifts to others for the sake of extending that communion.

Put differently, in the offering we experience God's desire for us, a desire that takes the form first of Christ given to and for us but also of all the material gifts that flow from God's hand. And as we experience that desire, our desire is quickened, renewed, and restored. Subsequently our desire flows with Christ, as his body, as an expression of that charity, in the service of extending the divine gift of communion even further, and our hands are opened, reaching out with all that we are, including our material goods, for the sake of reconciling (2 Cor. 5:18–19), of renewing the communion fractured by sin, including the sin that is capitalism.

But should we give to the point of impoverishing ourselves? Yes, if Jesus tells you, "Give all that you have to the poor." But then can we really be impoverished? After all, we have Jesus. We have Christ's body, the church. We have the promise of the resurrection. We simply cannot give more than God will provide. We cannot outgive God.

Conclusion

In the economy of salvation, Christ is given not to pay a debt or appease an angry God but so that God's desire for communion is satisfied. Christ gives, even to the point of death on the cross, that desire might recover its rest, its true end, its enjoyment in the communion of charity that is the divine life. For this purpose, this mission, in Christ we are empowered to give ourselves—all that we are and all that we have—in love of God and service of our neigh-bor. In Christ our life is so ordered economically that we reflect the divine economy of ceaseless generosity, of unending charity. The Christian (economic) life is a matter of living life as the gift that it is.

How does the body of Christ live so that its life is one continu-ous offering? How does our life reflect God's unceasing generosity? Are we producing and using and enjoying all to the glory of God? Does the way we are tilling and keeping, using and giving, serve the common good—the communion of all in the good that is God? Such questions bring us to the brink of Christian economics.

7

Christian Economics

Deleuze and Foucault help us to see that capitalism is more than a mode of production, that it is an economy of desire. This is implicitly acknowledged by capitalism's advocates as they note capitalism's revolutionary impact beyond the narrowly economic field, including the social, political, and cultural fields. I have suggested this revolution is nothing less than theological, disciplining desire so that it does not flow in accord with the divine creative intent, that is, in communion with God and others.

The present chapter continues this argument by completing the contrast between capitalism and Christianity begun with the treatment of capitalist theology in chapter 4. It does so in parallel fashion, considering how the Christian economy of desire shapes humanity in its relation to others and God, as well as how it construes the good life.

Creatures: Receiving the Gift of Ourselves

In the beginning God created humanity. In the beginning was the Word, and all things came into being through him. All that Christianity confesses about the human being and its place in the order of God's household, in the divine economy, is premised on this most fundamental claim. Beginning with the confession that we are creatures, Christianity declares that the true nature and end of human desire is found in the Creator's purposes for humanity. Furthermore, it declares that God graciously has provided various means of grace whereby our desire might be healed of its sin-sickness and flow once again in accord with the divine economy. Thus we find ourselves living at odds with an economy of desire that produces *homo economicus*.

Joined to Christ's body, under the influence of Word and water, bread and wine, the disciplines of the faith and the examples of the saints, *homo economicus* dies, and a new creation, a new subject of desire, is Spirit formed. Unlike its capitalist counterpart, this is a corporate, ecclesial subject that is neither self-interested nor relates to others as commodities in an endless (business) cycle of competition and conflict driven by scarcity, but instead participates in the divine gift economy of abundance and ceaseless generosity in the hope of nurturing communion.

Persons in Communion

Whereas capitalism produces the independent, autonomous, self-made individual, Christianity professes that we are persons in communion. Humanity was created for communion, and in the waters of baptism the corporate self that was shattered by sin into warring individuals is re-membered. Because there is one loaf, we who are many are nurtured as one body at the Lord's Table. For this reason, Paul notes, when one suffers, all suffer, and when one rejoices, all rejoice (1 Cor. 12:26); likewise, he warns that what we do to our bodies is done to the corporate body that is the church (1 Cor. 6:15).

It follows, then, that we are not individuals in the autonomous, independent, alienated sense of the capitalist *homo economicus*. Whereas capitalism's advocates may denounce the life of the "hive, herd, or flock," Christianity has long recognized and proclaimed that redemption is indeed a matter of being joined to the flock— Christ's flock. Redemption is a matter of communion, of the renewal of the community shattered by disordered desire in the fall. Accordingly, the redeemed subject is not an individual. It is rather a constellation of persons in communion—a corporate, ecclesial subject called the body of Christ.

Moreover, this subject is creaturely, which means that it is intrinsically dependent on God and others for its welfare. Unlike the capitalist self, who is formed to see her welfare as dependent on her success or failure in the struggle that is the capitalist market, Christians are formed in humble vulnerability to depend on God's providential provision through the gifts of others. Accordingly, dependency on and responsibility for others is a chief characteristic of the Christian person (Gal. 6:2). Likewise, in Christ we are freed from the almost reflexive impulse for security from the other perceived as a threat, a competitor for resources, and instead are open to reconciliation and communion. In other words, we are not self-made, and alienation from one another is not our proper, natural condition.

Likewise, we are not "possessive" in the sense that capitalism is marked by a possessive individualism. Because neither the outcome nor the meaning of our life depends on simply our abilities, we need not be driven by the passion to acquire and possess. Instead, because we have come to see that all we have and all we are is a gift given to us for the sake of being given to others in love and service, because in Christ our desire is to become ecstatic—moving outward toward the other in charity, justice, and generosity—we are a people who hold things loosely, who give to all who ask and who do not fear even being defrauded (Matt. 5:42; 1 Cor. 6:7). For nothing, finally, can be lost to those who are in Christ (Rom. 8:35), who never ceases to give all that we need for life and faithfulness.

This sense of providential dependence, of humble vulnerability, is behind the church's long-standing ban on the taking of interest. Building on passages like Deuteronomy 23:19–20 and Luke 6:35, the church long held that it was wrong to collect interest on one's wealth. To do so was to be guilty of the sin of usury. It is not uncommon for the church to be criticized for this prohibition on the grounds that the church, believing that money was sterile, failed to appreciate the character of money and its potential for making more money.[1] Yet when the likes of Aquinas denounced the taking of interest, they did so not because they failed to understand the character of money but rather because they understood the character of humanity, which was created to depend on divine provision

---

1. Michael Novak, "Root of All Evil No More," Beliefnet, accessed May 22, 2000, http://www.beliefnet.com/Faiths/2000/05/Root-Of-All-Evil-No-More.aspx.

instead of seeking to secure the future (which interest attempts by demanding payment regardless of what befalls the borrower).[2]

Free in Christ

One of the celebrated hallmarks of capitalism is the freedom to choose, a freedom that is negative and formal in the sense that it promises nothing beyond the opportunity to attempt to acquire what(ever) one desires. This notion of freedom shares little with the Christian faith, where freedom is intrinsically connected to Christ. "Where the Spirit of the Lord is, there is freedom" (2 Cor. 3:17). Indeed, this notion of freedom as autonomous choice more closely resembles that which is condemned in Scripture. For example, we read in Judges 17:6 that "the people did what was right in their own eyes" and so incurred judgment.

Freedom in the Christian tradition is the ability to worship and glorify God (Gal. 5:1–2, 13). To be free is to be released from the bondage of sin and to be Spirit-enabled to follow the good that is God (Rom. 6:22). Freedom is consenting to the good; it is accepting the call of the good. Thus Augustine writes, "There is no true liberty except the liberty of the happy who cleave to the eternal law," and Anselm writes that freedom is the ability to pursue the good for its own sake.[3] Freedom is life in Christ. We are free not because we can choose but because God chose us (John 15:16).

Bondage, however, is choosing and pursuing other than the good. Bondage might be described as "doing whatever I want," whereas freedom might be described as doing the will of God. Thus what is celebrated as freedom under capitalism—autonomous choice—is but a form of bondage.

Although it is not always recognized and can be resisted, when persons are gathered by the Spirit into the church and taught to bend their knees, bow their heads, and lift their hearts to God in worship, their desires are being reoriented. The various disciplines of the Christian life are means through which the Spirit redirects desire outward toward God and so toward the neighbor. As we

2. Christopher Franks, *He Became Poor: The Poverty of Christ and Aquinas's Economic Teachings* (Grand Rapids: Eerdmans, 2009), 71–76.

3. Augustine, "On Free Will," in *Augustine: Earlier Writings*, ed. J. H. S. Burleigh (Philadelphia: Westminster, 1953), 1.32, 2.37. Anselm, *On Free Will* 3.13.

study Scripture, engage in corporate worship, imitate the saints, serve our neighbors in our vocations and the works of mercy, love our enemies, and so forth, our desire is being drawn out of its self-absorption so that it may flow as it was created to flow—toward God and neighbor in the love that desires communion.

Thus when the congregation prays, "Thy will be done," it is asking for nothing less than that its desires be set free from all those things that would prevent it from desiring God and the things of God. And as a prayer of submission to the will of another, One who wills communion, it is working against the capitalist fragmentation of desire into individualistic channels.

Seeking the Common Good

The economy of desire that is capitalism forms human desire so that it is quintessentially self-interested. Rejecting the notion that there is a shared good or common purpose that ought to shape how we labor and use material goods, *homo economicus* is an interest maximizer. In contrast, Christianity proclaims that there is indeed a good that unites all of humanity, that there is a love in which we are all invited to share. This common good is the end or purpose for which we were created, namely, communion in the divine life. Moreover, it is this common good that shapes our labor and our consumption, how we make use of the goods God provides.

For this reason, when Christians contemplate our life's labors, we do not rightly think in terms of how our interests may be maximized or in terms of what we *want* to do. Rather, our work is a matter of vocation, of calling. We are called to work for the common good. Therefore, our various rolls and jobs ought to be describable/narratable in terms of service to the common good (1 Cor. 12:7). Many churches currently aid some of their members in this kind of discernment—primarily professional religious workers. But insofar as baptism ordains all Christians to the mission and ministry of Jesus Christ, all Christians are called to work for the common good, and the church should aid all in such discernment. Such a practice is an integral part of the redemption of desire.

Seeking the common good also has implications for how Christians value material goods and resources. Capitalism treats material goods as deterritorialized commodities that come to us with no purpose other than that which our autonomous wills choose. In contrast, the practice of offering forms us to recognize the universal destination of material goods. In other words, whereas capitalism encourages us to treat goods (and persons) as of no intrinsic value, but rather to assign value based on their exchange value,[4] Christians discern value in accord with the role of goods and services in relation to the common good, which is to say, the divine economy.

From the orientation of Christian desire toward the common good, it is evident that the Christian self is not self-interested. After all, the gospel is clear that we can do nothing to advance our interest; rather we are saved by grace. Indeed, until recently the Christian tradition was uniform in denouncing seeking our own advantage as sin (1 Cor. 10:24; Phil. 2:3–4; Rom. 12:1–2). Instead, as recipients of the gift of life in Christ, Christians are freed to live life as a surplus, to be Christ to one another, as Luther had it. Redeemed desire gives freely to and for others, without fear of loss (Matt. 22:39; Mark 12:31; Luke 9:24).

This orientation of Christian desire outward, it should be noted, is not simply a matter of supplementing or tempering self-interest or self-love with regard for the other. It is not uncommon for Christian advocates of capitalism to suggest that capitalism need only be reformed by the inclusion of the interests of others into the moral calculus of the market.[5] There are several difficulties with this argument. First, it fails to recognize the ways in which the capitalist market is incompatible with love and other-regard. The much lauded efficiency and productivity of the capitalist market would be crippled by the unintended consequences that accompanied efforts to incorporate the interests of others.[6] Moreover, the characteristics of *homo economicus* and the relations fostered by the capitalist market actively work against not only the demand but also the supply of traits like love and generosity.[7] In other

4. Nancy Ruth Fox in D. Stephen Long and Nancy Ruth Fox, *Calculated Futures* (Waco: Baylor University Press, 2007), 70.

5. Rebecca M. Blank, "Market Behavior and Christian Behavior," in *Faithful Economics*, ed. James W. Henderson and John Pisciotta (Waco: Baylor University Press, 2005), 42.

6. Friedrich A. von Hayek, *Law, Legislation, and Liberty*, vol. 2, *The Mirage of Social Justice* (Chicago: University of Chicago, 1976), 68, 91; see also Stephen A. Marglin, *The Dismal Science: How Thinking Like an Economist Undermines Community* (Cambridge, MA: Harvard University Press, 2008), 65–66.

7. Albert Hirschmann, "Against Parsimony: Three Ways of Complicating Some Categories of Economic Discourse," in *Why Economists Disagree: An Introduction*

words, the capitalist economy of desire economizes love.[8] As Hayek notes, the division of labor renders altruistic motives "literally impossible."[9] This holds true beyond the market as well insofar as the self-interested behavior encouraged by the market is not so easily confined to the market, especially in a situation where the market is ever more extensive and "free."[10] In sum, there can be no coexistence of the capitalist market and the virtue of charity. One cannot serve both God and capital.

The second problem with the notion of supplementing self-interest is the erroneous equation of "interest" with love. Self-interest is not synonymous with the divine call to self-love except perhaps in the sense that self-interest may be a disordered or corrupted form of genuine and proper self-love. As Aquinas explains, our love is properly directed toward God, and we love other things (including ourselves) only subsequent to and as a refraction of that love for God.[11] This is to say that our love for ourselves as well as for others is indirect, a consequence or extension of our loving God.[12] We do not love ourselves first and then love God and perhaps our neighbors. Rather, we do not love *either* ourselves or others properly *unless and until* we love with the love that is rightly directed toward God. In other words, while interests might be divided between self and other and then weighed and balanced, such is not the case with the rightly ordered desire that is charity or love. When Scripture exhorts us to love our neighbors as ourselves, we are not being told to balance or coordinate two competing interests or loves. Rather, the love of self and the love of others, including God, is a single, unified love. As Scripture

to the *Alternative Schools of Thought*, ed. David L. Prychitko (Albany: SUNY Press, 1998), 340–44; Samuel Bowles, "Endogenous Preferences: The Cultural Consequences of Markets and Other Economic Institutions," *Journal of Economic Literature* 36 (March 1998): 92, 95, 99.

8. Dennis H. Robertson, *Economic Commentaries* (Westport, CT: Greenwood, 1978), 147–54.

9. Friedrich A. von Hayek, *The Fatal Conceit* (Chicago: University of Chicago Press, 1988), 81.

10. See Robert H. Nelson, *Economics as Religion: From Samuelson to Chicago and Beyond* (University Park, PA: Penn State Press, 2001), 3, 6, 167, 231, 268; Duncan K. Foley, *Adam's Fallacy* (Cambridge, MA: Harvard University Press, 2006).

11. Thomas Aquinas, *Summa Theologiae* (Westminster, MD: Christian Classics, 1981), 2-2.25.1.

12. I owe this insight to Franks, *He Became Poor*, 117.

says, we are to love God with our whole heart (Luke 10:27), and when we do so, there is nothing left to parcel out and balance between self and neighbor. Instead, desire, when it is purified by Christ into the wholehearted, all-encompassing love of God, is like a laser directed at a prism: as it is focused on its proper object (God) it finds itself dispersed (toward self and others). Hence Augustine argues that when we love others rightly, we are loving them in God.[13]

Thus the economic question is not how to supplement self-interest with regard for others, but whether a given economic order economizes on love or encourages it, whether it resists desire deformed into self-interest or embraces it.

Homo Adorans: *Our Desire Rests in God*

Capitalism distorts the creative power that is human desire by constantly creating new objects/idols for its fascination. It entices desire with an endless array of distractions. The enchantments of capitalist production are distractions precisely because they cannot satisfy our desire. And as far as capitalism is concerned, this is a good thing, for satisfied desire would spell an end to capitalism, which depends on the frenetic power of unquenched desire to drive its productive engines.

In contrast, Christianity proclaims the good news that we can indeed find rest from the rat race that is the conflict of the capitalist market. Our desire finds its true home, its rest, its delight in communion with God. Desire's true fascination is the radiance of love that is the glorious life of the blessed Trinity. For this reason, humanity might rightly be called *homo adorans*—worshiping beings. We are not beings caught in an endless cycle of trucking and bartering (*homo economicus*) but beings inclined to worship and enjoy the divine love that provides all that we need. In other words, because the Lord is our shepherd, we shall not want (Ps. 23:1). We need not strive endlessly but can be content.

As desire learns in worship to rest in its true end, the capitalist economy of desire is exposed for what it is: an economy that normalizes the disordered desire that is properly named greed. Capitalism makes a virtue of what the tradition denounces as one of the seven

13. Augustine, *Confessions* 4.12.

deadly sins: avarice or greed—a restless, possessive, acquisitive drive that is lauded as the entrepreneurial spirit of *homo economicus*.[14]

The disordered desire that is avarice or greed is frequently identified with a desire for money and wealth, but it encompasses more than that. Greed is first and foremost about wanting *more than enough*. Furthermore, it encompasses not just wealth or material goods but intangible objects as well, like honor, knowledge, and even life itself. In short, as Augustine observes, greed concerns "all things which are desired immoderately, whenever someone wants absolutely more than is enough."[15] Thus even the unbounded creativity celebrated by capitalism's courtiers is a vice insofar as it is not directed by the shared love that is the common good.[16]

Greed would characterize as well the desire that has become self-referential, the "desire for desire" that celebrates not consumption but the endless pursuit of an object that goes by the name of "shopping."[17] This is to say, the disordered desire that seeks stimulation by exposure to ever more and novel commodities is but a form of avarice, a further symptom of capitalism's enchantment of desire.

In defense of capitalism, on occasion its advocates will attempt to redefine greed as hoarding and point out that capitalism does not encourage hoarding, that the wealth of the wealthy circulates.[18] Capitalism, it is rightly pointed out, would not long survive in a world where hoarding was widespread. The wealth of the wealthy does circulate via consumption and investment.

Such a defense is beside the point. While hoarding may well be a species of avarice, the church's condemnation of avarice is not rooted in the mere fact that goods do not circulate. Rather, avarice concerns goods and services failing to circulate in accord with their divinely ordained universal destination. This happens as goods and services either do not circulate or circulate in a manner

14. Alasdair MacIntyre, *Whose Justice? Which Rationality?* (Notre Dame, IN: University of Notre Dame Press, 1987), 111–12.

15. Augustine, "On Free Will," 3.17.48.165–66.

16. See Paul J. Griffiths, "The Vice of Curiosity," *Pro Ecclesia* 15, no. 1 (2006): 47–63.

17. See Bernd Wannenwetsch, "The Desire of Desire: Commandment and Idolatry in Late Capitalist Societies," in *Idolatry*, ed. Stephen C. Barton (New York: T&T Clark, 2007), 315–30; and Peter H. Sedgwick, *The Market Economy and Christian Ethics* (New York: Cambridge University Press, 1999), 149.

18. Novak, "Root of All Evil No More"; Novak, *The Catholic Ethic and the Spirit of Capitalism* (New York: Free Press, 1993), 29–30.

that does not foster communion. In other words, avarice is a sin not merely for the way desire clings too tightly to things, like an Ebenezer Scrooge, but also for the way desire wants more than it should, thus disrupting the circulation of goods for the sake of the communion God intends.

The Divine Gift Economy

Given how human desire is shaped by capitalism, it is unsurprising that humanity finds itself in conflict, or as Novak put it, wandering on a field of battle.[19] Capitalism orders human relations agonistically; hence we must compete for resources, for employment, for access to the market, for the time for friendship and worship. Human relations become contractual, narrowly limited by clearly defined obligations and responsibilities that we voluntarily accept, and human worth is increasingly measured in terms of efficiency, subject to cost/benefit analyses. Furthermore, the goods and services we consume are increasingly commodified, with the relations that make them accessible to us concealed by distance, marketing, and so-called trade secrets, thereby encouraging desire's moral apathy.

In contrast stands the divine economy, which functions according to the economic logic embodied in Christ's atoning work. This economy is ruled by God's desire for communion. Thus, as we receive the gifts of Christ in humble vulnerability, as we are received into Christ's communion, our desire is sanctified, healed, so that it flows in accord with God's desire, both entering into communion and seeking to extend communion to others. Accordingly, the marks of this divine economy are not struggle, competition, and strife but sharing and solidarity; noncompetitive, complementary exchange; and mutuality.[20]

In this divine economy humanity is valued without regard for its ability to participate in the market processes of production and consumption. People are valued as recipients of the gift of life and dignity by the Creator, who desires to share the communion of the divine life with them and who deems it good that we are not alone

19. Michael Novak, *The Spirit of Democratic Capitalism* (New York: Touchstone, 1982), 54; see also 53–55.
20. Karl Polanyi, *The Great Transformation* (Boston: Beacon, 1944), 58, 60. Franks, *He Became Poor*, 97; D. Stephen Long in Long and Fox, *Calculated Futures*, 203.

(Gen. 2:18). In other words, people are not properly regarded as either merely means or obstacles to the attainment of self-interest; they are gifts from God and for each other and are valued as such, irrespective of efficiency calculations and their market "worth." Indeed, it is precisely the care extended to those who are considered of little value by the capitalist market that is an indicator of the divine economy's orientation toward the common good.[21]

Furthermore, in the divine economy, human relations are understood covenantally rather than primarily contractually. Whereas capitalist contracts narrowly delimit relationships in terms of responsibilities and their duration, the covenants that characterize the divine economy entail mutual responsibility and care that are not so easily delimited or terminated. Desire renewed as the love that seeks communion creates bonds of solidarity that exceed any contract. This does not abolish all contracts, but repositions them within an economy that does not limit (economic) relations to the contractual form.[22]

In a similar manner, within this divine economy, everything is not simply a commodity or potential commodity to be used without regard for any purpose other than that imposed by the unfettered will as expressed in exchange value. Instead, material resources, no less than people, are properly regarded as gifts from God that come with a purpose attached. Thus exchange value is subordinated to use value, which is determined in the context of the divine intention that goods be used for the flourishing of all in communion.[23]

Finally, this divine gift economy disrupts the blissful ignorance and moral passivity that accompany capitalist commodities and the division of labor. Given by God for the sake of drawing us together in friendship, in solidarity, in pursuit of the common good, the material gifts that come to us prompt us to follow the lines of production and distribution in care for our near and distant neighbors. In contrast with the suggestion that capitalist consumers "don't need to know," the gifts we consume feed our

21. Jon Sobrino, *Where Is God?* (Maryknoll, NY: Orbis, 2004), 84, 88.
22. Luigino Bruni, "Common Good and Economics," trans. Michael Brennen, 7, accessed July 13, 2010, http://michaelbrennen.com/common-good-and-economics/. Antony Black, *Guild and State* (New Brunswick, NJ: Transaction Publishers, 2003), 155–57.
23. See Franks, *He Became Poor*, 68.

desire for connections, for the expansion of relations marked by love and justice. In this way, markets, as well as the division of labor (appropriately transparent), can be means of serving and so extending communion, of turning enemies and strangers into friends and neighbors.[24] Additionally, the desire for communion precludes dismissing either the harmful effects of the production and consumption of commodities as "externalities" or the concerns of stakeholders who are not stockholders or clients.

At this point it is important to be clear about what has *not* been said. The divine economy does not condemn production, consumption, private property, profit taking, contracts, the division of labor, or markets in themselves. To the contrary, the divine gift economy may encompass all these practices. Whether it does depends on the nature of those practices in a given economy.

For example, certainly the economic vision sketched thus far entails the production and consumption of goods and services. The divine economy is neither antiproduction nor anticonsumption. Without production there would be little to give, and without consumption we would not long survive. After all, humanity may not live by bread alone (Deut. 8:2–3; Luke 4:4), but we do nevertheless require bread. In other words, this divine economy should not be confused with the idyllic utopias that envision a paradise where the domination of nature has attained such a level that we no longer need labor. Although a theology of work exceeds the scope of this work, Scripture's vision of the new creation clearly includes labor, whether that is in the vision of the final consummation of things (Isa. 65:21–23) or it is the labor of those who follow Christ in this time between the times in a host of callings/vocations.

Labor in the divine economy, however, differs from the way work is experienced by many under the capitalist regime—as sheer drudgery and/or a necessary evil that is a means to acquire commodities for the sake of survival and self-expression. It differs from work disconnected from the divine end or purpose of all labor—serving communion/community. For this reason, labor in the divine economy is a vocation or calling. This means that whether or not it is connected to "earning a living" (e.g., unpaid work in a variety of forms, from caring for families and friends to what is recognized

24. Luigino Bruni and Stefano Zamagni, *Civil Economy: Efficiency, Equity, Public Happiness* (New York: Peter Lang, 2007), 94, 167; see also 163.

as "volunteer" work) or the attainment of "status" in an economy driven by the quest for distinction (e.g., serving the common good through unglamorous and undistinguished work), it is always connected to our God-given purpose. A corollary of this is that insofar as it is a vocation and not merely a career or a job, it will, even if it is difficult and often feels like drudgery, nevertheless partake of a certain delight insofar as it participates in and contributes to nurturing communion.

Likewise, the divine economy does not call for the abolition of private property. Although the disavowal of all property and mendicancy (begging) are faithful possibilities (callings actually, to be discussed in the next chapter), the church has long recognized private property as part of the divine economy. However, the Christian practice of private property is different from the laissez-faire notions common today. As one theologian has put it, the church espouses a kind of nonproprietary ownership.[25] This is to say, the holders of private property cannot do with that property whatever they will. Rather, even though property may be private, it is not thereby removed from circulating in God's economy; it is still to be used in a manner that serves the common good, that nurtures the life of all in communion. Indeed, as the likes of Aquinas note, private property is simply a means of serving the common good in situations where common ownership might lead to neglect, confusion, and strife.[26] Ownership, then, is not license but responsibility.

Along the same lines, the divine economy is not adverse to all profit taking. The divine economy is not simply a repristination of the slogan "production for use, not profit." Use and profit need not be set against one another; they can meet in service to the common good. In keeping with what has been said thus far, the measure of legitimate profit is not naked exchange value and the insatiable desire for increase but use value, which is measured in relation to the common good, the universal destination of things.[27] This is to say, profit that can be articulated in terms of service to the common good, and God's intention that material goods circulate to provide

25. Franks, *He Became Poor*, 59.
26. Aquinas, *Summa Theologiae* 2-2.66.2; Franks, *He Became Poor*, 61.
27. For a brief but helpful reflection on executive compensation in this regard, see Michael J. Naughton, "The 'Stumbling and Tripping' of Executive Pay," *New Oxford Review* 68, no. 11 (December 2001): 27–32.

a livelihood for all, with the "all" encompassing the livelihood of
both the buyer and seller, is legitimate.[28]

Redeemed Justice

Under capitalism, justice is reduced to its commutative form.
That is, justice is a matter of rendering what is due in accord with
the provisions of contracts freely entered into. There is, as Hayek
insists, no such thing as social justice, by which he means any kind
of moral norm that should guide the distribution of resources in a
society beyond the commutative justice of market exchanges. Or, as
another economist has put it more directly, "an unfettered market
system shows no mercy."[29]

This understanding of justice is quite common. Even in Christian
circles it is often thought that justice and mercy are distinct and
sometimes opposing acts. But this is a distortion of what justice is in
the divine economy. Here Aquinas is helpful. While he does discuss
justice in terms of its commutative and distributive operations, he
follows an older, classical vision that subordinates the commutative
and distributive operations of justice to a more general, overarching
sense of justice as the nurturing of solidarity in the shared love that
is the common good. Yet, Aquinas and the Christian tradition do
not simply adopt this older, classical vision but transform or redeem
it by repositioning justice within the divine order of charity/love.
According to Aquinas, charity is the form or end of justice. That
justice has its end or form in charity means that justice is about the
communion of humanity in God—for communion with God is, as
we have seen, the end of charity. Thus justice is about building up
the communion of all in the circle of love that is the Trinity.

This repositioning of justice within the divine order of charity
drastically changes the way the commutative and distributive operations of justice function. So informed by charity, those operations are
no longer enacted with the ruthless efficiency that characterizes an
economy of debt, equity, and retribution. Justice is no longer principally a matter of calculating and distributing what is due among
strangers; rather, it is concerned with maintaining the unity that
God establishes with and among humanity as humanity is liberated

28. Franks, *He Became Poor*, 101–3, has a helpful discussion of Aquinas on this point.
29. Alan S. Blinder, quoted in Long and Fox, *Calculated Futures*, 36.

from sin. Justice is, as Scripture suggests, about the renewal of right relations.[30] In other words, justice is part and parcel of the divine economy's fostering of communion. In contemporary parlance and practice, we might say justice is restorative.[31]

Accordingly, the distributive and commutative operations of justice are determined in accord with what, under the impact of the Spirit, is discerned to best promote the communion of humanity in the divine love. Thus at times justice may entail mercy and forgiveness, forgoing a strict accounting of what is due. For this reason, Aquinas, like Anselm, insists that there is no conflict or opposition between divine justice and forgiveness; they are but two names of the single love of God that draws humanity into communion. Justice and mercy are not opposing logics; rather they share a single end—the return of all love, the sociality of all desire, in God. Justice attains its end by enacting mercy to overcome sin. Mercy overcomes sin to attain its true end, which is justice. In this way, mercy implements perfect justice (Aquinas), and the rule of God's justice is mercy (Anselm). Hence, human justice is truly just when it is guided, not by a strict accounting of what is due, but by the mercy that would see all redeemed in the fellowship of love. Thus justice is in fact social.

It follows from this that justice in the divine economy entails obligations and responsibilities to care for others in the hope of fostering human flourishing in the communion of divine love, and that persons who are poor, far from being viewed as a threat, become an opportunity to continue the circle of gift giving and receiving initiated by God and into which we are drawn by Christ.[32] Indeed, as the scriptural vision of justice as particularly attuned to the plight of the widow, the orphan, and the poor makes clear, justice is not a blind proceduralism that merely enforces voluntary contracts but is a matter of deliverance, of liberation from all that obstructs the communion of humanity in God.[33]

---

30. Moshe Weinfeld, *Social Justice in Ancient Israel and in the Ancient Near East* (Minneapolis: Fortress, 1995).

31. See Christopher Marshall, *Beyond Retribution: A New Testament Vision for Justice, Crime, and Punishment* (Grand Rapids: Eerdmans, 2001).

32. For a profound treatment of this, see Kelly Johnson, *The Fear of Beggars* (Grand Rapids: Eerdmans, 2007).

33. Weinfeld, *Social Justice in Ancient Israel*; J. R. Donahue, "Biblical Perspectives on Justice," in *The Faith That Does Justice*, ed. J. C. Haughey (New York: Paulist, 1977), 68–112.

The Living God: The God Who Gives

The difficulties with capitalism's deformation of desire do not end with its twisting desire into the agony of self-interested individuals competing for scarce commodities. If humanity reflects the image of God, then the image of God reflected by *homo economicus* suggests that capitalism's God is not the God that Christians profess to worship.

The Trinity, Giver of Perfect Gifts

Capitalism construes God as the hidden God of the free market, who through the magic of the market transforms the agony of the self-interested pursuits of discrete individuals into the interest of the whole. Over against this, the Christian faith worships and proclaims the God from whom all blessings flow, the giver of every perfect gift (James 1:17), who enacts the divine gift economy of eternal giving to and receiving from others.

Accordingly, the invisible hand of the capitalist market is not the hand of God. It is not even a law of nature; rather, the total market of capitalism is a contingent human practice. More than this, it is unnatural, contrary to nature insofar as nature is ordered toward the communion of all in divine love. As such, it is an act of rebellion, a form of sin.

Even as it is opposed to the capitalist market, however, the divine economy is not intrinsically opposed to all markets. To the contrary, markets can be part of how we receive God's provision and serve our neighbors. What this divine economy does challenge is a market that is untethered from virtue, from the common good, from the universal destination of all things. It challenges a market that economizes on love and capitulates to vice, denies that there is a common good, and surrenders the circulation of goods to the clash of human wills. The divine economy embraces a market where efficiency does not have the last word,[34] and where notions of a just wage and a just price are welcomed as integral components of a truly moral market.[35] It is worth noting that much of the Christian tradition's animosity toward merchants and trade can be traced

---

34. D. Stephen Long in Long and Fox, *Calculated Futures*, 29. Blank, "Market Behavior and Christian Behavior," 44.
35. See Franks, *He Became Poor*, 84–97.

to these concerns—whether it is a matter of trade in luxury items that defied their universal destination or the tendency to capitalize on others' misfortune, need, or ignorance in order to buy cheap and sell dear.

The divine economy also challenges markets that are or aspire to be totalitarian, encompassing every dimension of life. As theologian Doug Meeks writes, "Christian theology should call into question the logic of the market, not to overcome it (such would be preposterous), but to put it in its place."[36] In other words, the divine economy is compatible with a limited market. In the divine economy, not everything can or should be given a price tag and exchanged on the market. Traditionally this limitation has taken the form of restrictions on the marketing and sale of such things and services as blood and body parts, children (i.e., adoption and child labor), persons (i.e., slavery, sex industry), church positions, political influence, and so forth.[37]

Finally, the God who is not reducible to the invisible hand of the market but is the giver of gifts for the sake of communion is also the God of the downtrodden and oppressed. Scripture consistently proclaims that God is the stronghold of the oppressed, the one who upholds justice, who hears the cry of those who are poor. This is not in addition to seeking communion but an expression of the desire for communion.

Holiness: God Is Redeeming Here and Now

The central theological issue regarding the moral legitimacy of capitalism concerns what God is doing in history now to redeem humanity from sin. Capitalism's proponents argue, in effect, "not much." God manages sin. God motivates us to do the lesser evil, and God pardons sin. God is *not* redeeming us from sin here and now. So the God of capital ends up resembling the God of Stoicism or Deism.

In contrast, the God that Christianity has long worshiped and proclaimed is the living God who is active here and now, struggling

36. M. Douglas Meeks, *God the Economist* (Minneapolis: Fortress, 1989), 38–39.
37. For more on this, see Margaret Radin, *Contested Commodities* (Cambridge, MA: Harvard University Press, 1996). See also Michael J. Sandel, *What Money Can't Buy* (New York: Farrar, Straus and Giroux, 2012).

against sin, graciously redeeming creation by gathering all into a new community where the means of grace heal desire so that it flows once again as the sociality of love. This is to say, Christian worship is not a protracted memorial of a dead person or a distant God on the sidelines or edge of history, but the announcement of "God with us," of the real presence of the One who is able to make us better than we otherwise would be, a celebration that happens in the Spirit. Hence the good news the church proclaims is that we are *not* stuck in our sin; we are not only forgiven (justified) but also healed (sanctified). Sin does not have the last word; we can live otherwise. Even here and now we are being set free from sin and for holiness. Even now our desire is being healed of its disorder and redirected toward God and so toward our neighbors in love. Through the Spirit-empowered disciplines of faith we have been given everything we need to be faithful followers of Christ. After all, the saints among us are not virtual personalities or online avatars but real, live sanctified flesh-and-blood persons whose desire has been freed of its capitalist chains and instead now fosters bonds of love.

Thus the capitalist validation of self-interest runs counter to faith and trust in God. It denies the work of Christ and the work of his disciples as they are conformed to Christ (Phil. 2:3–4), and it runs against the grain of the moral teaching of the church, which has consistently taught that one may not do evil for the sake of good or to avoid a greater evil (see Rom. 3:8).

Thus capitalism is not revealed to be realistic, as its supporters often claim, but nihilistic—surrendering to the power of sin and death as it denies the reality of the gift of the Spirit to sanctify us, of the real presence of the One "who by the power at work within us is able to accomplish abundantly far more than all we can ask or imagine" (Eph. 3:20).

God's Abundance: There Is Enough

The driving force of capitalism is scarcity—limited resources to meet unlimited desires. Scarcity warps desire into a grasping, acquisitive power and so prepares it for the agony that is the capitalist market. Thus the God of capital is revealed to be a stingy deity who parcels out only enough to stimulate the agony of the market, where we are forced to compete like economic gladiators in the hope that the fickle favor of the invisible hand will bestow its blessings on us.

In contrast, Christianity has long proclaimed that God has given and continues to give abundantly; there is enough. God provides for all our needs. As Chris Franks observes, there is a providential coincidence between the requirements for human flourishing and nature's provision.[38] The Lord is our shepherd; we do not need more (Ps. 23:1). The abundance of God is proclaimed throughout Scripture,[39] and when Christians place themselves under the discipline of the Word, allowing their imaginations to be formed by its vision of God and the world, their desire is graciously released from the capitalist discipline and freed to flow generously.

That the liturgical act of offering is properly placed after the proclamation of the Word points to this: receiving the Word excites the desire to serve, to give, to share the divine abundance. Likewise, formal services of Christian worship ordinarily conclude with a sending forth in love and service to the world. Such a sending forth to give is not premised on one's acquisitive power or capital holdings. Rather, it is expected that all will give because all—rich and poor, able bodied and otherwise, the young and old—have received of God's abundance and so have more than enough to give and serve, be it in the form of material wealth, time, wisdom, strength, compassion, presence, prayers, need, or even life itself, in the case of the martyrs. In the Gospels, Jesus feeds the multitudes with a few loaves and fishes. Through the means of grace such as worship, study of Scripture, prayer, fasting, the works of mercy, and the guidance of the saints, Jesus does the same thing with the broken and bent desire of sinners. He takes what is foolish and weak and low and despised, he takes our poverty (physical and spiritual), and brings forth from it great riches, an abundance of love sufficient to reconcile the world (1 Cor. 1:26; 2 Cor. 5:18).

Care should be taken, however, not to mistake the character of God's abundance. The opposite of scarcity is not "unlimited" in the sense that God will satisfy our avarice, gluttony, and lust—all the cravings of our disordered or fallen desire. Rather, the abundance

---

38. Franks, *He Became Poor*, 96.

39. Gen.1:29–31; Ps. 23:1; Isa. 55:1–3; John 6:35. See Walter Brueggemann, "The Liturgy of Abundance, The Myth of Scarcity," *The Christian Century* (March 24–31, 1999).

that God gives is a matter of enough. God graciously gives all that we need for flourishing. Therefore, God's abundant provision should not be confused with a "prosperity gospel." God's abundance is not about meeting our wildest consumer dreams. Rather, God's abundance takes form in the disciplines that heal our desire so that it moves in accord with its true end, so that we desire what and how we should desire.

In this regard, it is sometimes noted that in an economy where desire is insatiable, where wants are unlimited, wants and needs become indistinguishable. So there is no difference between my wanting a second home and an impoverished *campesino* in Honduras desiring clean water. And there is no moral problem with an economy that delivers to me (and thousands like me) that home while the *campesino* (and millions like him) languishes without potable water. Hence, receiving the gift of God's abundance is not necessarily about receiving more (for many it will mean consuming less) but about the reordering of desires such that we can properly recognize (and enjoy) enough and share the abundance we have been and continue to be given.

If God's abundance is not synonymous with the fulfillment of capitalist dreams, neither does it mean that scarcity is not a reality. The juxtaposition of God's abundance to capitalist scarcity is meant to counter the suggestion that the material poverty that afflicts humanity is a consequence of nature (and so implicitly the fault of the Creator). Proclaiming God's abundance does not deny the reality of scarcity.

What it does is locate the origin of scarcity where it belongs, namely, in sin. Scarcity is not a natural condition but the consequence of sin. Indeed, capitalism has been implicated in the generalization of scarcity, such that it is no longer isolated and occasional but the structure of our existence.[40] That many languish in misery today because they lack access to things like adequate food, shelter, employment, and sundry forms of care is not due to nature or a perverse God but to the distortions of human desire that first shaped and now is shaped by an economic order that fails to use the gifts of God properly.[41] Material scarcity, we might say, has its roots in the scarcity that is the lack of faith (Luke 18:8).

40. Marglin, *Dismal Science*, 215.
41. See Bruni and Zamagni, *Civil Economy*, 200.

Furthermore, to say that scarcity is not a fact of nature and to assert that God provides is not to suggest that we may never suffer or go hungry. Clearly in this time between the times, God's provision does not preclude hunger, suffering, and even death, and there is no simple or easy answer as to why this is the case. Nevertheless, what God's provision does make possible is a kind of asceticism, a hope that nurtures faithful endurance and struggle against sin-inflicted scarcity. Here we would do well to recall Christ's suffering obedience to which we are conformed as we are joined to his body. In this time between the times, God's abundance may take the form of martyrdom and resurrection, and the assurance that in giving our life, we actually receive life, and that although we may die, we will not perish (Matt. 22:39; Luke 9:24).

Christ Is God with Us

The capitalist vision of providence endows corporations with a significance that is almost messianic and suggests that they should be revered as the church. Moreover, Adam Smith is not infrequently elevated above Jesus Christ when it comes to guidance regarding the economic order, because, it is said, Jesus appreciated neither the power of production nor the ability of money to make money.

That the corporation would be elevated to almost messianic standing makes sense if one begins with the premise that God is not active in sanctifying us now and so we are left to our own devices. In a world where capitalism reigns, it makes sense that the corporation would be king. As Deleuze and Foucault argued, and as is becoming more evident every day, even states bow before and serve the mandates of capital and the corporation.

However, if Jesus is Lord here and now and if the Spirit is healing desire so that we may participate in the divine economy, then the corporation does not merit such exaltation. If Christ is present sanctifying his body, the church, so that it might enact the divine economy, then the corporation cannot claim such a status or role in our lives. It, like the market, properly has a more limited role.

But it does have a role. That the corporation is not sacred does not mean that it ought simply to be rejected. Rather, like property and profits or markets and exchange, how the corporation is theologically evaluated depends on what a corporation is and does in a given context. A genuinely good corporation will "produce virtue explicitly or implicitly" and deliberately avoid vice.[42] Yet the current capitalist configuration of corporations in both national law and international trade agreements can make this difficult. For example, US law mandates that corporations operate "in the best interests in the corporation," which is understood in terms of increasing shareholder value, or "shareholder wealth maximization."[43] In other words, corporations are capitalist individuals writ large—self-interested and profit maximizing. Thus when Milton Friedman famously wrote that corporations do not have any social responsibility, he was espousing not only his opinion but also the law, with one significant caveat. Corporate social responsibility is permissible so long as such responsibility can be shown to contribute to maximizing shareholder wealth, that is, when it is a means to advancing the corporation's best interests, or as Friedman puts it, when social responsibility is "hypocritical window dressing" meant to sell a product.[44]

Such a vision of the corporation is problematic because it is not directed toward virtue, toward the common good of nurturing communion. Any genuine goods toward which it contributes are only incidental/instrumental to shareholder wealth maximization, and so any virtue it appears to display is deficient, for genuine virtue has as its end the common good. This is not to suggest that all who are involved with such corporations are thereby necessarily devoid of virtue but rather that such an institutional culture militates against virtue and so presents a particular moral challenge to those who would do good work there.

If the corporation does not merit its exalted status, Adam Smith and his disciples fair no better. Indeed, when viewed in light of the divine economy, Smith comes across neither as a prophet nor as particularly wise. Rather he is symbolic of the capitalist economy's rejection of the Triune God in favor of the deistic or Stoic hand of the capitalist market. Like the blind man at Bethsaida before Jesus healed him, Smith sees nothing of the perfect gifts that God gives.

42. D. Stephen Long in Fox and Long, *Calculated Futures*, 130.
43. See Joel Bakan, *The Corporation* (New York: Free Press, 2004), 28–59; Alan R. Palmiter, *Corporations*, 6th ed. (New York: Aspen Publishers, 2009), 213, 216.
44. Bakan, *The Corporation*, 34.

Being Recognized and Reconciled: The Good Life

Capitalism encourages desire to strive for distinction and survival through the struggle of the market. To this struggle there
is no end, only tenuous victory for the fortunate. It is tenuous
because the invisible hand that rules the capitalist market is fickle.
It neither makes nor keeps promises. Thus even the celebrated
entrepreneurial spirit and creativity do not guarantee success, for
while the market may demand that we render one another what is
contractually due in accord with commutative justice, the market
adheres to no such canons of justice in its bestowal (or not) of
either distinction or wealth/value. (The most creative, productive,
and efficient do not always succeed or prosper.)

In contrast, Christianity proclaims the end of all struggle and
strife and begins to enact that end here and now as desire is
renewed in the form of the charity, generosity, and justice that
seeks to extend communion. Accordingly, the good life in the
divine economy challenges the capitalist hope for distinction and
survival.

Justification by Grace

Like many of the components of the capitalist economy of desire,
the desire for distinction is not in and of itself wrong. After all,
humanity was created to be in communion with God, creation, and
one another, which entails recognition and regard. The error lies in
the means and ends of the capitalist market's desire for distinction.
This is captured well in the passage from Smith cited previously
regarding the end of capitalist "toil and bustle" as vanity, which
is "to be observed, to be attended to, to be taken notice of with
sympathy, complacency and approbation."[45]

Desire rightly finds its value outside of itself in others; it rightly
seeks, as Smith noted, recognition, sympathy, and approbation.
But it does so not on the basis of its powers of production and
acquisition, attaining victory over others in the struggle that is the
capitalist market. Regard is not something that one can purchase,
produce, or otherwise earn. Capitalist regard is at best fleeting,

45. Adam Smith, *The Theory of Moral Sentiments* (Indianapolis: Liberty Fund,
1984), 50.

lasting as long as it is profitable, until it has been surpassed by the next fad, fashion, or upgrade. Furthermore, the capitalist desire for distinction does not finally sustain the turn outward toward others. Indeed, it cannot, given the character of *homo economicus*. Thus the capitalist desire for distinction is always a matter of pride or envy, or in the case of those battered and broken by the capitalist market, perhaps despair and loathing.

In contrast, the distinction that we rightly desire is not rooted in the self and its accomplishments at all but is a gift of God that is utterly gratuitous. We cannot justify ourselves; salvation is by grace (Rom. 3:24). The regard that desires to draw us into communion, that recognizes and welcomes us, is not produced or earned by us. Rather the distinction that is ours is a matter of the dignity bestowed by the love of God that creates, sustains, calls each of us to our labors, and redeems. Moreover, as such, it is inalienable (Rom. 8:38–39; 11:29). Although it can be defaced by sin, it cannot be bartered or battered away in the agony of capitalist life; it is not subject to the inscrutable whims of an invisible God's merciless hand.

Furthermore, insofar as this distinction is rooted in the goodness of God and not in commodities and distinction won as trophies of the market, it is a matter of holiness. It is the goodness of God that creates human dignity and worth, and it is that goodness to which we are restored (recall Anselm's pearl) as the Holy Spirit sanctifies human desire and fits it for communion in the divine economy. And while this holiness does indeed entail practices of production and consumption, albeit now rightly ordered in accord with the divine economy, it also encompasses goods and practices that are not properly marketized and that are neither productive nor consuming, such as prayer and fasting, worship and study of Scripture, friendship, and so forth.

This holiness that is to distinguish our lives as good lives is manifest as our desire is conformed to Christ's humble vulnerability and is displayed in virtues such as charity, generosity, and justice. Thus the distinction that marks the good Christian life is a matter of ceaseless giving to (and receiving from) others or, as Scripture says, of provoking one another to love and good deeds (Heb. 10:24). This is a distinction of service, not exaltation, unless it is the exaltation of being lifted up on the cross as we follow Christ in self-giving service to and for others.

Salvation and the End of All Struggle

Insofar as capitalism is driven by scarcity, it rightly recognizes the problem created by desire shorn of its divinely given purpose or end. However, capitalism's solution is no solution at all to the extent that it does not seek to heal desire of that wound but instead exploits that disordered desire, harnessing its productive energy by means of the enchantments of the market. Yet one cannot produce one's way out of the conflict fueled by the endless desire that capitalism nurtures and by which it profits.[46] Not only is the effort proving destructive of creation, but for many the promise of security achieved through accumulation of goods, capital, or distinction also remains elusive. Yet even where relative security is achieved, it falls far short of human flourishing, for the victors remain in the clutches of a desire that is still unsatisfied and so in conflict with their neighbors. Accordingly there is neither peace nor rest from the agony of the market.

Here again the contrast with Christianity revolves around that truth that salvation does not come through our efforts and the market's whimsy but through the love of God that befriends us, undoing the pernicious effects of the fall; bringing the conflict of humanity with itself, creation, and God to an end; and reestablishing communion. Christ is our peace, breaking down the walls of hostility, putting an end to the agony of sin (Rom. 6:11; Eph. 2:14). As we are joined to Christ and infused with the virtues of faith, hope, and love, our desire is released from the fear of the other and the restless search for more that drives the conflict at the heart of the capitalist economy of desire.

This, however, does not mean that Christians are freed from all risk. Again capitalism is correct in recognizing that life in the midst of desire shorn of its divine end is risk-laden. But again its insight is only a parody of the truth insofar as the risk it enjoins on desire is not reconnected to the divine purpose of reconciliation and the renewal of communion. In the divine economy, desire risks much in the world of sin. We are called to take up the cross. But redeemed desire risks not in order to secure itself. Whether it is the risk of the market, of extending hospitality to the stranger, of lending and sharing, or of serving in the blighted and broken spaces of this world, desire that is caught up in the divine gift economy risks for the sake of others, for the sake of extending communion.

46. Marglin, *Dismal Science*, 216.

Moreover, unlike its capitalist counterpart, redeemed desire does not seek an end to risk, or more accurately, to the humble vulnerability that renders desire open to the neighbor. Instead, part of the freedom of a Christian is the freedom to live in holy insecurity, trusting that God will provide and that even if we or our loved ones die, neither we nor they will perish, for the gifts of God are inalienable and inexhaustible.

Conclusion

Having completed the comparison of capitalist theology and Christian economics that underwrite capitalism and Christianity as economies of desire, we now turn to the works of mercy as the form of the diaspora or pilgrim economics that characterizes the Christian economy of desire as it makes its way through this world.

8

The Work of Mercy

Peter Maurin, modern-day beggar and intellectual force behind the
birth of the Catholic Worker Movement, once asserted that "the
basis for a Christian economy is genuine charity and voluntary
poverty" and that the works of mercy were central to a Christian
society.[1] These two claims mark the parameters of this chapter.

Thus far we have traced the outline of the Christian economy of
desire, arguing both that it is fitting that Christianity be construed as
an economy of desire and that it is an economy that forms human
desire and its relations very differently from the capitalist economy.
The task that remains is to spell out more concretely and specifically
what the Christian economy of desire looks like. Of course, this
is not an entirely novel move insofar as already a number of practices have been named, from the prohibition of usury/interest, to
recognizing just price and just wage, limited markets and contracts,
inalienable (nonmarketable) goods, and use values, to recovering a
sense of "enough" and striving for the common good. Add to this
the disciplines involved in reordering or sanctifying desire from the
self-interested orientation of the free market toward other-directed
generosity, and already we have enough to keep the church busy
reordering its economic life and witness for a long time.

1. Peter Maurin, *Easy Essays* (Chicago: Franciscan Herald Press, 1961), 123; Peter
Maurin, "Christ the King Alone Can Reconstruct the World: The Practice of the Seven
Corporal and Spiritual Works of Mercy Is the Basis of Christian Society," *Catholic
Worker* 2 (October 1934): 1, 6.

Nevertheless, the focus to this point has been on painting with broad strokes a general vision or perhaps even "spirit" of the divine gift economy. Certainly the practices and virtues named thus far do not amount to a full-blown economic vision or blueprint for a comprehensive alternative to the regnant capitalist (dis)order.

Hence, in this chapter, we turn more directly and deliberately to some of the concrete practices and disciplines that characterize the divine economy. As Maurin suggests, these practices can be gathered under the umbrella of charity (almsgiving) and voluntary poverty (begging). As he also suggests, they can be approached in terms of the works of mercy as well. Accordingly, this chapter proceeds considering the callings of voluntary poverty and charity and concludes by considering the works of mercy as a manifestation of the divine economy.

A Diaspora or Pilgrim Economics

Before turning to those tasks, however, it is important to recall what has already been said about the expectations regarding the articulation of a complete economic blueprint for an alternative to capitalism. First and foremost, the divine economy is a gift that God gives and not something that humanity in general or Christians in particular engineer or construct. Thus when Christians lend without expecting anything in return or pay a just wage or suggest that the market should not be total and "free," the church is not assembling something so much as it is accepting that which it has been given; it is living into the life "which God prepared beforehand to be [its] way of life" (Eph. 2:10). Moreover, even as Christians live in accord with the divine economy now, they do not expect that economy to be manifest *in its fullness* until Christ returns in final victory. In other words, in this time between the times, so long as sin remains, Christianity expects the divine economy to remain, in the words of Deleuze, fugitive or nomadic.

In other words, that the Christian alternative to capitalism is incomplete is not indicative of Christianity's failure to articulate a viable alternative, and in pointing out the incomplete character of this alternative I am not trying to *lower* expectations. Rather, what is at issue is *changing* expectations in accord with the humble vulnerability that properly characterizes human desire in the divine gift economy. In this time between the times, Christians do *not* expect the kingdom in its catholic fullness.

This, however, is not a counsel of resignation or passivity, as if all the church can do is sit and wait for the kingdom to arrive. Rather, it points toward the opportunity or mission that the divine economy of desire sets before the church—which returns us to the notion of a diaspora or pilgrim economics raised briefly in the introduction. That the divine economy appears in the world in fragmentary fashion is not a sign of failure or an indication that there really is no alternative to capitalism. Rather, the ad hoc embodiment of the divine economy is a deliberately missionary posture. Just as Jeremiah encouraged the Jews to embrace exile and diaspora (scattering) as an opportunity to evangelize and witness (Jer. 29:7), so too the unfinished character of the divine economy's appearance now is a missionary or evangelistic opportunity to redeem the time.

Augustine proves helpful in making sense of this. As the Roman world was being overrun, Augustine penned his famous work *The City of God* in defense of Christianity against those who attributed Rome's fall to the abandonment of the pagan gods for Christ. In that work, Augustine juxtaposes the city of God with the earthly city. This juxtaposition of two cities, however, is not a matter of two distinct sets of institutions or economies, each occupying separate geographical territories, like, for example, New York City and Quito. Rather, Augustine defines the cities according to their loves. The city of God is constituted by those whose desire or love is properly directed toward God and neighbor, whereas the earthly city consists of those ruled by a disordered desire that relates to others agonistically, that strives for dominion and conquest. To contemporary readers, who are used to thinking of cities (and economies) in terms of distinct institutions and territories, this cannot help but strike us as odd. Yet it paves the way for appreciating the pilgrim or diaspora character of the Christian life (and economy) in this time between the times.

Explaining how these two cities interact, Augustine says in words that echo the prophet Jeremiah:

> Miserable, therefore, is the people which is alienated from God. Yet even this people has a peace that is not to be lightly esteemed, though, indeed, it shall not in the end enjoy it, because it makes no

good use of it before the end. But it is our interest that it enjoy this
peace meanwhile in this life; for as long as the two cities are com-
mingled, we also enjoy the peace of Babylon.[2]

The two cities are intermingled. They do not exist in separate and
distinct institutions and territories, as though Christians lived in
their own cities and operated their own economies while others
lived in other cities and ran different economies. Rather, the two
cities overlap, if you will. Elsewhere Augustine speaks not only of
the two cities being intermingled but of the church itself being a
mixed body, that is, a community that includes both believers and
nonbelievers.[3] Furthermore, Augustine exhorts the members of
the city of God to make good use of the peace of the earthly city.
    Some read this as a sign of Augustine's corruption, of his wedding
the church to empire and compromising the purity of the faith for
the sake of imperial privileges, but such a reading misses his point,
which is not imperial but evangelical. He is merely spelling out the
consequences of God's desire and the church's calling to see the
circle of communion extended. The earthly and heavenly cities are
purposefully entangled in this world; the citizens of the heavenly
city are properly found in the company of the citizens of all earthly
cities as nomads, refugees, exiles, sojourners, and pilgrims. That
they are is a reflection of the heavenly city's desire for and means
of accomplishing universal filiation—the renewal and expansion of
human communion, without exclusion, "to the ends of the earth."
Thus Augustine writes:

> Let this city bear in mind, that among her enemies lie hid those who
> are destined to be fellow-citizens, that she may not think it a fruit-
> less labour to bear what they inflict as enemies until they become
> confessors of the faith. So, too, as long as she is a stranger in the
> world, the city of God has in her communion, and bound to her
> by the sacraments, some who shall not eternally dwell in the lot of
> the saints. . . . But we have the less reason to despair of the recla-
> mation even of such persons, if among our most declared enemies
> there are now some, unknown to themselves, who are destined to
> become our friends.[4]

2. Augustine, *The City of God*, trans. Marcus Dods (New York: Random House,
1950), 19.26.
    3. Ibid., 1.35.
    4. Ibid.

Christians do not occupy their own city or country, because doing so would require withdrawing from the earthly cities and defending borders, thereby diminishing the opportunity to convert enemies into friends, to offer the grace of God that frees desire from its capitalist bondage and renews communion.

In other words, in this time between the times the Christian economy does not take the form of a separate and distinct economy alongside the economic blocs of this world, as though there should be a "Christian economic zone" next to the capitalist order. The practices that characterize the divine economy in this time between the times do not constitute an entire economic order unto themselves precisely because the economic mission of the church is to intermingle with the economies of the earthly cities, making good use of them, as Jeremiah and Augustine remind us—making better use of them than *homo economicus* and the messianic corporation can—by offering a just wage, refusing usury, accepting responsibility for the common good, limiting the reach of the market, and so forth. Thus the divine economy does not reject the market entirely, denounce the division of labor out of hand, or renounce currency, investment, and profit. Instead, Christian economics is about redeeming such practices, that is to say, properly ordering them toward the end of the renewal of communion in God's household.

In this regard, recall the social map of desire that Deleuze and Foucault trace. Notwithstanding what capitalism's chaplains and spokespersons want us to believe, capitalism and its state-forms have not succeeded in subduing desire entirely. Rather, capitalism's victory is always unstable, tenuous, contested. At any time and in any space, alternative and oppositional forms can be at work. As Augustine suggested long ago, in any space multiple economies of desire can be at work. To the forms of the divine economy at work in the midst of the earthly economies we now turn.

Why Not Be a Beggar? Two Callings

Specifically, we turn from two cities to two callings, which Maurin described as poverty and charity and in a preceding chapter were described as renunciation of material goods and almsgiving, or what we might call stewardship.

Naming the two callings thus, however, is not without its problems. After all, those called to poverty are moved by the virtue of charity and engage in acts of charity. For example, St. Francis gave his clothes—his *only* clothes—to a fellow beggar. Likewise, what is meant by the practice of charity or stewardship in the divine economy is at risk of being misunderstood because the modern practices of giving to persons who are poor and needy that go by those same names actually bear little resemblance to what the church has long meant by charity and almsgiving.[5]

Furthermore, those who are called to practice stewardship and almsgiving are not absolved of a certain asceticism or practice of renunciation. Think, for example, of the renunciation of greed and of the call to give for the sake of the renewal of communion to which all Christians are called. Chris Franks identifies this universal renunciation with "poverty of spirit" and observes, "All are thereby called to a pattern of renunciation that can have many forms."[6]

Traditionally these two callings have been related to one another as precepts and counsels. Precepts were thought to apply to all Christians, while counsels, sometimes called "counsels of perfection," were thought to apply to those who desire to be perfect. More specifically, the counsels of perfection were thought to apply to those who took the vows of the professional religious life and joined monasteries or the priesthood. Accordingly, almsgiving or stewardship was regarded as a precept or command that was applicable to all Christians, whereas renouncing all possessions and embracing voluntary poverty was regarded as a counsel of perfection, appropriate for those who joined religious orders.

It is well known that the Protestant Reformation rejected this two-tiered ethic, which appeared to privilege the life of professional religious types while simultaneously diminishing the legitimacy of the life of laity who toiled at worldly tasks. Furthermore, it is widely held by descendants of the Reformers that as Protestantism abolished the monastic life founded on these counsels and blessed the worldly activity of laity, the counsels of perfection were likewise discarded. Hence, among Protestants, mendicancy has disappeared,

5. For a critique of modern stewardship, see Kelly Johnson, *The Fear of Beggars* (Grand Rapids: Eerdmans, 2007).

6. Christopher Franks, *He Became Poor: The Poverty of Christ and Aquinas's Economic Teachings* (Grand Rapids: Eerdmans, 2009), 114.

clergy take no vows of lifelong celibacy or poverty, and even the meaning of obedience has become more fluid.

There are, however, several problems with the wholesale rejection of the counsels of perfection. To begin with, there is the historical problem that the Reformers, such as Luther and Calvin, did not discard the counsels. When they rejected the two-tiered ethic, they did not simply lop off the higher tier in favor of having everyone follow the less rigorous standard articulated in the precepts. To the contrary, what the counsels relegated to the few, the Reformers insisted were applicable to all Christians. In effect, what they cut off was the *lower* tier of the medieval ethic. Rejecting the distinction between the counsels and precepts amounted not to lowering the moral bar for everyone but raising it. Luther makes this clear in a passage where he criticizes St. Francis, the founder of the mendicant order:

> He made the universal gospel intended for all the faithful into a special rule for the few. What Christ wanted to be universal and catholic, Francis made schismatic. When a Franciscan takes his vow he vows nothing more than that which he already vowed at the start in his baptism, and that is the gospel.[7]

The problem with the distinction between counsels and precepts is not that they ask too much of professional religious types but that they excuse the majority of the church from the life to which they were called in their baptisms.[8] This suggests the second problem with simply discarding the counsels of perfection.

The theological problem with abolishing the counsels is that doing so diminishes the moral function of the commandments called precepts.[9] The precepts alone are insufficient for desire to return to communion with God and neighbor. This is the case because one can obey them and still not love God and neighbor. One can do what the commandments require not out of the desire for communion but out of fear or some base desire, like pride. Herein lies the importance of what were called counsels of perfection.

7. Martin Luther, "The Judgment of Martin Luther on Monastic Vows," in *Luther's Works*, vol. 44, ed. James Atkinson (Philadelphia: Fortress, 1966), 255.

8. The exception is lifelong clerical celibacy. This was not regarded as an obligation for any Christian.

9. What follows relies on Franks, *He Became Poor*, 120–31.

First, the counsels were important for some as instruments for healing desire. As Aquinas puts it, all are called to love God and neighbor, and both the precepts and counsels aid in attaining this end, albeit in different ways.[10] The precepts are directed at acts that are *contrary* to this love. For example, murdering one's neighbor or stealing from her are *contrary* to the love that desires communion. These acts are prohibited for everyone. In contrast, the counsels are directed at acts that are *not* contrary to love but may nevertheless *hinder* or *obstruct* love. For example, while marriage is not contrary to love, it can be an obstacle to the love of God, as the cares of this world draw one's desire and attention away from God (1 Cor. 7:32–34). The vow of celibacy is directed at this potential obstacle. Likewise, material possessions are not *inherently* contrary to the love of God and neighbor; nevertheless, they can be an obstacle to communion as they create divisions, hence the vow of voluntary poverty. Because the counsels are not directed at acts contrary to love, they are not obligatory; nevertheless, some find them helpful in overcoming obstacles in the moral life and directing their desire toward its true and proper end.

Second, the counsels were important insofar as they were exemplary. They were exemplary, however, not in the sense that those who adhered to them were necessarily morally better than those who did not. After all, as Aquinas makes clear, one can love perfectly without making the vows, and one who makes the vows does not thereby necessarily love more perfectly than one who does not.[11] Rather, they are exemplary in the sense that they help all Christians see at what the precepts or commands aim. The counsels, in other words, assist in understanding what the point of the precepts is. How did they do this?

Even though not everyone was required to take vows of celibacy, poverty, and obedience, the presence of persons who did served to remind the church that merely satisfying the law as a kind of moral minimum was insufficient. The counsels reminded the church that the point of the moral law lies not in fulfilling the letter but the spirit, that is, not simply in doing *outwardly* what the law requires but rather in the *inward* renewal of the desires of the heart.

10. Thomas Aquinas, *Summa Theologiae* (Westminster, MD: Christian Classics, 1981), 2-2.184.3.
11. Ibid., 2–2.184.4.

In this regard, consider the practice of tithing. It is not uncommon in Christian circles to suppose that tithing is a sufficient expression of economic stewardship. But almsgiving or stewardship involves all that we have and all that we are. Stewardship is about the reordering of our desires in accord with the divine gift economy that seeks to extend communion. The counsel of voluntary poverty reminds us of this, that God claims *all* that we have and that we are. Therefore, when the counsel of voluntary poverty is dismissed, when the church is deprived of the example of those called to the vow of poverty, it can more easily forget that tithing is not the end but the beginning of stewardship. Likewise, voluntary poverty reminds the church of its calling to humble and even cruciform vulnerability, trusting in the Lord and not in the power of its earnings or the size of its bank account. Thus that we will have persons who are poor with us always is a constant invitation and reminder from God to embrace the divine economy. Maurin calls persons who are poor "ambassadors of God" and notes, "That is what the poor are for, to give the rich occasion to do good."[12] The presence of persons who are poor is an opportunity for desire to be healed as it is called outward in love toward the other (see Matt. 25:31–45).

Hence the heading of this section, "Why Not Be a Beggar?" which is borrowed from another of Peter Maurin's poems.[13] As we consider the work of mercy, there is little question that, at least among Christians not suffering from involuntary poverty, almsgiving or stewardship has been the dominant calling in the church.[14] Indeed, much of the modern church no longer seriously considers, supports, and so listens for the call to voluntary poverty. Yet such deafness has important repercussions for how stewardship is practiced. Thus the importance of recognizing the call to begging, to voluntary poverty, before considering the work of mercy that is stewardship. Voluntary poverty is, no less than almsgiving/ stewardship, an important dimension of the economy of desire that is Christianity. As Martin Luther said, echoing Christ, when God calls, then we must be ready and willing to give everything away,

12. Maurin, *Easy Essays*; see, e.g., 8, 167. Maurin is repeating a common understanding of the medieval church.

13. Maurin, *Easy Essays*, "Why Not Be a Beggar?" 77.

14. Although it might be worth pondering the fact that many Christian institutions exist in large part by begging, even if they often lament that fact and seek to avoid it.

even to the point of being poor.[15] If the church would be about the work of the divine economy, then it would do well to recognize and support that call. Indeed, to close one's ear to the call to voluntary poverty may seriously impair the church's ability to hear and follow the Spirit's direction with regard to almsgiving or stewardship.

The Works of Mercy

In the midst of a discussion of the sacrificial nature of the Christian life, Augustine notes how participation in Communion shapes our desires. He observes that as the church celebrates the sacrifice of Christ at the altar in Communion, it is joined to that sacrifice and so receives the form of a servant. It then goes forth to make true sacrifices, which are works of mercy that relieve distress and draw persons into communion with God.[16]

The work of mercy is a fitting name for what the Christian economy of desire sets Christians to doing in this world, for mercy is the virtue that responds to the distress of another, and it captures as well the church's call to participate in Christ's self-giving for the sake of renewing communion.

Within the Christian tradition there has developed a set of practices known as "the works of mercy." Although they do not explicitly address every dimension of the divine economy, they are nevertheless a good starting point for outlining the practices that constitute that economy in everyday life. The works of mercy were inspired by passages of Scripture like Matthew 25:31–45 and as they came to be formally identified over the centuries include seven corporeal (bodily) and seven spiritual works. According to Aquinas, they are the following:[17]

Corporeal works	Spiritual works
feed the hungry	instruct the ignorant
give drink to the thirsty	counsel the doubtful
clothe the naked	comfort the mourning

---

15. Martin Luther, "The Sermon on the Mount," in *Luther's Works*, vol. 21, ed. Jaroslav Pelikan (St. Louis: Concordia, 1956), 14–15.

16. Augustine, *The City of God* 10.6.

17. Aquinas, *Summa Theologiae* 2-2.32.2.

shelter the homeless	reprove the sinner
visit the sick	forgive injuries
ransom the captive (minister to prisoners)	bear wrongs patiently
bury the dead	pray for all

Although this tradition has been largely forgotten by modernity, it was at the heart of what has been called "the Christian revolution," the profound change that the birth and spread of Christianity effected in the Roman world and beyond. For whereas the practice of beneficence was not foreign to ancient Roman and Greek cultures, it was a beneficence specifically directed toward the city and citizens.[18] Furthermore, the precepts of classical morality considered mercy and unearned aid to be immoral and unjust.[19] Into this world came the good news of a merciful God whose followers were about the work of extending this mercy beyond their own, beyond family, tribe, and city, to include the stranger and persons who are poor.[20] Indeed, it has been said that Christianity invented "the poor" in the sense that its work of mercy not only brought visibility and recognition to a population that previously was marginalized and ignored but insisted as well that such persons be integrated into community.[21]

As a consequence, as the church spread and developed, the works of mercy took shape in a host of charitable institutions and practices that encompassed laity, religious orders, church leaders, and institutions.[22] Bishops had a special responsibility to care for persons who are poor in their jurisdiction, and they did so by founding

18. Peter Brown, *Poverty and Leadership in the Later Roman Empire* (Hanover, NH: Brandeis University Press, 2002), 4–5.

19. Rodney Stark, *The Rise of Christianity* (San Francisco: HarperSanFrancisco, 1997), 212; Edwin Judge, "The Quest for Mercy in Late Antiquity," in *God Who Is Rich in Mercy*, ed. Peter T. O'Brien and David G. Peterson (Grand Rapids: Baker, 1986), 107.

20. Christianity followed Judaism in this regard. See Ramsay MacMullen, *Christianizing the Roman Empire (A.D. 100–400)* (New Haven: Yale University Press, 1984), 54.

21. Brown, *Poverty and Leadership*, 1–44.

22. See James F. Keenan, *The Works of Mercy* (Lanham, MD: Rowman & Littlefield, 2005); James W. Broadman, *Charity and Welfare: Hospitals and the Poor in Medieval Catalonia* (Philadelphia: University of Pennsylvania Press, 1998); James W. Broadman, *Charity and Religion in Medieval Europe* (Washington, DC: Catholic University of America Press, 2009); John Henderson, *Piety and Charity in Late Medieval Florence* (Chicago: University of Chicago Press, 1994); Antony Black, *Guild and State* (New Brunswick, NJ: Transaction Publishers, 2003); Michel Mollat, *The Poor in the Middle*

shelters and providing food. Hostels, hospices, and hospitals were founded by the church and laity for the sake of sheltering persons who are poor, the traveler, the sick. Nursing, the idea that one would care for instead of abandon the gravely ill, was a Christian invention.[23] Homes for children, orphans, lepers, ex-prostitutes, the elderly, widows, and mentally ill were established. Schools were erected for persons who are poor; legal aid was provided them as well. Professional, civic, and religious groups (orders, fraternities, guilds) were formed for the sake of establishing and sustaining such institutions and practices, for ransoming captives, for paying the dowries of poor women, for supporting public works such as roads and bridges. In sum, in ways and to an extent that is difficult to imagine today, given both the capitalist deformity of desire as well as modernity's self-justifying caricaturing of the church before modernity, the works of mercy permeated Christian society.[24]

The extent and effect of the works of mercy were such that the pagan emperor Julian complained in 362 CE that the withering of the pagan faith was connected to Christianity's benevolence to strangers and care for persons who are poor, even the pagan poor.[25] We might recall as well Adam Smith's comments about the church's practice of the works of mercy cited earlier, where he observed that those practices constituted the most formidable obstacle to the advancement of the free market.

Notwithstanding the widespread practice of the works of mercy in earlier eras, the suggestion that they constitute a concrete form of the divine economy today faces several objections, which revolve around the extent to which they actually embody an alternative to the current capitalist order. After all, one might argue that the works of mercy have not been forgotten but rather have taken form in what today is called private philanthropy and public (i.e., governmental) welfare, and that neither practice is clearly counter to capitalism but in fact may be crucial to the perpetuation of capitalism as they ameliorate the effects of "market failures."

Certainly the works of mercy can be co-opted by the capitalist order and reduced to philanthropy or welfare. The important point,

Ages (New Haven: Yale University Press, 1986); Brian Tierney, _Medieval Poor Law_ (Berkley: University of California Press, 1959).

23. See Stark, _Rise of Christianity_, 73–94.
24. This is not to absolve medieval Christian practice of its failures and abuses.
25. Stark, _Rise of Christianity_, 84.

however, is that when that happens, that is a *reduction* of the works of mercy. Notwithstanding their superficial similarity, when the works of mercy are engaged as private philanthropy or migrate to the governing authorities in the form of welfare, they are no longer the same acts; they are no longer part and parcel of the divine gift economy that is the church's witness and work in the world, but instead have become very different practices in a different economy of desire. Benedict XVI suggests as much when he writes:

> The Church's deepest nature is expressed in her three-fold responsibility: of proclaiming the word of God (*kerygma-martyria*), celebrating the sacraments (*leitourgia*), and exercising the ministry of charity (*diakonia*). These duties presuppose each other and are inseparable. For the Church, charity is not a kind of welfare activity which could equally well be left to others, but is part of her nature, an indispensable expression of her very being.[26]

Unlike philanthropy and welfare, the works of mercy are an integral dimension of the church's very essence. They are, in the pope's words, inseparable from Word and sacrament, from proclamation and worship. They are, in other words, an intrinsic expression of the economy of desire that is the church's life.

Beyond Philanthropy

That they are an intrinsic expression of the economy of desire that is the church's life distinguishes the works of mercy from philanthropy in at least two ways. First, private philanthropy offers no critique of the capitalist discipline of desire. Philanthropy is extraeconomic, operating "outside the market"—that is, it entails no critique of current market arrangements. Instead, by picking up after the market, so to speak, it relieves pressure on the need for more fundamental solutions. It does this by creating a false sense that the problems are being addressed, thereby relieving the consciences of those who prosper under the current market arrangements.[27] Furthermore, philanthropy sustains the system insofar as

26. Benedict XVI, *God Is Love* (San Francisco: Ignatius, 2006), 60.
27. See Janet Poppendieck, *Sweet Charity? Emergency Food and the End of Entitlement* (New York: Penguin, 1999).

it is a means of "laundering" the profits of the current order. This is to say, ordinarily no questions are asked about the source of the wealth given to sustain philanthropy.[28] Philanthropy, like stewardship, is giving that has become disconnected from any question of justice in earnings. Indeed, philanthropy becomes a means of shoring up the image of capitalism's beneficiaries. Like the Rockefellers and Dukes of old, individuals and businesses can engage in philanthropy today, confident that questions of justice will not be asked of those gifts. Indeed, philanthropy can insulate one from questions of justice as such acts bolster one's image as generous and caring. This was the one concession Milton Friedman made to corporate social responsibility. One may engage in such charitable practices hypocritically, that is, not out of a genuine commitment to the common good but for the public relations and marketing value of such acts.[29]

In contrast, the works of mercy embody a critique of the capitalist system insofar as they are part and parcel of the divine gift economy that works to renew and extend communion. In this regard, the works of mercy are not synonymous with philanthropy as private choice, unexpected, optional. Rather, the works of mercy are not private, voluntary, or free in the popular sense of those terms at all but are part of the just ordering of public, communal life in accord with God's will, in accord with the universal destination of material goods. In other words, they are neither private nor optional but public and expected. It is for this reason that the early church used to speak of almsgiving not as an act of pity but of justice.[30] As public acts of justice, they have everything to do with political economy.

Granted, this can be difficult to discern in a world where the church has largely acquiesced to its marginalization as an apolitical, cultural space. Yet even without knowing the history of the works of mercy, how they were shorthand for an ecclesial (churchly) political economy encompassing an array of institutions and practices that embraced clergy, monastics, individuals, families, businesses, and professional groups, the list of practices itself suggests broadly

---

28. See Johnson, *Fear of Beggars*, 71–100.

29. Not that all philanthropy is hypocritical. The point is that philanthropy does not require justice and concern for the common good.

30. Boniface Ramsey, "Almsgiving in the Latin Church: The Fourth and Early Fifth Centuries," *Theological Studies* 43 (1982): 230–37.

systemic concerns. In other words, on the face of it the works of mercy do not appear apolitical, extraeconomic, or even necessarily outside the market. After all, feeding the hungry, sheltering the homeless, caring for the sick, and clothing the naked have everything to do with what political economy is about. There is no reason, apart from the modern privatization of Christianity, that the works of mercy should be equated with the philanthropy that leaves capitalism untouched.

In a related vein, the works of mercy may be thought to deal only with redistribution and to ignore production. Focused as they appear to be on giving, they would seem to comport well with modern notions of stewardship and philanthropy that are divorced from questions of production, from matters of justice in earning. However, as was the case with the claim that the works of mercy ignore the need for systemic or structural change, the suggestion that the works of mercy are merely about (re)distribution and not production is a misunderstanding. It is a misunderstanding born of confusing the philanthropy of a spiritualized and domesticated modern church with the robust economy of desire that challenged first pagan Rome and then, as Smith noted, the emergent capitalist economy. Indeed, the modern market economy did not appear suddenly, as if from scratch and in stark opposition to what preceded it, but instead was a mutation of a Christian "civil economy" that united charity and economy, gift and contract, virtue and the market.[31] After all, the works of mercy did not just take shape in the redistributive practices of almsgiving and hospitals but also in the confraternities and guilds of economic producers, which oversaw not merely distribution of alms but also such things as productivity, quality of products, and just prices.[32] Recall as well that matters of just price, just wage, and usury were all part of this ethos. In other words, the works of mercy reflect an economy of desire that treats both production and distribution; only when the capitalist discipline of desire succeeds in severing economy from virtue and in reducing justice to voluntary exchange—and the church embraces these developments—do the works of mercy begin to look like merely redistributive philanthropy.

31. See Luigino Bruni and Stefano Zamagni, *Civil Economy: Efficiency, Equity, Public Happiness* (New York: Peter Lang, 2007), 30; see especially chaps. 2–4.
32. See Black, *Guild and State*.

The ways in which the works of mercy address the systemic and productive dimension of economy are not exhausted by the corporeal works but are manifest as well in the spiritual works of mercy. Although they are as susceptible to privatization as the corporeal works, practices such as instructing the ignorant and correcting sinners certainly can (and should) entail Christians addressing those who influence the shape of the economic system. The appropriateness and effectiveness of this kind of intervention is captured well by Hélder Câmara in his well-known observation, "When I give food to the poor, they call me a saint. When I ask why the poor have no food, they call me a Communist."[33] As the Latin American liberationists, among others, suggest, where the works of mercy are rightly engaged as an expression of the Christian economy of desire, giving inevitably leads to "asking why," to questioning the practices and systems that contribute to the conditions that the works of mercy address.

This leads to the second way the works of mercy are properly distinguished from philanthropy. Not only is philanthropy devoid of systemic critique, but it is also finally only about the giver.[34] As a private, voluntary act of pity, shorn of any social expectation or justice claim, philanthropy is an extraeconomic expression of the commodity form. This is to say, just as the commodity comes to us from the market with no history and no moral strings attached, and so no meaning or purpose other than what the purchaser's will imposes on it, the object of the philanthropic act—be it money, time, labor, or other resources—is similarly naked until clothed by the will of the giver. Philanthropic giving is an expression of private ownership.[35] It is giving that is first and foremost an act of self-expression. It is born in the need of the giver, and, even if it is quite public, philanthropy is still the expression of private interest or desire.

All of which is to say that philanthropy severs giving from mutuality. While it may meet some needs—of the giver first and foremost but, hopefully, of the recipients as well—it does not build community. It does not create, extend, or renew human relations beyond

33. Hélder Câmara, *Essential Writings*, ed. Francis McDonagh (Maryknoll, NY: Orbis, 2009), 11.
    34. What follows is drawn from Stephen H. Webb, *The Gifting God* (New York: Oxford University Press, 1996), 17–22.
    35. Ibid., 17.

the capitalist form. To the contrary, the goal of much philanthropy is the opposite of community. Givers—when they care at all about the recipients—hope that recipients will become self-sufficient or self-sustaining. In other words, they will become fully functioning capitalist individuals, *homo economicus*, available to the market.

The works of mercy, however, as an expression of the divine economy of desire that seeks to gather all into the communion of love, are not simply personal expressions of private ownership, nor are they directed at self-sufficiency and autonomy. More will be said about this after we consider how the works of mercy exceed welfare.

Beyond Welfare

If the works of mercy do not correlate with private philanthropy, perhaps they are more compatible with public welfare. Indeed, the history of the works of mercy in the early and medieval Christian eras show them institutionalized in the government, both as government was exercised by the church and as it took the more secular forms familiar today. This is as it should be insofar as government properly serves the common good (Rom. 13). Nevertheless, there are several issues that render contemporary state welfare problematic.

First, as was the case with private philanthropy, government welfare may not challenge capitalism. Instead it may support the capitalist economy by tending to the victims of market failures without addressing the cause of those failures. In this regard, notwithstanding much popular rhetoric, neoliberal capitalism is not opposed to all government welfare.[36] Rather, it is opposed to welfare that interferes with the market, for example, by imposing the demands of social or distributive justice on it or by offering assistance that fosters behaviors and cultures that obstruct the market or render persons less fit for entering it.[37]

This leads to the second problem with welfare, particularly in its contemporary bureaucratized form. It does not nurture community. Contemporary government welfare mediates the care and responsibility of society for its members by means of supplying a

36. Friedrich A. von Hayek, *Law, Legislation, and Liberty*, vol. 2, *The Mirage of Social Justice* (Chicago: University of Chicago Press, 1976), 87; see also 136.

37. See, e.g., Michael Novak, *The Catholic Ethic and the Spirit of Capitalism* (New York: Free Press, 1993), 178–94.

minimal level of basic goods that may or may not be adequate to individuals. In this provision, however, individuals remain strangers, disconnected. As Michael Ignatieff observes, the mediation of government welfare "walls us off from one another" such that we are in a sense "responsible *for* each other, but we are not responsible *to* each other."[38] In contrast with philanthropy, welfare is focused on the recipients but does not integrate them into community. In this regard, consider the commonplace concern about welfare creating dependency. To counter this, welfare is dispensed in a manner that is impersonal and bureaucratic, thereby minimizing or eliminating altogether any kind of enduring mutual obligation or responsibility that normally characterizes community. Accordingly, welfare remains an act of pity, not justice; a luxury indulged in by societies that have, in the words of Hayek, "reached a certain level of wealth,"[39] not an essential expression of the common good that properly animates communities.

Moreover, governmental welfare can actually inhibit community. It is widely recognized that the development of governmental welfare in the twentieth century has undermined the sense of responsibility that neighbors and communities have for others; it has contributed to the withering of neighborhood ties. Because the government provides, we feel no obligation to do so.

Along these lines, although it is frequently suggested that the central political conflict of our time is between the individual and an overbearing state, the real conflict is between the state and any community or group that would challenge its direct access to individuals.[40] As Deleuze's history of capitalism suggests, the state-form has become a crucial tool in capitalism's freeing desire from communal ties so that desire is available to the capitalist market. In other words, the modern capitalist state is not *against* the individual. Rather, it is devoted to sustaining the capitalist individual against communities and associations that would embed persons in networks of relations, goods, and purposes that resist the presuppositions of *homo economicus*. There can be little doubt that governmental welfare has served an important role in the advance of the capitalist economy of desire against alternatives. Just as the

38. Michael Ignatieff, *The Needs of Strangers* (New York: Penguin, 1985), 10.
39. Hayek, *Mirage of Social Justice*, 136.
40. See Robert A. Nisbet, *The Quest for Community* (New York: Oxford University Press, 1973), 102–8.

modern state emerged by displacing the political presence of the church, so too state welfare displaces ("crowds out" in economic parlance) the efforts of other communities to engage in the works of mercy as an alternative to capitalism.

It is worth noting that this critique may apply as well to ecclesial efforts insofar as they mimic their secular counterparts. The history of at least some church social ministry efforts is the history of gradually replacing the labors of local communities with bureaucratic institutions whose only ties to those communities are financial. The result is that in the process of meeting basic needs efficiently, the importance of needs of flourishing—encompassing human and divine communion—have diminished. Persons are served, but they are not integrated into the church community. As Christine Pohl notes, one consequence of the development of such institutions is the reduction of human relations to the roles of caregiver and recipient, professional and client.[41]

In this regard, we would do well to recall that historically even where the church established the works of mercy as part of its governing authority, such governmental establishment did not *replace* other efforts initiated by persons, parishes, professional organizations, and so forth. Where Christian governing authorities engaged in works of mercy, it was complementary to the broader economy of mercy rather than a substitute for it.

The Labor of Communion

The deficiencies of philanthropy and welfare can be summarized in the failure to nurture communion. As Luigino Bruni writes, "Entrusting the reality of agape [love] to the philanthropist or to the State cannot be considered a satisfactory solution (though without desiring to negate the many positive aspects of either the welfare State or philanthropy) as in such a solution two fundamental elements of Christian agape are normally lacking."[42] Those elements are community and mutuality. What distinguishes the works of mercy from contemporary philanthropy and welfare is that the

41. Christine Pohl, "Hospitality from the Edge," *Annual of the Society of Christian Ethics* 15 (1995): 130.
42. Luigino Bruni, "Common Good and Economics," trans. Michael Brennen, 6, accessed July 13, 2010, http://michaelbrennen.com/common-good-and-economics/.

works of mercy are ordered toward the renewal of communion. There are several aspects of this labor of nurturing communion that bear emphasizing for the way in which they further distinguish the works of mercy as an economy of desire distinct from philanthropy and welfare.

First, this labor of communion is personalist in the sense that it is about bringing persons into relationship. The Christian tradition has long recognized that the works of mercy entail reciprocity between giver and recipient that is not self-evident. Yet if we recall their scriptural basis in Matthew 25 or the tradition's claim that persons who are poor are a means of grace to those who are rich, the reciprocity becomes clearer. As those with material resources provide for those who are lacking, those who are lacking give in the form of prayers for their benefactors. And, as Scripture points out, God hears the prayers of the poor and distressed (Job 34:28; Isa. 25:4). So Ambrose refers to the prayers and "redemptive tears" of the poor, and Jerome (d. 420) can contrast the material gifts of the wealthy with the spiritual gifts of the poor, writing, "The poor person gives more than he receives. We give bread, which is eaten up on the same day. For that bread he gives us the kingdom of heaven in return."[43] Recognizing the mutual gifting that marks this communion, John Wesley could urge wealthy Christians to resist the trend toward philanthropy and not simply donate money, but to meet and spend time with persons who are poor, which is echoed by Latin American liberationists today when they insist that it is not sufficient to do things *for* the poor but that one must befriend the poor, and that the church must be not only *for* but *of* the poor.[44] The works of mercy are a means of grace whereby desire is renewed in the sociality of love.

Second, although the works of mercy are personalist, they are not private or extraeconomic. Rather, they comport well with what Latin American liberationists call "integral liberation," that is, redemption in its personal, spiritual, *and* social-political aspects. However, what may not be as clear is how this call for the works of mercy is distinguished from the call of some for the spread of voluntary associations as the custodians of the moral values

43. Both cited in Ramsey, "Almsgiving in the Latin Church," 256. See also Bruni and Zamagni, *Civil Economy*, 42–43.
44. See especially Jon Sobrino, *The True Church and the Poor* (Maryknoll, NY: Orbis, 1991).

needed to temper capitalism. The difference is that the works of mercy are more holistic than voluntary associations in civil society. This is to say, the pilgrim economy manifest through the works of mercy does not assume that civil society *rather than* the market or the state is the proper place for the nurture of virtue. After all, as Deleuze and Foucault suggest, desire is shaped by the market, state, and civil society. Thus the healing of desire as justice and generosity cannot be relegated to a single social site. Virtues like justice cannot be "outsourced" to social sites other than the market. Rather, the market and the state, no less than civil society, should nurture virtuous desire and be ordered toward the common good. Neither regulation alone, the market alone, nor civil society alone is sufficient.[45] The history of the works of mercy suggests as much. While they were practiced by what today would be called civic associations, they were also part of government and economy. To locate virtue and the desire for communion in voluntary civic associations as a corrective to the capitalist market is to reduce the labor of communion to philanthropy. Said differently, the works of mercy, as more than philanthropy and welfare, reveal the divine economy's call not for morals *and* the capitalist market but for a moral market, for an economic order that serves the desire for communion.

Granted, until Christ returns and establishes the divine economy in its fullness, the church on pilgrimage through this world's economies will not be surprised if the government and economy resist justice, generosity, and the common good. This, however, is no reason for the church to cease witnessing to this economy in its life and interactions with others. After all, this is precisely its mission as a pilgrim or diaspora economy.

Third, the works of mercy, as a labor of communion, are about more than meeting basic needs. Both philanthropy and welfare are typically conceived in terms of addressing basic needs. Capitalism, likewise, is often assessed in terms of its success or failure in meeting basic needs. In an economy devoid of a common good that orients human desire, this is understandable. In a society lacking consensus on the good, it is thought that agreement might be reached at least on "basic needs."[46]

45. On this point, see Rowan Williams, "Theology and Economics: Two Different Worlds," *Anglican Theological Review* 92, no. 4 (2010): 613.
46. M. Douglas Meeks, *God the Economist* (Minneapolis: Fortress, 1989), 165.

The works of mercy are not about basic needs because the way basic needs are typically understood does not escape, but reinforces, the capitalist discipline of desire. Because they are disconnected from any particular vision of the end or common good of humanity,[47] needs function much like "rights" do in the capitalist economy of desire. They are tantamount to claims of individuals *against* society for access to certain resources so they may pursue private interests or goods. In this way, they conform to the agony of capitalist relations.

Furthermore, basic needs are expansive, mimicking the insatiable character of desire under the capitalist discipline. Economists draw a distinction between absolute and relative needs.[48] Absolute needs are generally associated with necessities, with the basic means of survival, whereas relative needs are those felt in relation to others, and could be equated with what we might call luxuries. For example, basic shelter might be regarded as an absolute need, whereas a home a little nicer than one's acquaintances would be a relative need. The distinction between absolute and relative needs, however, is tenuous. Absolute needs expand as relative needs tend to become absolute over time.[49] Thus whereas at one time indoor plumbing was an extravagance, today few offering assistance to the impoverished would regard it as such.

The point is that insofar as the logic of needs does not escape the capitalist discipline, meeting needs does not adequately name the goal of the divine economy as displayed in the works of mercy. Rather, as the labor of communion, the works of mercy strive for more than meeting basic needs. They are about human flourishing or abundant life (John 10:10) and not merely sustaining bare biological life.[50] This means the works of mercy exceed needs, be they absolute or relative, to encompass relational goods. They are about the good of renewed relations, the bonds of love that unite all in the divine economy. Accordingly, they embody the truth that life does

47. Ignatieff, *Needs of Strangers*, 14.

48. John Maynard Keynes, *Essays in Persuasion* (New York: Norton, 1963), 365.

49. Stephen A. Marglin, *The Dismal Science: How Thinking Like an Economist Undermines Community* (Cambridge, MA: Harvard University Press, 2008), 206–22; Juliet B. Schor, *The Overspent American* (New York: Harper, 1998), 3–21.

50. Steve Corbett and Brian Fikkert note that defining needs in narrowly materialist terms—ignoring relationships, dignity, and belonging—is typical of wealthy Western persons. See *When Helping Hurts* (Chicago: Moody, 2009), 68.

not consist of an abundance of possessions (Luke 12:15), that the solution to poverty (of body and spirit) is not simply the provision of more, but of solidarity and friendship, generosity and mutuality. In this regard, it should be noted that the works of mercy as a labor of communion are no less expansive than needs, but they are expansive in a much different sense. Works of mercy produce and provide, not for the sake of empowering the insatiable desire of autonomous individuals to pursue private goods and interests, but for the sake of expanding communion. The goal of the works of mercy is not self-sufficiency but participation in the circle of giving and receiving (cf. Eph. 4:28).[51] Unlike commodities in the capitalist order, material goods circulate in the divine economy as a means of drawing us together, a reality reflected nowhere more clearly than in the liturgy of Communion, where bread and wine by the power of the Holy Spirit bring we who are many together as one body (1 Cor. 10:17).

Fourth, the works of mercy do not operate according to a strict logic of merit and desert. Recall the prior discussion of the redemption of justice. Questions of desert have no place in the works of mercy for the simple reason that God gave to us sinners and continues to give, while we were and are undeserving. In the same way, sharing in the divine work of mercy, we are called to give, even to the undeserving.

Granted, we ought try to give in ways that are truly helpful, that truly contribute to the common good. But this judgment is different than that of worthiness or desert. It is akin to discerning fraud. And there is much in the tradition that affirms discerning who genuinely needs help and who does not.[52] But even here one must be careful. After all, Paul says, "Why not be defrauded?" (1 Cor. 6:7; cf. Heb. 10:34; Luke 6:29–30).[53]

51. Although treating the complex topic of class exceeds the parameters of this work, it is worth noting that Michael Zweig's work on class as a matter of relations of production and agency rather than simply income stratification illuminates one dimension of what I am calling the labor of communion. See Michael Zweig, "Class and Poverty in the U.S. Economy," in *Religion and Economic Justice*, ed. Michael Zweig (Philadelphia: Temple University Press, 1991), 196–218; Michael Zweig, *The Working Class Majority* (Ithaca, NY: ILR, 2000).

52. Tierney, *Medieval Poor Law*; Brian Tierney, *Church Law and Constitutional Thought in the Middle Ages* (London: Variorum Reprints, 1979), 360–73.

53. Two of the best discussions of the dynamics of Christian assistance to others is provided by Corbett and Fikkert, *When Helping Hurts*, and by Christopher L. Heuertz

This is the context for hearing Paul's exhortation: "Anyone un-willing to work should not eat" (2 Thess. 3:10).[54] Paul is not draw-ing a bright line between the deserving and undeserving poor, nor is he exhorting us to be autonomous and entrepreneurial *homo economicus*. Rather, Paul's concern is the use of material goods for the sake of the extension of communion. Those who are able but do not contribute simultaneously withdraw themselves from the circle of mutuality and reciprocity and detract from the commu-nity's labor of communion. Hence, even this seemingly coldhearted statement is an expression of generosity, of how the church's life is rightly ordered so that it can best serve its mission of extending communion by sharing material goods.

What Do You See? The Divine Economy Today

As we reach the end of this work, the suspicion may yet linger that escape from capitalism is not possible, that the capitalist economy of desire is too effective, its hold on our desires too deep and all-pervasive. Of course, as I have suggested, this is less a matter of the strength of the capitalist discipline than it is a question of what God is doing here and now to heal desire of its capitalist corruptions.

In the Gospel of Matthew, the disciples of John confront Jesus with the question of whether he is the long-awaited Messiah. Jesus responds to the skeptics of his day by pointing out what they see and hear: the blind see, the lame walk, the lepers are cleansed, the deaf hear, the dead are raised, and the poor have the good news brought to them (Matt. 11:2–5).

So we might ask with regard to the divine gift economy on pil-grimage in this world, what do we see? Are the works of mercy being embodied in the midst of the capitalist order as an alternative to that order? Is desire being healed of its capitalist distortions?

The answer is yes—if we have eyes to see, if we have eyes not for the kingdom in its fullness but rather for glimpses of the kingdom in its pilgrim form that is its lot in this time between the times. If we

and Christine D. Pohl, *Friendship at the Margins: Discovering Mutuality in Service and Mission* (Downers Grove, IL: InterVarsity, 2010).

54. See Allen Verhey, *Remembering Jesus* (Grand Rapids: Eerdmans, 2002), 292.

have eyes to see, then all around us, in the midst of the economies of this world, the divine economy appears in a variety of practices and forms challenging the capitalist order of things and freeing desire to flow in the joyous conviviality of love. Thus, in a manner not unlike the medieval works of mercy, today the divine economy appears in our midst in an array of institutions and practices that encompass lay and ordained, congregations and intentional communities, as well as institutions and initiatives organized by both church leaders and laity.

The divine economy is present in the initiatives that have emerged from the practices of simplicity and solidarity. Exploring the discipline of simplicity, Christians are resisting the consumerist culture of capitalism and reordering their lives in accord with the common good and the universal destination of material goods. In the practice of solidarity, Christians are exercising hospitality,[55] sanctuary, and—in efforts like the Jubilee campaign—calling for the restructuring of the global economy. They are using the division of labor and alternative markets as opportunities to pursue and establish just relations and fair trade with persons around the globe as they reconnect the goods and services they use with the conditions of their production and distribution.

Congregations and intentional Christian communities—like the Catholic Worker Movement, what is called the "New Monasticism,"[56] Focolare, and others—likewise are embodying the divine economy as they establish small groups for the sake of strengthening economic discipleship by means of accountability and support.[57] They are developing alternative markets, like Seeds of Hope and Church Supported Agriculture, and supporting fair trade in an increasing array of products. They are moving beyond philan-

55. See Heuertz and Pohl, *Friendship at the Margins*; Christine D. Pohl, *Making Room: Recovering Hospitality as a Christian Tradition* (Grand Rapids: Eerdmans, 1999); Elizabeth Newman, *Untamed Hospitality: Welcoming God and Other Strangers* (Grand Rapids: Brazos, 2007); Luke Bretherton, *Hospitality as Holiness* (Burlington, VT: Ashgate, 2006).

56. Jonathan Wilson-Hartgrove, *God's Economy: Redefining the Health and Wealth Gospel* (Grand Rapids: Zondervan, 2009); Wilson-Hartgrove, *New Monasticism* (Grand Rapids: Brazos, 2008); The Rutba House, *School(s) for Conversion* (Eugene, OR: Cascade, 2005).

57. See James Halteman, *The Clashing Worlds of Economics and Faith* (Scottdale, PA: Herald Press, 1995); Relational Tithe, Shane Claiborne, and Isaac Anderson, *Economy of Love* (Kansas City: The House Studio, 2010).

thropy as they reach out beyond the handout in an effort to develop communities.[58]

The divine economy is also being revealed in more traditional business enterprises such as the Economy of Communion and the Mondragon Co-operative Corporation, both of which are shaped by the Christian economy of desire. The former encompasses over eight hundred "for-profit" business firms around the world that are committed to the common good by means of gratuity, charity, and care for those in need.[59] The latter is an initiative organized around Christian teaching in the 1950s that is now one of the largest business groups in Spain and a significant player in the European market.[60]

Although these efforts are not widely recognized and lauded, the divine economy is active in them, as well as in countless others like them. God is present here and now healing desire of its disorder, using the circulation of the gifts of material goods to renew communion.

Conclusion: Little by Little

Yet given the depth of capitalism's hold on us, the extent of its discipline in a marketized society and world, and the pilgrim or fugitive character of the divine economy, we may find ourselves at the end of this work perhaps like the blind man of Bethsaida touched once by Jesus. That is, we may catch a glimpse of a different ordering of desire, we may sense the attraction of a different economy, but

58. John M. Perkins, *Beyond Charity: The Call to Christian Community Development* (Grand Rapids: Baker, 1993). See also John McKnight and Peter Block, *The Abundant Community: Awakening the Power of Families and Neighborhoods* (San Francisco: Berrett-Koehler, 2010).

59. Luigino Bruni, "Experience of the 'Economy of Communion' and Its Relation to the 'Civil Economy,'" *Communio* 27 (Fall 2000): 464–73; Luigino Bruni and Amelia J. Uelmen, "Religious Values and Corporate Decision Making: The Economy of Communion Project," *Fordham Journal of Corporate and Financial Law* 11, no. 3 (2006): 645–80; Lorna Gold, "The Roots of the Focolare Movement's Economic Ethic," *Journal of Markets & Morality* 6, no. 1 (Spring 2003): 143–59.

60. See Race Mathews, "Mondragon: Past Performance and Future Potential," The Capital Ownership Group, October 2002, accessed October 30, 2010, http://cog.kent.edu/lib/MathewsMondragon_(COG)_g.htm. See also http://www.mondragon-corporation.com/ENG.aspx.

things still remain so foggy. All we see are walking trees. Capital's hold is still so strong.

Dorothy Day, one of the great practitioners of the works of mercy of the last century, as well as a keen observer of the unfolding of the divine economy in our midst, wrote of her lifelong struggle to inhabit that economy.[61] Appealing to the example of St. Francis, she notes that it can begin with much fear and trembling, even tears and hiding. That one may only gradually begin to see clearly and live differently. That one may take it "little by little," that change may not be a matter of one great leap or stride but many steps, many very small steps.

Maybe it begins by calling one's bank and canceling an interest-bearing account. Maybe it means stopping for a few minutes to talk with the homeless person before giving her your loose change, or asking your pastor to lead a study on the works of mercy or the Christian tradition of a just price and a just wage. Perhaps that small step is a matter of turning over the label on your shirt or blouse to see where it was made and then tracing the commodity chain back to the persons who sewed it and the conditions in which they did so. Or doing the same thing with the food on your plate—tracing how it was grown and prepared and delivered to you. Perhaps it is a matter of a Sunday school class or youth group finding out more about local possibilities for supporting fair trade, alternative markets, or church-supported agriculture, or making connections with local efforts like the New Monasticism or the Catholic Worker Movement. The possibilities are multitude, because the Spirit blows where it will, in unexpected ways and places (John 3:8), touching us with God's grace, that we might see clearly the new creation and live faithfully, even in the midst of the passing economies of this world.

61. Dorothy Day, *Dorothy Day: Selected Writings*, ed. Robert Ellsberg (Maryknoll, NY: Orbis, 1993), 109–12.

Conclusion

Dishonest Wealth, Friends, and Eternal Homes

> Make friends for yourselves by means of dishonest wealth so that when it is gone, they may welcome you into the eternal homes.
>
> Luke 16:9

In the sixteenth chapter of Luke, Jesus tells a parable about a dishonest steward. It is well known because of the closing exhortation, "you cannot serve God and wealth" (v. 13). The parable is a difficult one because it appears that notwithstanding this exhortation, Jesus endorses the dishonest steward's dealings, to the point that he encourages disciples to imitate the dishonest steward's shrewd economic practices. It is as if Jesus acknowledges that the world of money, business, and economics is not pure, but that is okay so long as you do not let it dominate your life, so long as you do not put your trust in riches, so long as you use dishonest wealth for good purposes.

I have argued that the possibility of an alternative to the capitalist economy of desire hinges on what God is doing in the world today. If this reading of the parable is correct, then clearly God is *not* healing desire now, and perhaps capitalism is the best we can

215

do in this time between the times. It is the best use we can make of dishonest wealth and the dirty world of wealth and business.

Everything hinges on verse 8 in the parable: "His master commended the dishonest manager because he had acted shrewdly; for the children of this age are more shrewd in dealing with their own generation than are the children of light." Who is praising the dishonest steward? Who is this master? The parable begins with the dishonest steward being visited by his wealthy employer. In other words, it is *not* Jesus who praises the dishonest steward for his clever wickedness. Rather, the point Jesus makes is laid out in the second half of verse 8. Specifically, Jesus is encouraging his disciples, the children of light, to be as shrewd or as wise as are the children of "this age." Jesus lifts up the steward, not as a sanction for dirty hands in the inevitably dirty world of business and finance, but as an example of a child of this world who responded wisely when visited by his lord, his master. What Jesus is telling his disciples is that they should be just as wise when they are visited by their Lord.

In other words, because disciples have been visited by their Lord, because their Lord is present in the means of grace, in the practices and disciplines of the Christian life, disciples are set free from the struggle for wealth and set free for service to God, to use wealth wisely, faithfully.

What does it mean to use wealth wisely? Jesus is quite explicit that disciples are to use this world's wealth and resources to make friends. In other words, this world's wealth has a universal destination—to nurture relations, friendships, communion.

However, Jesus says more than this. He says disciples are to make friends so that they may be welcomed into eternal homes. In the midst of a political economy where wealth attracts friends and is a source of influence, this is an important clarification.

But who are these friends who have eternal homes? Who is it that Luke tells us throughout his Gospel has eternal homes? The lowly, the hungry, the poor and outcast, the despised. Think of Mary's Magnificat (1:46–55): praise the Lord who lifts up the lowly and brings down the proud and mighty. Think of the Sermon on the Plain (6:20–25): "Blessed are you who are poor, for yours is the kingdom of God" (v. 20), or the parable of the rich man and Lazarus (16:19–30). The rich man has the home in this world as Lazarus starves, while in heaven it is Lazarus who has an eternal home as the rich man languishes in hell.

In this parable Jesus is telling those who are full now that if they wish to be welcomed into eternal homes, they will welcome the lowly, the poor, the downtrodden into their homes, their community, here and now. Disciples will share the gifts God has given for the purpose of befriending those in need and extending communion. Because they have been visited by their Lord, because their desire has been set free of the bonds of capital, they will use the material resources of this world—producing, distributing, consuming—to extend communion. They will be about the works of mercy, the labor of communion.

Index

219